LEADERSHIP
FOR THE AGES

Delivering Today's Results,
Building Tomorrow's Legacy

DAVID P. HANNA

Executive
Excellence
Publishing

For permissions requests, contact the publisher at:

Executive Excellence Publishing
1366 East 1120 South
Provo, UT 84606
phone: 1-801-375-4060
toll free: 1-800-304-9782
fax: 1-801-377-5960
www.eep.com

For Executive Excellence books, magazines and other products, contact Executive Excellence directly. Call 1-800-304-9782, fax 1-801-377-5960. Visit our Web site at www.eep.com.

Printed in the United States

Printed by Publishers Press

10 9 8 7 6 5 4 3 2 1

Cover design by Heidi Lawson

Cover image: *Splendor of the Tetons* by Peter Ellenshaw. Artwork courtesy of the artist and the art print publisher. Mill Pond Press, Inc.; Venice, FL 34292-3500; 1-800-535-0331.

Library of Congress Cataloging-in-Publication Data

Hanna, David P.
    Leadership for the ages : delivering today's results, building
tomorrow's legacy / David P. Hanna
        p. cm.
Includes bibliographical references.
    ISBN 1-930771-00-2 (hardcover : alk. paper)
    1. Leadership.   I. Title.
    HD57. 7 .H357 2001
    658.4'092—dc21

                      2001001976

Advance Praise for
Leadership for the Ages

"Dave Hanna has captured the lessons we learned at Saturn, coupled them with lessons learned from other successes, and presented them in an easy-to-read and understandable guide for leaders in fast-paced times."

—Richard G. "Skip" LeFauve
Former President, The Saturn Corporation

"This is a book about achieving business excellence! Not just a book about the difference between revenues and expenses, but a textbook about leadership driving values, personal conduct, and systems thinking. David Hanna can teach at my 'university' any time."

—Patrick Mene, Vice President, Quality
The Ritz-Carlton Hotel Company

"In over 35 years of reading business books, none has been as insightful or so in tune with what is happening in today's business environment as Dave Hanna's new book, *Leadership for the Ages*. This book is a must read for any individual or organization who wants success in the new business environment."

—Ted W. Dodge, CLU,
Chairman and CEO, The Boardwalk Group

"This is a compelling guidebook for leaders at any level in any organization who care about sustainable change! The general principles are illustrated with such practical examples and solid insight that readers will be moved out of their comfort zones to face what is really possible as a result of their leadership."

—*Kate Kirkham, Masters of Organizational Behavior Program Director, Brigham Young University*

"Many people talk about how the rules of business are changing in the Global Age. Dave Hanna has written a book that is one of the few to capture the essentials for succeeding under those new rules while understanding that the leadership principles of customer value and healthy organizational culture have remained constant. This is a must read for any manager who would like to move beyond buzz words and sound bites to really make a difference and return to the leadership fundamentals that can restore faith in our institutions."

—*Charles H. Roadman II, M.D. President and CEO, American Health Care Association*

*In memory of William G. Dyer and Richard Beckhard.
Their influence has encircled thousands and will
continue to grow for ages to come.*

Contents

Preface

This book is written for managers and leaders who want to do great things—not merely survive—in their environment.

The coming of the computer has revolutionized how each of us lives, works, plays, thinks, and relates to others. It has given us possibilities our predecessors only dreamed about. And it has opened up the world to become more than just a collection of isolated cultures. We have become a toddling global economy, taking our first steps toward new freedoms and opportunities.

The new global arena has fueled the desire for "more with less." Customers delight in a world that offers more for less. Employees have learned to fear its potential impact on their jobs. Managers have been forced to learn how to strategize, reengineer, outsource, and merge in an attempt to improve their bottom line. "More with less" has truly brought the best of times and the worst of times to those who work in organizations.

Slowly, almost imperceptibly, another force has been gaining momentum in the workplace. This is the force of individualism, or "look out for yourself." Get more for less yourself and don't worry about things you can't control—how the organization is run, how leaders lead, how others are affected, what it all means. Metaphorically, just plug in your earphones, turn on your personal Walkman, and make the most of the day.

So beginning in the 1980s, people in organizations single-mindedly pursued "more with less" and tried to numb themselves to some of the pain around them. Thousands of people lost their jobs, were uprooted, and tried to land on their feet in new settings. Too many cases of greed and excess caused many to take out their earphones and ask, "Why are we doing this?" Now they are cautious in giving their trust to senior managers and public officials and the institutions these leaders represent.

My consulting work with organizations in the past three decades has brought me face to face with the best and worst of this scenario. The original inspiration for this book was the hope I saw bloom in companies when their leaders decided to truly lead. *When "more with less" is consciously applied to more than self, more stakeholders get even more with even less.* But this requires great changes in how leaders think and what they do. These changes can only be fueled by a recommitment to one's own highest values and to those natural laws that govern our ultimate effectiveness.

The work with many of my clients has produced the hope you will find in these pages. Together we have experienced:

• Recommitting yourself to your highest values can be invigorating and earn trust in the midst of cynicism.

• Being passionate about a vision of the future is contagious when that vision makes life better for others as well as yourself. Then the vision becomes more compelling than self-interests.

• Designing or redesigning your organization according to natural laws can correct many of the flaws of today's bureaucracies.

• Building trust in your work culture can be the catalyst to create something that lasts beyond the moment.

My understanding of Leadership for the Ages has emerged from these experiences. Through the years I have worked with leaders who not only got great results at the time, but also revolutionized their work cultures. Studying the lives of great leaders in ages past has reaffirmed the few things that make leadership live on, even after these leaders have retired. That is the reality—and the hope—you will find in this book.

Acknowledgments

Space does not permit adequate recognition of the thousands who have contributed to *Leadership for the Ages*.

My own family has been the most fun, challenging, and rewarding forum for leadership development. My wife, Charlee, is the real change agent in our family. I learn daily from her intuition and courage to simply do what is right. Our children Ben, Melanie, Angie, Beth, and Scott are not only great research assistants and movie scouts, but also have been patient with me as we have counseled together about life's opportunities and transitions.

Someone recently asked me, "How have you developed your own leadership?" I owe it to the good fortune of being around wonderful leaders—beginning with parents, two brothers, and a sister who all taught me that "overachievement" is normal. I am grateful also to many church leaders who have guided my "postgraduate" studies in high performance.

The organizational behavior department at Brigham Young University has been the guiding light of my professional development from the moment it first touched my life. Bill Dyer, Gene Dalton, Bonner Ritchie, and Stephen Covey have been influential mentors. The students and faculty at BYU are a source of continuous stimulation and improvement in my work.

Other important mentors have been Herb Stokes, Laurence Megson, Richard Walton, Dick Beckhard, and Chris Bartlett. Our work together has turned my intuition into processes and frameworks that have made a difference in many settings.

I am indebted to many friends and colleagues at Procter & Gamble, the Covey Leadership Center, Franklin Covey, and Confluence Consulting for profound work experiences. I am grateful for clients who have proven themselves to be men and women of principle and ability. They have taught me the natural laws and practices summarized here.

The content of this book has been influenced importantly by many wonderful individuals. Arthur Jones, Mike Crowther, Holger Krug, Roger Merrill, Blaine Lee, Jim Stuart, Keith Gulledge, Pam Walsh, and Craig Pace have contributed important concepts and case examples. Adam Merrill and Matt Townsend provided research, dialogue, and ideas that helped firm up many important elements. Brent Anderson contributed the Hillenbrand Industries case study in chapter 5. Nancy Brown-Jamison carefully read my manuscript and worked with me to improve it significantly.

Working with the Executive Excellence Publishing team has been a real joy. Ken Shelton, Steven Townsend, Elisabeth Lamb, Chad Hutchings, and Heidi Lawson have contributed vision and heart—as well as professionalism—to improve the raw manuscript I first handed them. I am grateful for their excellent work.

The inspiring people at Shell Oil; the city of Mapleton, Utah; the Ritz-Carlton Hotel Company; the Saturn Corporation; and the Broward County School District, as you will see, are heroes for our age.

Experiences with all these individuals and organizations have proven to me that there are many others out there who, with some solid coaching, can take our collective quality of life to much higher levels. If you will learn from them as I have, then you will love what happens in your life!

David Hanna
Mapleton, Utah

Section

1

Leadership and the Test of Time

1
The Seeds of Leadership

"You can buy a man's time; you can buy his physical presence at a given place; you can even buy a measured number of his skilled muscular motions per hour. But you cannot buy enthusiasm. . . You cannot buy loyalty. . . You cannot buy the devotion of hearts, minds, or souls. You must earn these."

—Clarence Francis

"The voice of conscience is so delicate that it is easy to stifle it: but it is also so clear that it is impossible to mistake it."

—Madame de Stael

EVERYTHING IN THE GLOBAL AGE IS SUBJECT to change—and everything is on schedule! As computers, satellites, and the Internet have shrunk our world and brought together people who have been isolated for centuries, have you experienced changes in the way you do your work? Do your customers have different needs? Are you partnering with more organizations to deliver your product or service? Do you have different competitors? Do you personally have new and different career aspirations?

We live in one of the great transitional periods in the history of the world. Just as leadership was challenged by the move from the Agrarian Age to the Industrial Age, those who lead today's organizations must find new ways of doing things in the Global

Age. Information technology has created one market out of countless suppliers and customers in different lands. Competition is no longer just around the corner, but may come from any corner of the world from any size enterprise.

All this means today's leaders often must bring together geographically dispersed people, materials, and technology to create goods and services for a global market that now offers—and demands—more for less. It also means organizations must operate better, faster, and cheaper than ever before. And, they have to adapt to a myriad of changes as they adjust to the new competitive realities.

At the same time, those who work in and with these organizations also want more for less. They want more income, more personal freedom, and more challenge and excitement in their employment. And, the global market now offers them multiple options for satisfying their needs.

As a leader, you are expected to bridge all of these organizational and personal needs while remaining competitive day to day. Wouldn't it be nice if all this energy would somehow flow together naturally? Like this scenario:

• • •

On July 19, 1989, United Airlines Flight 232 crashed into a cornfield just yards short of a runway at Sioux City, Iowa's Gateway Airport. The mammoth DC-10 flipped over twice and ripped apart as it skidded through the rows of corn, spewing out passengers and crewmembers before coming to rest upside down. With 296 people aboard, this was clearly an extraordinary emergency. And, as the world soon learned, there was an extraordinary organization waiting to conduct the rescue operation.

Even before the giant plane skidded to a stop, ham radio operators were on the scene calling for help. Fire trucks and a dozen ambulances appeared within minutes, along with police, fire, and National Guard units who began locating bodies—many of whom were still alive!

Then other volunteers pitched in. Doctors and nurses—some retired, some living 70 miles away—helped out at Marian and St. Luke's medical centers. At one point there were two doctors for every injured passenger. At the local blood bank, more than 300 people came in and donated three times the amount of blood needed. Counselors showed up voluntarily.

Many local companies also did whatever they could. Local contractors donated portable toilets. Jolly Time popcorn and Sioux Bee honey, along with other businesses, gave food, clothing, and flowers. One store stayed open until after midnight so Red Cross workers could buy clothes for survivors. Restaurants donated food without being asked. Briar Cliff College opened its dormitories to 54 survivors and relatives. Other people offered their homes as the town's 1,500 hotel rooms filled quickly.

The rescue organization even transcended the borders of Sioux City. After learning of the crash, four relatives of victims of the Pan Am crash in Lockerbie, Scotland rushed to Philadelphia airport—Flight 232's final destination—to console those waiting for word.

In the end, 110 passengers and crewmembers died, one of the worst airplane disasters in U.S. history. But, largely because of the efforts of Sioux City's volunteer organization, 186 people miraculously survived.

Captain Alfred Haynes, a 33-year United Airlines veteran, was one of the many heroes who helped accomplish the miracle. Trying to steer a crippled plane whose hydraulic steering systems had been severed in flight, the captain used heart and soul as well as skill to bring the plane in nearly perfectly. While others congratulated him for his superhuman effort, the captain could only weep as he thought of his passengers and crew who had perished in the crash.

• • •

Can you picture this high-performing organization accomplishing its work? Hundreds of people putting aside other things and coming together in a rescue effort that saved 186 lives? What motivated these individuals to do what they did? What held this organization together? What explains the speed and efficiency with which things were done? Such a coming together of people and resources is not just coincidental. To understand what happened in Sioux City is to comprehend what holds any organization together.

The Essence of Organization

You might say to yourself, "Sioux City was extraordinary. It was a one-time crisis. You can expect people to extend themselves for one event. But keeping that magic alive in an everyday work organization is an entirely different matter."

Why do we make it so different?

The Sioux City organization dramatically illustrates the core elements—the essence—of any successful organized endeavor:

1. A compelling, common purpose. People will volunteer their best efforts if the purpose is compelling enough. A purpose is compelling when individuals benefit importantly from its fulfillment. Why don't we make sure we have a compelling purpose before expecting everyone to be committed to it?

2. Organizational processes and systems that align each person's contribution with others. People often know intuitively what needs to be done day to day, but are prevented from doing so by human-crafted policies and rules. Perhaps you've seen in your own organization in times of crisis that performance rises to a new level because standard operating procedures are temporarily suspended. Why do we then go back to those procedures (and lower performance levels) once the crisis subsides?

3. A culture in which mutual trust and commitment to the purpose are unquestioned and where each individual sees what needs to be done and then does it. Unfortunately, most organizations operate in a culture of low trust and self-commitment rather than commitment to a compelling, common purpose. Culture is a dynamic that emerges naturally from the alignment of purpose and systems. Why do we expect to have a high trust culture when we haven't created the conditions in which trust can flourish?

4. Results that exceed expectations, especially in trying situations. One of the main premises of this book is Arthur Jones' insightful observation that "all organizations are perfectly designed to get the results they get." Why do we expect daily results to differ from a one-time crisis? Why don't we organize to capture the Sioux City phenomenon every day?

There is another very critical element in the Sioux City episode. It is the most important element of all because it is the force that caused everything else to flow together. It is the element of committed, visionary leadership.

Two years before Flight 232's crash, rescue agencies in Sioux City and surrounding Woodbury County conducted a mock air disaster rescue in which 150 "survivors" were treated. The leaders who organized this dress rehearsal were looking beyond the day-to-day pressures of their assignments. They called upon all community resources to consider the possibility of an emergency situation and to practice the appropriate response. The practice experience helped the city better align its processes and systems so it would be ready when a crisis occurred.

No doubt some people criticized these community leaders for wasting time and money to practice something that might never be needed in Sioux City. But these leaders were not to be deterred, sacrificing their personal comfort out of commitment to what they saw as a greater purpose.

In the end, the proactive Sioux City leaders couldn't have anticipated the real depth of the organization during a disaster. The retired doctors and nurses weren't part of the dress rehearsal. Neither were the volunteers in Philadelphia. And there were no phone calls to summon the many citizens and corporations who helped when the plane actually crashed. No government decree ordered the stores and restaurants to stay open all night. Yet, doctors, volunteers, stores, and people only remotely tied to Flight 232 found out about the situation and did whatever it took to help out.

When people have a compelling purpose and follow visionary leaders, work can be natural, spontaneous, and exciting. The organizational elements of purpose, processes, systems and culture all flow together to create an organization that is breathtaking and beautiful. This formula for organizational vitality has remained the same through the Agrarian Age, the Industrial Age, and our present Global Age. Look around, and you will find there have been compelling purposes and visionary leaders that have shaped some of today's most exhilarating organizations. Consider, for instance:

• Steven Wozniak and Steven Jobs' vision, passion, and technical skills as they created the first personal computer while working in a California garage. The two inventors haven't always seen eye to eye, and the company they started, Apple Computer, has been anything but a smooth-sailing enterprise. But, those at Apple have followed the founders' dream, reviving it from near-death experiences more than once in the volatile new industry they helped create.

• Founders Don and Deyon Stephens of Mercy Ships have turned dreams and prayers into reality by delivering health care to those who could never afford their services. Since 1978, their four "floating hospitals" have visited over 70 ports, performing more than 6,000 operations; providing medical, dental, and optical care to over 122,000 patients; and delivering more than 16.5 million pounds of medical supplies, equipment, and relief goods. The crew and staff of these ships (including doctors and nurses) all volunteer their time and raise their own financial support. This enables Mercy Ships to give relief at no cost to the patients and to operate at a total cost of less than $10 per person served. Their mission is truly life changing—for both the providers and the patients.

• Cisco Systems has grown into a $25 billion corporation in only 17 years by dramatically altering its operating assumptions and work systems as the Internet industry has exploded onto the scene. Cisco has found ways to shrink its product delivery cycle time through a constant willingness to question and then reshape who does what. This, coupled with a keen eye for new partnerships, has kept Cisco fast afoot in the high tech race. People at Cisco share the optimistic view of CEO John

Chambers that they can continue to set the pace for an Internet industry that has been growing at a staggering rate of more than 60 percent per year in recent years.

• Herb Kelleher, stepping in to be CEO of infant Southwest Airlines, has won loyal followers in his quest to save a good idea from the garbage heap. Others have had the vision of operating a successful low-fare airline. But only the people at Southwest have brought everything together—lowest passenger fares; more than two decades of unbroken profitability; a 300 percent growth in their stock price in the past 20 years; best-in-industry results in safety, service, on-time performance, and employee retention; and a consistent rating as one of the best companies to work for in America.

This organizational excitement isn't the exclusive domain of new start-up companies. I have worked with leaders who have achieved this same magic in companies like Procter & Gamble, Saturn, Ritz-Carlton, Shell, Eastman Chemical, S.C. Johnson, and Metro Cash & Carry. Their vitality is not diminished whether they operate in the Americas, Europe, Asia, or Africa. The purpose of this book is to review the leadership elements that have created such high performers. It is Leadership for the Ages because, as you will see, great leaders in different cultures throughout all ages have utilized the same fundamental elements of the Sioux City episode. Process-wise, Leadership for the Ages looks like this:

1. The leaders are personally committed to a worthwhile vision, often times sacrificing their personal preferences and comfort for it.

2. The leaders' vision becomes a compelling, common purpose for all those who have an important stake in the organization's success because fulfilling it improves their quality of life.

3. The stakeholders work together to shape organizational processes and systems so that each person's contribution is aligned with others.

4. A culture of high trust emerges in which each person does whatever it takes to fulfill the purpose.

5. The outputs are results that exceed expectations, especially in trying situations.

These leadership fundamentals have shaped organizations that are unlimited by periods of crisis or product lifecycles. And, so it can be with you and your organization. As you cultivate the elements of Leadership for the Ages, you will not only deliver today's results, but also build a legacy that lives on through time.

The Bottom Line of Leadership

The place to begin understanding Leadership for the Ages is to get in touch with the dynamics of leadership. What is it that separates real leaders from those who merely have the title "leader"? The best way I've found to do this is to picture yourself in a situation where someone comes to you with a special request: "We are facing a serious problem! I will need you to give everything you have over the next several weeks to help us solve it. I'm afraid you won't sleep much or be able to spend much time with your family until things are back to normal."

Would you follow this person with enthusiasm? Before you choose your response, let me put a face on the one making the request. Which of the following individuals would you enthusiastically follow in this situation?

- Marie Curie
- Bill Gates
- Genghis Khan
- Nelson Mandela
- Henry Ford
- Joan of Arc

Each of these individuals has (or had) a formal leadership position in an organization. But just because they have subordinates doesn't necessarily make them a leader. *Bosses have subordinates; leaders have followers.* That's been the bottom line throughout the ages. By this definition, each of these individuals is also a leader. Some people have sacrificed or are sacrificing much to follow their lead.

But the question to you is a very personal one. Would **you** be willing to forego sleep and family relationships and give everything you have for several weeks for any one of these leaders? The seeds of leadership are found in the relationship between the leaders and their followers. Colin Hall, CEO of Wooltru Ltd. in South Africa, puts it this way, "We've forgotten that leadership is really about followership. We've never had the followership of 85 percent of the people in this country. We've had compliance, but we've never had followership. Leadership is about earned followership."

The full magic of the leader-follower relationship blossoms when the followers themselves exert leadership over their part of the system—pursuing the common purpose, holding themselves and others accountable for results, seeking ways to improve how they operate, and upholding the values of the culture. Thus leadership multiplies and intensifies—and will live on in others once the original leader has left the scene.

Now consider your relationship with each of these six individuals. What do some of them lack? Or what do some have that would cause you to volunteer your best efforts to carry their banner? The bonding agent is trust—a trust that can only be earned by trustworthy people. Trustworthiness is a function of two factors:

• *Character—do the leaders share your vision and values?* This element causes us to examine the would-be leaders' integrity and motives. *Character is what a leader is.*

• *Competence—can they deliver on their promises?* This causes us to look at the leaders' skills (technical, strategic, teamwork, etc.) to see if they can effectively mold individuals into cohesive and competent teams. *Competence is what a leader does.*

Again, the critical test is how you perceive them to measure up in these two areas. Your perception is based not only on your experience with the leader, but also with your experiences with other leaders in a variety of settings. So many leaders disappoint us these days that it has become a reflex to view new leaders with some degree of skepticism. And, this is most likely how others are viewing you now. They are assessing who you are and what you can do. Can you confidently expect them to follow you?

The Inside Out Process

The seeds of leadership are within you. Your character and competence are the keys to overcoming skepticism and attracting and holding on to enthusiastic followers. But how can you cause these seeds to grow and lead to greater, even timeless results? It's a process that Stephen Covey describes as "inside out," or as Mahatma Gandhi put it, "You must become the change you seek in the world." This inside out process begins in the personal arena—with your work to strengthen your own character and competence. The measure of your personal effectiveness is the amount of trust you build with others. The inside out process reaches its zenith in the organizational arena when your organization is able to deliver more for less to your key

stakeholders (owners, shareholders, customers, suppliers, associates, and communities). Your organization's effectiveness is found in its alignment with the ever-changing global market place as measured by such things as bottom-line results and stakeholder satisfaction.

This book will follow this inside out sequence in discussing the elements of Leadership for the Ages. As you think about what you have read in this chapter, ask yourself three questions:

• Do I want to accomplish something truly great in my work?

• Does the global market require more than my organization has historically delivered?

• Do I need enthusiastic followers to reshape how we work together?

If the answer to any of these questions is "yes," then read on.

2
Natural Laws and Lifecycles

"There is the Moral of all human tales; 'Tis but the same rehearsal of the past. First Freedom, and then Glory—when that fails, Wealth, vice, corruption—barbarism at last. And History, with all her volumes vast, Hath but one page."

—Lord Byron

"What experience and history teach is this—that people and governments never have learned anything from history, or acted on principles deduced from it."

—Georg Wilhelm Friedrich Hegel

TRUE LEADERS HAVE FOLLOWERS, NOT JUST subordinates. However, a leader's ultimate success is tied to his or her ability to deliver results. Whether you are in business, government, education, or in a volunteer agency, leaders—and organizations—haven't survived in any age unless they achieved some critical, expected results. With this in mind, consider what the following organizations all have in common:
- Cambria Steel
- Guggenheim Exploration
- Lehigh and Wilkes-Barre Coal
- Intercontinental Rubber
- Schwarzchild and Sulzberger
- Central Leather

Each of these institutions was one of the top 100 U.S. firms in 1909, but none exists today as an independent entity. They are either out of business or a minor player in some larger corporation. Some were quite large in their glory days (Central Leather was *number seven* on the 1909 list). Unfortunately, they were not able to maintain their successful beginning. In a few management generations they have disappeared. These six are certainly not unusual: of the top 100 U.S. industrial firms in 1909, only 14 are still in the elite group today. Only 23 are still around at all! On the other hand, think about what the following corporations have in common:

- U.S. Steel (now USX)
- Eastman Kodak
- E. I. Dupont De Nemours
- Standard Oil (now Exxon)

These companies were also in the top 100 in 1909, and they (or the organization of which they play a leading role) are still there based on the latest *Fortune* Magazine list of the top 500 Industrial firms. But even those in today's top 100 are anything but secure. Each of the four companies listed above has been undergoing serious business shakeups and downsizing in an attempt to remain competitive in the global market. And other giants such as General Motors, IBM, and Sears have experienced severe economic problems in recent years as profits have been down and thousands have lost their jobs. They are straining to do more with less just like everybody else.

The struggle for life isn't something peculiar to large corporations. Research indicates that approximately 700,000 people in the United States start their own businesses each year. Unfortunately, by the end of the first four years at least 51 percent of them will be out of business. And more than 80 percent of the small businesses that survive the first five years will fail in the second five. Is this what the global market will be known for: creating countless shooting stars that burst onto the scene and then fade as rapidly as they appear?

These alarming trends aren't just in businesses. Budget cutters are trimming whole departments in government. Schools from kindergartens to universities are scaling back as the educational structure reshuffles. Everyone is looking for ways to deliver more with less.

Organizational Lifecycles

Both the top 100 companies and the small entrepreneurial businesses—indeed, all organizations—share a common lifecycle. Though one organization may extend its peak phase more than others, most organizations' bottom line over time looks like this familiar bell-shaped curve:

The lifecycle tells us that whenever people come together, certain dynamics emerge. They unite themselves and grow. Then something happens and they degenerate over time. Yet, organizations are the only living systems that have the potential to live on indefinitely. They don't have to follow the up-and-down slope of the lifecycle.

Leadership for the Ages offers the potential to extend your organization's lifecycle through the Global Age and beyond. That doesn't mean perpetuating everything you are doing today. It will require many changes and evolutions over time, but Leadership for the Ages is about doing what is required for your organization to be alive and healthy for generations to come.

To extend an organization's lifecycle, we first need to better understand its dynamics. What accompanies an organization's rise to peak performance? What drags it down? What must leaders keep in mind if they are to stand the test of time? To answer these questions, let's consider two organizational applications— the lifecycles of civilizations and product innovations. Both are extremely relevant to our present society and global economy.

My intent in reviewing these lifecycles is not to make you a social anthropologist or research scientist. Examining their common patterns can help us better understand the natural laws and principles that govern both the ascent and descent of complex organizations. The following is a summary of thousands of years of human experience as documented by renowned historians. As you read this material, see if you can determine why, as Arnold Toynbee said, "Nothing fails like success."

Lifecycles of Civilization

The world's great civilizations, such as those in Sumeria, Egypt, India, Greece, Rome, China, and Mesoamerica, all share a common lifecycle: they started from almost nothing, flourished, declined, and then either disappeared or lingered on as shadows of their former selves as others overtook them. Robert Muntzel summed it up best, "Great nations rise and fall—the people go from bondage to spiritual faith, from spiritual faith to great courage, from courage to liberty, from liberty to abundance, from abundance to selfishness, from selfishness to complacency, from complacency to apathy, from apathy to dependency, from dependency back again into bondage." Building on this description, I offer this lifecycle with the following nine stages:

1. Bondage. All great civilizations start in bondage to others and either overthrow another group or emigrate to a new home. One key to moving out of bondage is tribal loyalty. The tribe is one. There is no dissent. There is democracy, but it is characterized not by freedom of opinion and dissension so much as by equality of duty.

2. Faith. Moral or religious faith has accompanied the early rise of each civilization. The element of faith provides an overarching value system to which individual desires are subordinated.

3. Courage. All members courageously pursue the group's objectives to protect themselves from enemies and to expand their culture beyond its initial boundaries.

4. Community. City-states often expand the tribal loyalty to ever-wider circles of followers. Though the population may be quite large, the common values make citizenship a personal and fulfilling experience.

5. Abundance. Each civilization reaches a point where it becomes the envy of its neighbors. Abundance means there is plenty for everyone; that the quality of life is high for most people and not artificially constrained.

6. Selfishness. After arriving at the pinnacle, unfortunately, most of the great civilizations have also followed a predictable path to ruin. The people begin to be selfish rather than courageous in defending their cause. Subtly, the power of moral or religious faith diminishes. There is no longer an overarching set of values, freeing the people to glorify themselves and gratify their own desires. Divisions in beliefs and wealth become more pronounced. Cooperation breaks down; the central power of the state is weakened.

7. Greed. The quest for self gratification leads to greater materialism, colonialism, and imperialism—an ever increasing escalation of exploiting other groups for the benefit of a select few. Social problems grow, such as crime, family break ups, and poor leadership. Younger generations lack social concern. In the words of one historian, "Wealth corrupts, not immediately, but invariably."

8. Dependence. Since inequality grows with greed, each civilization has found itself divided between an advantaged minority and a deprived majority. As this majority grows, it slowly begins to restrain the progress of the privileged elite. The majority's ways of speech, dress, recreation, feeling, judgment, and thought infiltrate upward in society. Civilization remains only as strong as its weakest link.

9. Bondage. Weakened civilizations eventually give way to other groups. Thus, the lifecycle has come full circle: from bondage to bondage; or, in Byron's words, "a rehearsal of the past."

"Throughout the history of civilization, societies have been conquered by barbarians whenever they grew weak," writes historian Charles Brough. "The inescapable conclusion has been that there was a strength in the social structure that enabled them to conquer more civilized people. This, in turn, has led to the conclusion that a civilization that could resist invasion or could even conquer barbarians must have had a social structure similar to that of the barbarians." Note that Brough is saying it is the strength of the social structure (culture) that explains why civilizations rise or fall.

From the writings of Will and Ariel Durant, Émile Durkheim, Neville Kirk, Albert Schweitzer, Adam Seligman, Pitirim A. Sorokin, Oswald Spengler, Alexis de Tocqueville, Arnold Toynbee, and George M. Wrong emerge the following characteristics of a declining civilization:

• A declining sense of community and national pride (evidenced by political apathy) as people become more concerned with only their own private affairs (selfishness)

• A preponderance of great cities

• A worship of money and material wealth (greed)

• Religious values replaced by disparate and contending secular values and a resulting moral confusion

• A lack of emphasis on the family, marriage, and the proper training of children, leading to further moral and social fragmentation

• The rise of dictators

• A cumulative weakness and chaos in the social fabric that leaves the population open to exploitation and/or decimation (dependence/bondage)

The dynamics of this civilization lifecycle are profound because they transcend individual people, cultures, and even epochs of time. Each of these civilizations can be likened to an organization—a group of people working toward some common purpose over time.

I invite you to think of your organization as if it were one of the great civilizations. At which point in this lifecycle does your organization find itself? Are you ascending, on top, or sliding downhill? Do these attributes describe where your culture has come from, where it is now, and where the current trends will lead you?

The Product Lifecycle

The civilization lifecycle closely resembles another lifecycle—that of the product innovation process. The rise and fall of today's industrial organizations are due to dynamics that are very similar to those of civilizations. The lifecycle of developing innovative goods and services frequently looks like this:

1. Debt. The initial context for all innovations is debt, meaning they are dependent on other organizational resources for their sponsorship and execution.

2. Vision. Every innovation is sparked by a vision of a better solution (product, technology, or service) to someone's need. The light bulb, the computer, and overnight courier services all began as some individual's vision of a better world.

3. Persistence. This vision leads a product champion to go through the arduous incubation period of product development. Persistence is required by the innovator to move the vision to reality against a tide of opposition from the status quo.

4. Divergence. The search for the right means to achieve the product vision results in a period of great uncertainty in which many different paths may be explored. This stage calls for experimentation to test the validity of the concept and to choose an operational prototype. An important attribute in this stage is the ability to explore different alternatives without prematurely judging any as "good" or "bad."

5. Convergence. Out of the many options explored in stage four, a single prototype is selected to introduce into the marketplace. Now, all of the organization's departments must come together to make the introduction successful. This is a brief period of stability as product and production processes are standardized, marketing strategies are chosen, and early market responses are closely monitored.

6. Market Share. This is a period of growth. The market evaluates the new innovation and determines its relative value compared to other available offerings. Abundance follows when the desired market share is realized.

7. Inward Focus. The downward spiral for products and services is not unlike that of the great civilizations. Following a successful debut in the market, every innovation has slowly faded from the top. There are several reasons for this gradual decline. First, prosperity brings with it a typically greater emphasis on production costs and economies of scale. This, in turn, increases pressure to standardize production to minimize the cost of expansion. The frequent result of all these forces is to infect the innovators with "Internal Myopia," meaning they stop focusing on the external market needs and become preoccupied by their own concerns. This causes them to lose touch with the market at a crucial moment, for the introduction of a real innovation inevitably promotes a whirlwind of competitive activity. Competitors begin to imitate and improve upon the new innovation. Customers' preferences may be reshaped and raised as a result.

8. Win-Lose Strategy. As time passes, the market becomes established and the product is standardized. Competition's innovations are still unproven; new customer needs are unexpressed. Mass production prevails and costs dominate the competitive scene. There is little innovation in this stage beyond superficial product differentiation as the strategic focus subtly drifts toward the competition and away from the customer. Continuing this trend leads to Win-Lose strategies that attempt to maximize self-interests at the expense of competition.

9. Follow Competition. Ignoring the market place brings the inevitable downfall in an ironic turn of events. By focusing on the competition almost exclusively, the innovator eventually loses the competitive edge. Competitors invariably introduce new offerings, which erodes one's competitive position and requires the organization to play "catch up" with the newer innovations. The leader now becomes the follower.

10. Out of Business. The product dies or is replaced by a newer form. This newer form may come from within its own organization or from competition.

A good example of the dynamics of this product lifecycle is the saga of "Product X" from the annals of one of America's premier companies:

• • •

The Saga of "Product X"

Year 1: A concept is tested—stimulated by intellectual curiosity, not by any project objective. (Vision)

Year 7: The research division abandons the concept. Working part time, a lone investigator in another department continues the work. When his supervisors are told of his involvement, they ask, "Why are you working on that?" The investigator stops reporting his activities.

Year 9: Numerous attempts to produce a feasible prototype end in failure. (Persistence)

Year 11: The major product defect is solved. However, the new form presents a heretofore non-existent performance problem. The vice president says to the director, "How can your fellows fiddle around with a product we haven't even thought of making when we've got more unanswered problems out here in the factories? You're just not giving us the right kind of service! You've got to stop it!" The associate director tells the section head, "Don't let it interfere with anything else he (the investigator) is doing, but do whatever he can on it. But don't put it in your weekly report."

Year 12: The director decides to drop the project after extensive work by the research division shows no merit in the basic concept. The investigator and his managers use new test methods (quite different from the approved methods used in the past) to argue for their concept. The director reluctantly reverses his stand and allows work to continue. Testing is hampered by manufacturing's unwillingness to make product samples. Only one out of three requests is actually processed.

Year 13: The number of potential product options seems endless. No single formula appears to have a clear edge over the others. (Divergence)

Year 14: The vice president is favorably impressed by the latest review of Product X. He schedules a review downtown with top management. Members of company management are in favor of beginning a test market. The normal two-year cycle is viewed to be a problem due to fear of competitors making a preemptive response. It is proposed to roll out immediately, bypassing normal blind, shipping, and advertising tests. The CEO's response is, "We've never done that!" (Convergence)

Year 15: The product fails to win a paired-comparison blind test before entering the test market.

Year 17: The CEO reports to the stockholders, "In our judgment, there is small chance of [Product X] replacing our existing products to any marked extent. It is a marvelous product in some fields, but limited in others, and will supplement rather than supplant our products in most homes." The president of a major competitor, noting the modest results of the new product in test markets, claims, "This product is a flash in the pan. It won't last!"

• • •

What is Product X? It is something that has influenced every one of us. It is Tide, the first synthetic laundry detergent introduced to consumers by Procter & Gamble in 1948. After a modest debut, it gradually ascended to the number one market position (Market Share). The product lifecycle dynamics of vision, persistence, divergence, and convergence take on a new meaning when we consider it was largely one man, supported by a few sponsors, who created this breakthrough technology against the entrenched procedures of a large and successful company!

The story of Tide's development is not a criticism of Procter & Gamble. What this story illustrates is how powerful the forces are which shape or frustrate product/service innovation and development. Will and Ariel Durant point out the value of these conflicting forces:

"So the conservative who resists change is as valuable as the radical who proposes it—perhaps as much more valuable as roots are more vital than grafts. It is good that new ideas should be heard, for the sake of the few that can be used; but is also good that new ideas should be compelled to go through the mill of objection, opposition, and contumely; this is the trial heat which innovations must survive before being allowed to enter the human race. It is good that the old should resist the young, and that the young should prod the old; out of this tension, as out of the strife of the sexes and the classes, comes a creative tensile strength, a stimulated development, a secret and basic unity and movement of the whole."

After its initial introduction, the momentum on Tide swung over to mass production, cost efficiencies, and similar issues. This could have seduced P&G into the cycle of Inward Focus, Win-Lose, and Follow Competition. Through the years, however, Procter & Gamble has brought out new formulas, perfumes, packaging, and even new forms (today, there is a liquid Tide) in order to keep the product viable in a changing marketplace. Tide remains today the top-selling laundry detergent in America and its international cousin, Ariel, is the number one detergent globally. The original Tide product is out of business, but the brand name still lives on because the organization has continued to learn and adapt its product to the consumers' changing needs. Tide is an ageless brand franchise.

The saga of Product X has been repeated in a host of other product/service arenas. A similar story is told at 3M regarding the adhesive for the now famous "Post it" note. Company management first deemed the new adhesive a total failure because it wouldn't permanently hold things together. Who would want an adhesive that would stick and then release? It took a product champion, much like the one in the laboratories at Procter & Gamble, to pursue a vision for the product now used in hundreds of ways around the world.

Think of how we got the light bulb, penicillin, overnight courier services, personal computers, and countless other items that contribute to our standard of living. In each case the product lifecycle dynamics have been evident. Think further about companies, products or services that have become obsolete. Again, the lifecycle has been conspicuous as carriages gave way to automobiles, phonograph records have been largely replaced by compact discs, and conventional mail services have been frequently displaced by fax technology and the Internet.

Place your own product or service where you think it fits today on the product lifecycle. Are you just approaching the desired market share, already at the top, or falling from where you used to be?

In the midst of these lifecycle dynamics is the potential for your organization to "jump the curve"—to renew itself before obsolescence drags you down. Your products or services may need to change through the years, but your organization can endure any season. Now, let's examine the keys to fulfilling this potential.

Natural Laws Govern Longevity

Of course, your organization is not the Ming Dynasty and your conditions today are different than when Tide was developed. But, consider for a moment the common threads revealed in these two lifecycles—and what lessons you can apply from them to your own situation:

The similarities are striking and pose some serious questions. Why is it that with all our technical advances, with our unparalleled capacity to learn and store knowledge, with the coming of reengineering, balanced scorecards, and Quality management— why is it that with all this going for us we are unable to build organizations that can hold up over time? One wonders if any system can survive more than a few decades.

The most enduring systems are found in nature. The oldest life forms on this planet are California's redwood trees. Ecosystems of mountains, forests, streams, meadows, insects, and animals are amazingly resilient. These systems can survive physical calamities, destructive weather patterns and other major environmental shifts, and endure for ages unless humans intervene and attempt to "civilize" them. What these natural systems have in common with civilizations and product organizations is that they are all living systems, meaning some of their key elements are living, breathing entities. A review of the natural laws that govern the survival of living systems offers profound wisdom for understanding organizational longevity.

A natural law expresses a universal truth that governs the makeup of something or some dynamic process. An example from the world of physics is the natural law of gravity. Jump off a cliff and you will fall to the ground below. Natural laws are not subject to our desires or beliefs; we are always subject to their rules. In other words, natural laws govern our interactions whether or not we are aware of them, agree with them, or follow them. We must align ourselves with these laws to arrive—and remain—in a desirable place.

How do you know if something is truly a natural law, or merely someone's value or preference? A practical way to determine the difference is to look at the universality and timelessness of the value. If the value leads to success in a wide variety of circumstances, in diverse cultures, in all ages, then it qualifies as a natural law. Values, on the other hand, may serve us well in some specific situations, but not in others.

Since the following seven characteristics are always present in living systems that survive over time, they also qualify as natural laws:

1. Ecological order—each element of the ecosystem must fit into the order of things. Living systems are all part of a larger network of elements. They either fit into this ecosystem in a way that maintains balance of the greater whole, or they perish.

2. Purpose—everything else is subordinated to the highest purpose: survival for self, group, and species. Natural instincts lead to self-preservation and preservation of the species. Failure to be concerned with anything beyond self ultimately leads to ecological imbalance and death.

3. Steady state—survival is maintained via steady processes that follow a proven, functional routine. The steady state is a pattern of habits that assures daily survival and stores energy for meeting critical challenges. Without a steady state, the system uses more energy than it can obtain from the environment.

4. Mobilization—threats to survival and the steady state are sensed and met. The dynamic of mobilization is a two-edged sword. It certainly protects the steady state. On the other hand, it can actually attack a force that would cause constructive change to occur.

5. Complexity—systems develop more complex, specialized functions. We humans often misunderstand this law. In nature, greater complexity generally leads to expanding skills or functions and a greater ability to adapt to the environment. In human organizations, greater complexity usually translates into creating steeper hierarchies and narrower spans of control.

6. Synergy—the whole is greater than the sum of its parts; synergy comes from new relationships. Synergistic breakthroughs occur when different elements come together in new ways. The challenges and opposition posed by a diverse environment are the very forces that shape the beauty of nature, the survival of a species, and an organization's competitive advantage.

7. Adaptation—processes change as necessary when environmental changes threaten survival. Effective living systems subordinate processes to purpose. They are able to grow and adapt in remarkable ways when new environmental conditions require them to do so.

These seven natural laws govern all living systems—from sagebrush, to barn swallows, to bison, to human organizations. They identify for us the characteristics an organization must possess if it would endure for more than a few decades. Now consider how these natural laws fit into the lifecycle patterns we have already reviewed. Adhering to these laws explains the ascent up the lifecycle and violating them explains why organizations fall from their peak.

Any organization must fit into the *ecological order* of the marketplace if it is to have the roots for growth and prosperity. Though the organization starts out in debt and "bondage," it can fit into the market ecology if it fills important needs. The organization's initial challenges are to develop a compelling, common *purpose; mobilize* all its resources in fulfillment of that purpose; and eventually develop a *steady-state* operation that reliably delivers the outputs valued by the market. Successful growth challenges the capacity of the new organization and requires greater *complexity* (e.g., greater functionality) to maintain its performance. When everything comes together successfully, there is a sense of community between the organization and its stakeholders, *synergy* emerges, and the results are an abundant market share. But the challenges of change are never ending; therefore, the length of the lifecycle ultimately is tied to the organization's ability to further *adapt* what it does as the environment changes.

The fragile nature of organizations comes from the fact that they are not always put together consistent with natural laws, but by human-crafted policies. To the degree these policies adhere to the natural laws described here, the organization's longevity is enhanced. But, if the policies conflict with natural laws, the system's lifecycle will be shortened. (I will examine some of these human-crafted organizational policies in more detail in chapter 10.)

As the lifecycle reviews have already demonstrated, most organizations fall from their peak because, instead of staying aligned with natural laws, they become internally focused and *fall out of the ecological order* that sustains their livelihood. At the very point when the competitive market is stimulated to produce something new, the organization suffers from Internal Myopia. Greed and win-lose obsessions (both self-serving) become *counterfeits for purpose*. In an attempt to further standardize and control the steady state, *human complexity* substitutes for natural complexity, further focusing everyone's attention only on their piece of the whole. The more fragmented the system's elements become, the more dependent they are on factors outside their control when attempting to make meaningful improvements. The bottom line of all this is that the instincts for further adaptation are blunted and the organization accelerates down the path of obsolescence.

This scenario has profound implications for many of today's newer, high-tech companies. I have often heard leaders of these organizations say something like this: "We are in a constant state of motion, just trying to keep up with everything. I don't spend more than 15 minutes reading or working on any one thing." Yet, as previously noted, the passion of start-up and technological challenge propel these organizations forward in exciting ways. The natural laws/lifecycle scenario points out the criticality of carefully shaping the characteristics of steady state, complexity, synergy, and adaptation before the wet clay hardens in these young companies.

Remember that planes, trains, and automobiles were once "high tech" start-ups, too. Remember that Central Leather was big in 1909. Remember that consumer products were glitzy in the post World War II era. Their leaders, too, were stretched to capacity just keeping up with the boom markets of their day. But, as each of these industries matured and became more competitive, those who were misaligned with natural laws suffered enormously. Those with "unsteady states" were overwhelmed by the Japanese quality juggernaut. Those who had built in human complexity with steep hierarchical pyramids and monotonous jobs were unable to innovate and synergize against new competition. And, those who did not adapt to the new order of things became extinct.

The root cause of all these problems has not been changing market conditions, new technology, or formidable competitors. The root cause of organizational obsolescence is always poor leadership. Leaders who are too busy to understand the evolving order of things, or design a competitive steady state, or shape adaptation as a cultural cornerstone will not be able to bring everything together when the heat is on. It would be a tragedy if, in a few decades, today's vision and passion in Silicon Valley became the latest version of a declining Industrial Revolution.

The Ageless Lifecycle

The conclusion to be drawn from this chapter is straightforward: *you must adhere to the natural laws of living systems if you would develop an organization for the ages.* It is straightforward, but certainly not easy to do (as history teaches us!). If an organization were to follow nature's script:

- It would always plan what it does in the context of the most important needs and expectations of its major stakeholders.
- It would develop a sense of purpose so that each member would instinctively act to fulfill it and to protect the organization from anything that might threaten it.
- It would develop quality work processes that consistently deliver high quality outputs.
- Daily problems would be solved competently by those closest to their source.
- It would grow over time in its skills and flexibility so that environmental changes could be handled without major trauma.
- The teamwork would be so synergistic that it would enjoy competitive advantages over others in terms of quality, unit costs, cycle time, innovation, and problem solving.
- Whenever the environment introduced new complexities, the organization would be able to draw on all of the other attributes to re-strategize and redeploy its resources to remain in an advantaged position.

If these characteristics were typical of the way your organization conducted itself, your lifecycle would look like this:

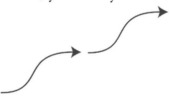

The critical point is at the end of the first arrow. If the organization were able to adapt at the peak of abundance and refocus on ecological order and purpose instead of being blinded by Internal Myopia, the lifecycle would begin a new upward spiral instead of sliding down. It is the capacity for continuous improvement and adaptation that critically influences organizational longevity.

An important thing to remember is that, in a sense, there is no such thing as an organizational mission or organizational behavior. Organizations don't have missions; people have missions. Organizations don't behave; people behave. Yet, when enough people share a mission or behave in the same ways, their pattern becomes an underlying structure for the organization. Thus, *organizations for the ages can only be developed by leaders who follow the success pattern of natural laws.*

Organizational Viruses

In all organizations there are some values that are not aligned with the natural laws discussed here. This is like placing a compass in a magnetic field. When this happens, one's direction is no longer determined by True North, but by local interference. When organizational politics interfere, for example, senior management's wishes might be given preference at the expense of natural laws. This causes the ecosystem to fall out of balance and all other relationships become distorted. The boss's wisdom supersedes True North.

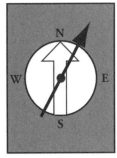

Indeed, the effect of diverting the organization away from natural laws is like that of a virus. Some viruses will attack and destroy the immune system that protects the body from common diseases. A sick organization (one not aligned with natural laws) no longer protects itself from unhealthy habits. The dysfunctional elements, like a virus, run rampant and eventually may control how the organization operates.

Organizational viruses explain why executive opinions may count more than market research; why unethical behavior becomes acceptable; why Wall Street paranoia may determine HR policy; why large departments may perpetuate themselves even if their function has become obsolete; why majority rule may kill the truly innovative idea. Here are some examples:

• A marketing group was reviewing its latest strategy with a senior manager when a serious disagreement arose. The senior manager said price wasn't an important factor in the purchase decision, but group members quoted market research to support the opposite point of view. The senior manager refused to be persuaded and finally said to his subordinates, "You aren't listening to me! We aren't going to drop the price." Against their better judgment, the marketing group followed orders. But *True North didn't budge!* Today, the product has all but disappeared.

• A well-known government contractor was caught diverting over $40 million in phony purchase orders for work and equipment it never delivered. Top executives talked about wanting employees to report wrongdoing, yet some employees said the corporate culture encouraged the opposite. Those who did report wrongdoing ended up labeled as troublemakers and were forced out of the company or shuffled into dead-end jobs. The company ended up paying more than $60 million in fines.

• A large company with an excellent track record in its industry was having trouble pleasing Wall Street. Despite the company's strong financial foundation and good growth record, stock analysts said its future was questionable because the operations were overstaffed. In due time the layoffs began.

• Another company had overhauled its entire accounting system in the late 1980s. Many functions were computerized and financial personnel were decentralized and assigned to each operating division. Yet despite all these modernization steps, the number of people in the central accounting department remained the same.

• Despite results that made it the most productive plant in its industry, an electronics plant was closed in 1992 as part of a company-wide cost-cutting effort. Why did the parent company close down its best plant? Pressure from both senior management and union leadership led to the decision. The plant was both non-union and unconventional in its approach. The other plants fit in better with the corporate culture. Meanwhile, the parent company is falling even further behind Japanese and American competitors in the marketplace.

When viruses like these are strong enough, organizations drown in puddles, and molehills become mountains. One manager gave a colorful description of the effects of an organizational virus, "We have an organization that utilizes excellent people to turn out mediocre results."

On the other hand, healthy organizations (those aligned with natural laws) are able to overcome dysfunctional individuals, practices, or operating cycles. Leadership for the Ages establishes the conditions whereby people freely choose, and work systems strongly facilitate adherence to natural laws on a daily basis. No matter whom you talk to in these organizations—top managers, associates, customers, suppliers, community representatives—they all agree that their association is an enriching experience. *Life for all is better because of what the organization is doing.*

As you can see, Leadership for the Ages presents us with enormous challenges. It humbles us to acknowledge we aren't in control; that natural laws govern our effectiveness. It overwhelms us to contemplate how we might influence others to align with these natural laws. And it reminds us how many things happen every day that are not aligned with natural laws—therefore requiring our leadership to put things right.

So how do you as a leader begin aligning your organization with these natural laws so it becomes ageless? You must work from the inside out, beginning with yourself. *Your leadership must first earn the enthusiastic followership of other people. When these people become aligned with natural laws, they will create an ageless organization.* The next two chapters address the starting point of the inside out process: how you can earn the devotion of hearts, minds, and souls.

• • •

Applying what you have learned:

Here are three suggestions to put into action what you have learned in this chapter:

1. Place your organization's culture on the lifecycle. What factors are pushing you up or pulling you down?

2. Examine how well your organization is presently aligned with natural laws. Rate your present performance on a scale of 1-5 (1=poor, 5=excellent) for each of the seven bullet points

on page 42. (Resist the temptation to rate through rose-colored glasses. A "5" means you are among the top 12 percent.)

3. Ask representatives of each stakeholder group (customers, suppliers, employees, shareholders, communities, etc.) to rate your performance as in #2.

Section

2

The Leader's Core

3
Earning Trust

"Many persons have a wrong idea about what constitutes true happiness. It is not attained through self gratification, but through fidelity to a worthy purpose."

—Helen Keller

"You can take my factories, burn up my buildings, but give me my people and I'll build the business right back again."

—Henry Ford

IN 1792, YOUNG ARTHUR WELLESLEY, THE fourth son of an Irish nobleman, purchased his commission as a lieutenant colonel in the British army according to the custom of the day. Arthur was only 23 years old. He was now an officer, but could he command his men's respect? During his initial battles, Arthur's troops were astoundingly successful. What was it that enabled him to be more than someone with formal authority; to be one who could lead his men to victory? This episode from his life is most revealing:

• • •

Once while visiting one of his camps, Arthur discovered his officers had taken over the recovery tent intended for those wounded in battle. "The heat is unbearable," his officers explained in defense of their actions.

"There is nothing more important than seeing to our wounded men!" Arthur fumed. He ordered the officers to return the wounded to their tent immediately. He supervised the transfer; then he and his staff rode off.

After riding some distance, Arthur and his party turned back and returned to the campsite. Just as he feared, the officers had again commandeered the tent once their leader had left the scene. Without delay, the officers were placed under arrest, new officers appointed, and Arthur led away his prisoners, satisfied at last that his wounded would be cared for properly.

• • •

Through this and many other similar experiences, Arthur earned his soldiers' trust and went on to have an admirable military career. At the battle of Waterloo, he met and defeated Napoleon himself. Yes, Arthur Wellesley was also known as the Duke of Wellington.

The Critical Importance of Trust

The Duke of Wellington is a role model of how to earn trust. The following diagram illustrates the roots and fruits of Wellington's leadership:

The camp episode spoke volumes about Wellington's character to those who served under him. Every soldier knew they could count on him to look after their needs. He could be trusted. This trust earned Wellington the followership of his British soldiers. Similarly, the roots of our own leadership effectiveness are in our character—our values, motives, and paradigms. Our character forges the difference between simple compliance and trusting, enthusiastic followership.

Growing from these roots are leadership's fruits. Wellington became skilled in the tasks of war and he helped his soldiers do the same. Likewise, effective leaders today must develop followers who skillfully pursue the same mission. Character (who we are) is essential to earn others' trust, but competence (what we do) must be added in order to maintain that trust. An honorable Wellington who lost every battle wouldn't have kept his followers' trust.

Renowned horseman Pat Parelli uses the formula of character and competence to teach would-be riders how to gain a horse's trust. He points out that a horse's instincts are to mistrust any creature that has two eyes in the front of its head, since these are nature's predators. People, lions, and wolves all alert the horse's instincts to danger. "First, you have to show the horse how much you care," says Pat. "Then you have to show it how much you know. Once you establish these two things, the horse knows you won't give any command that will endanger it. Then you can lead and the horse will follow." Pat's instructions also parallel our world in which leaders are viewed suspiciously because of reported layoffs, strategic blunders, dictatorial styles, and a host of other unpleasant actions. Many people have become conditioned to view leaders as selfish predators.

Imagine for just a moment what your life would be like if there were absolutely no trust between you and the people in your work group:

• What if you couldn't count on them to come to work on time or stay at their work when they were needed?

• What if you feared anything you said might be passed on to the press or to your competitors?

• What would the day be like if you couldn't trust anyone to do even the simplest task without making a mistake?

• What if you had absolutely no confidence in any judgment they might make?

And imagine what it would be like if the people in your group had absolutely no trust in you:

• What if they feared losing their job at your whim or without any warning?

• What if they feared anything they said might be used against them?

• What if they believed that you had invented the latest results summaries to manipulate them?

• What if they viewed you to be totally incompetent and spent considerable time second-guessing every decision you made?

• What if they knew from past experience that any order you gave would be forgotten by the next day?

It doesn't take too much reflection like this to appreciate how central (and perhaps overlooked) trust is in the work place. Stephen Covey uses a wonderful metaphor to symbolize the amount of trust in our relationships—the Emotional Bank Account. Just as with a financial bank account, we can make deposits and withdrawals from the Emotional Bank Account. Whenever we make more withdrawals than deposits from this trust account, people will be slower to pursue the mission and will get bogged down in their work. This dynamic is true for every stakeholder we work with—associates, senior management, various departments, customers, suppliers, government agencies, the public—everyone. Trust is both the glue and the lubricant of any organization. It is the glue because it bonds you and others together. And it is the lubricant because it enables all kinds of work—simple as well as complex—to move ahead with minimal friction. When the glue is weak or the lubricant is contaminated, though, our organizational efforts begin to stall.

How do you earn others' trust? Just like Wellington did—by living the values and developing the needed competencies to successfully fulfill your mission. Elijah Macon, a Procter & Gamble technician, best explained this concept when he said, *"People tend to be like their leaders."* Let's turn our attention now to some paradigms and processes that can help you earn trust.

Centering Your Life

One popular description of those who can't be trusted is, "They don't walk their talk." In other words, they say one thing and do another. My experience is that such untrustworthy behavior often is not conscious, but comes from handling situations one at a time, in the heat of the moment. Because situations and emotions can vary significantly, they do not produce consistency. Yet, one important contributor to trust is the consistency to "walk the talk"—to do what we say we will do and to live according to our beliefs. Maxwell Anderson, in his stage production *Joan of Lorraine*, described such consistency this way:

"Every man gives his life for what he believes. Every woman gives her life for what she believes. Sometimes people believe in little or nothing. Nevertheless, they give up their life to that little or nothing. One life is all we have and we live it as we believe in living it and then it's gone. But to surrender what you are—and live without belief—that's more terrible than dying, more terrible than dying young."

One of the great disconnects in today's organizations, and one of the greatest obstacles to establishing Leadership for the Ages, is the number of individuals who are not in tune with what they believe, i.e., what is truly most important in their lives. Such people are often described as "not centered." If you are not centered on what is most important, you may find yourself giving your time and energy for the sake of "little or nothing" as this model depicts:

Inject a stimulus (a cancelled airplane flight, for example) into such a person's life and what would you expect his/her behaviors to be? It might depend on the person's values concerning others. Or, it might depend on how important the appointment is at the destination. Or, it might depend  on the person's experience with that particular airline. Or, it might depend on how tired the person is, or whether or not the person is ill. Can you see how many potential forces could govern the person's response if his/her most important life values are unclear or hidden in the subconscious?

Years ago Earl Nightingale described what he called "The Strangest Secret in the World"—something that separates successful individuals from those who fail. It is the simple idea that "we become what we think about." Nightingale taught seminars on the dynamics of visualizing something important in the future and then working towards its fulfillment. Peter Senge teaches a similar idea and calls it personal visioning and mastery.

Remember that all effective living systems have a clear sense of purpose that fosters survival of self, group, and species. This is instinctive with plants and animals. Salmon swim upstream, lay their eggs, and die—thereby perpetuating the species. But we humans, with our more complex intellectual abilities, can ignore or rationalize away instinctive behaviors unless they are forcefully imprinted into our thinking. A mission statement has the potential to fulfill this function if we are committed to it and if we think about it every day. Study the life of great leaders in ages past and you will find they were centered on their personal mission.

If we become what we think about, then the personal mission has the power to help us handle any situation in life in accordance with our values. I have seen how important this is for people and organizations. And I have seen the high costs associated with not centering on your chosen mission. Consider the case of one of my clients, Louise, and her employer:

• • •

Louise was an impressive person. She had a Ph.D., a great family, and a career headed upward on a fast track! She was a very positive role model for many others in her company. But, one day she confided a personal dilemma to me. "I'm working 80 hours a week and hardly ever see my family any more," she began. "My son has learning disabilities and is having trouble in school. When I tried to leave a meeting the other day for a conference with his teacher, my boss jumped all over me. 'You are needed here!' is what he told me. So, I stayed and missed the teacher conference." Louise said she needed some advice on how to juggle all the demands upon her time. She was thinking of quitting her job and finding something that would enable her to be more available for her family. "I'd quit in a minute if I didn't know that so many people in the organization look to me as a role model," she confessed.

"You're right, Louise," I said. "But what are you modeling?" She suddenly understood exactly what she had been doing to herself and others. Then I recommended some ways she could step back and reflect more deeply on what her priorities were before making such a big decision.

Several weeks later Louise came back. She was much more relaxed this time. In the interim period, she had drafted a personal mission statement—a credo that focused her on balancing God, family, and work. Then she outlined several options that she felt would be aligned with her personal mission and also keep her in the company. She could (1) get more people on her team to handle the work load; (2) move to another department that wouldn't require so much time; or (3) move to another function.

Ultimately, her boss vetoed all three of Louise's alternatives. Her project was vital to improving the product, he said, and if the new product didn't succeed in the market, the whole department's profit goals wouldn't be met. According to him, "the company" felt that her suggestions were out of the question.

Louise resigned her position and used her experience and background to start her own business that she operates out of her home with great success. She has been able to restore balance in a very busy and rewarding life. (Remember, in the global market there are always alternatives!)

• • •

Think of the difference Louise's boss might have made to many stakeholders if he had been able to maintain her trust in this situation! His attempts to keep Louise on the project failed miserably. She refused to follow. Not only did she leave at a critical time, she did so without any transition to her successor. The company lost Louise's talents altogether! And the product ultimately fizzled after she left. As this experience illustrates, taking action without being centered on a carefully chosen mission lessens our effectiveness. And the damage to the bottom line from being off-center seldom can be traced to its real cause.

Centering Your Organization

The Mission-Centered Model has major implications for you as a leader. In the drive to do more with less, you are faced with countless situations where a number of factors might drive the behaviors of those involved. Let's look at an example of these dynamics. See if you can identify what this organization is centered on:

• • •

In late 1991, an automobile manufacturer sent a letter to thousands of owners of one of its models. "This notice is sent to you in accordance with the requirements of the National Traffic and Motor Vehicle Safety Act," the letter began. It then proceeded to outline in detail a problem with this model's seat belt retractors. Under certain conditions, the retractors could lock up and make the seat belt useless. The car owners were instructed as follows: "If you currently have a safety belt that is locked up, please call your dealer right away and schedule a time to have the safety belt replaced." For those who had not yet experienced the problem, the instructions were, "if you ever have this problem in the future—no matter when—contact your dealer for safety belt replacement. . . Please keep this letter in your car so that any future owners will also know of this situation."

The company provided the toll free numbers of its customer assistance center and the National Highway Traffic Safety Administration. Then the letter closed by saying, "We are sorry to cause you this inconvenience; however, we have taken this action in the interest of your safety and continued satisfaction with our products."

• • •

Where does a company get its sense for the right thing to do in a situation like this? From its values. What is a company centered on if it will repair a defective seat belt once it is broken, but not do anything until then? Not the customer's "safety and continued satisfaction." Is this action consistent with its corporate mission? As one of the recipients of this letter told me, "The Highway Patrol says it's illegal to drive a car without a seat belt. That means by law I'd have to have my car towed if the retractor ever jammed. If (the company) was *really interested* in my safety, they'd tell me to bring in the car and fix it before a problem came up!" Obviously, this company was centered more on cost savings and profitability than keeping trust! Its response to this problem was very efficient. But, whatever this manufacturer saved in seat belt replacement costs, it lost in trust. Coincidentally, this model chronically falls short of its sales targets.

Any time we allow one priority or need to dominate at the expense of other mission elements, we undermine our personal and organizational trustworthiness. Being truly mission-centered is a paradigm shift of major proportions. It changes the way we view everything around us. It shapes how we might deal with the issues of the day. And it requires deeper analysis and greater courage to be consistent over time.  Here is a wonderful example of what these ideas look like in real life. Let's visit the Ritz-Carlton Hotel Company.

Ritz-Carlton Hotels: Earning Trust Pays Off

The best way to appreciate the Ritz-Carlton organization is to experience it as a guest:

• • •

Imagine yourself caught in the middle of a travel nightmare. You are supposed to be enjoying spring break in Florida, but an unexpected snowstorm has canceled your connecting flight in Atlanta. Your bags are lost, you have no winter clothing, and the hotel you booked at the airport is nowhere in sight as you leave the subway station. The chilling winds take your breath away. You and your spouse are very concerned about your shivering four-month-old son.

This is what happened to a certain family a few years ago. Fortunately, Eric Smith, Rooms Executive at the Atlanta Ritz-Carlton Hotel, overheard their worried conversation. He volunteered his assistance. "We would be happy to have you stay with us over there at the Ritz-Carlton (just across the street). And we'll charge you the same rate you would have paid at the other hotel."

It didn't take long for the grateful family to accept Eric's offer. Once inside, they were checked in quickly and given a room on the club level. A full size crib was waiting for their son when they entered their room. Shortly thereafter a Ritz-Carlton employee known only as "Dan" volunteered to stop at a store and pick up some baby supplies. All this service—and for a room rate that was approximately one third of the normal price!

The husband summarized his feelings in a letter to Ritz-Carlton, "Words do not fully express our gratitude for the assistance given to us by Mr. Smith and Dan, as well as the entire staff of the Ritz-Carlton Atlanta, for making a very difficult situation into a pleasant stay at your hotel."

A one-in-a-million experience? Only if you have never stayed at a Ritz-Carlton. As impressive as this story is, it is typical of what Ritz-Carlton guests experience. Here are some other examples:

• • •

A Hong Kong businessman (let's call him Mr. Ho) was staying at the Ritz-Carlton in Marina del Rey, California. Mr. Ho checked out of his room, left his bags at the Bell Desk, and attended a meeting in the hotel. Later, he and his associates drove down to San Diego for another meeting. He planned to fly to Seattle via Los Angeles later that afternoon. Only when Mr. Ho entered the airport did he realize he had left his bags at the Ritz-Carlton! Suddenly panicked, he called the hotel to see if his luggage could be sent to Seattle. The Ritz-Carlton employee quickly saw another possibility—he had just enough time to drive to the Los Angeles airport and meet Mr. Ho personally. Timing was critical, but this employee drove to the airport, located the gate, presented Mr. Ho with his bags as he came through, and escorted him to the ticket counter to check the bags to Seattle. Mr. Ho proceeded on his next flight without delay.

• • •

What about a situation in which a guest is disappointed? One regular customer at the Pentagon City Ritz-Carlton wrote in to complain that his wake up call was missed during his last stay. He indicated the importance of the wake up calls since he could not rely on "terrible" hotel alarm clocks. The Ritz-Carlton team went into action. In addition to assuring this guest his future wake up calls would be reliable, they purchased the same alarm clock brand (and similar model) that this guest uses at home. Now, whenever this guest checks in, he is greeted by "his alarm clock" tuned to his favorite radio station. This guest's response? "I was surprised at the special effort you made in response to my note. Needless to say you have earned my continued loyalty as a customer."

• • •

Such things happen every day in 38 different Ritz-Carlton hotels in Canada, China, Egypt, Germany, Hong Kong, Indonesia, Jamaica, Japan, Korea, Malaysia, Mexico, Puerto Rico,

Singapore, Spain, the Virgin Islands, United Arab Emirates, and the United States. Uncompromising service, personal attention, near flawless quality, and continuously earning trust. At Ritz-Carlton, excellence is measured in moments like these.

And its excellent performance has paid off. Ritz-Carlton has the highest occupancy rates in the industry. Its customers prefer Ritz-Carlton by a margin of 73-10 over competition. Employee turnover is about one third of the hotel industry's average. And the company continues to open new hotels in an industry that many describe as "glutted." In 1992 and 1999, Ritz-Carlton won the prestigious Baldrige Award for Quality excellence. How do they achieve such excellence in vastly different cultures around the world?

It all began as one man's dream.

A Dishwasher's Dream

Horst Schulze could not have predicted where his career would take him when he began a cooking apprenticeship at age 14 in his native Germany. He started out washing dishes and helping in the kitchen. Through the years he worked for some of the finest hotels in Europe and the United States before helping to form the Ritz-Carlton Hotel Company in 1983.

Along the way, Horst developed a passion for service and excellence. "Service is a much misused word today," he says. "True service is very gratifying; it's a real gift to serve. In the hotel industry, most people sell food, beverages, and rooms. That is not our business. Service is our real business."

His appreciation for excellence came out of his experience while working as a room service waiter in the San Francisco Hilton. "I wanted to be promoted to Room Service captain. Someone else got promoted before I did. This hurt my ego. After three months I finally admitted to myself that the other fellow deserved the promotion more than I did. Then a second guy got promoted and it only took me 10 days to admit he deserved it. Finally, it dawned on me. If I truly deserve it, I will get promoted. So, I decided to create excellence every day."

Horst contends that most people think of success and excellence as something in the future. "There is a big problem with that thinking," he says, "because if success is in the future, how can you be successful? You're not there!" The young room service waiter resolved to be successful at whatever he was doing at the moment. "My accomplishment of today is success. The reward for success comes later. My first reward came when I knew I was the best room service waiter. My second reward came when others said, 'You do a good job.' My third reward came when I finally got promoted."

Horst left his vice president position at Hyatt Hotels and joined the Ritz-Carlton organization to pursue a dream—"to create a hotel company where people can create excellence. I gave up money and benefits for the sake of my dream. And others have joined me because they share the dream." Also joining Ritz-Carlton from the Hyatt organization were Siegfried Brauer, Herve Humler, Joseph Freni, and Edward Staros. These five remain the key leaders at Ritz-Carlton today.

Just spend a few minutes with any of these executives, or with any General Manager or staff member at any of the Ritz-Carlton hotels, and you will feel how deeply they share the values of service and excellence. Service and excellence are who they are. Everyone is centered on the company's Gold Standard—the Credo, Motto, Three Steps of Service, and The Ritz-Carlton Basics. Every employee carries his/her own pocket version of the Gold Standard:

The Ritz-Carlton Hotel is a place where the genuine care and comfort of our guests is our highest mission. We pledge to provide the finest personal service and facilities for our guests who will always enjoy a warm, relaxed yet refined ambiance. The Ritz-Carlton experience enlivens the senses, instills well-being, and fulfills even the unexpressed wishes and needs of our guests.

A more careful look at the Credo's three sentences reveals a powerful simplicity:

Sentence 1: *What* we are—a service organization.

Sentence 2: *How* we will live up to #1—by being:
- *Warm*—sincere and caring.
- *Relaxed*—being ourselves.
- *Refined*—respecting our guests and each other as ladies and gentlemen.

Sentence 3: *Why* we want to do #1 and #2—to have fun and excitement every day.

Building on this mission, the focus shifts to the fundamental role everyone at Ritz-Carlton needs to fill in order to make the Credo a reality. This role is expressed in the Motto:

"We are ladies and gentlemen serving ladies and gentlemen."

The important message in this motto is that while service is Ritz-Carlton's business, employees are not servants! They, too, are ladies and gentlemen serving their guests. Through the fulfillment of this motto, every employee is the recipient of a "warm, relaxed yet refined ambiance" and an experience that "enlivens the senses, instills well-being, and fulfills even the unexpressed wishes and needs." Employees are as important as their guests! The motto reduces the entire Gold Standard to a single, easy-to-remember sentence. As the 18,000 associates live this Motto every day, they build trust with each other and with their guests.

Building on the philosophy that success is what each person does right now, the three steps of service outline what success looks like:

Three Steps of Service

1. A warm and sincere greeting. Use the guest name, if and when possible.

2. Anticipation and compliance with guest needs.

3. Fond farewell. Give them a warm good-bye and use their names, if and when possible.

Anything a Ritz-Carlton employee does in a typical day can be categorized into one of these three steps. Finally, the company has identified 20 basics that describe what is required to care for each hotel's performance capacity and results. These include such standards as:

- Continuously identify defects.
- Any employee who receives a customer complaint "owns" the complaint.
- Guest incident action forms are used to record and communicate every incident of guest dissatisfaction.
- Uncompromising levels of cleanliness are the responsibility of every employee.
- Use the proper vocabulary with our guests. (Use words like "Good Morning," "Certainly," "I'll be happy to," and "My pleasure.")
- Escort guests rather than pointing out directions to another area of the Hotel.

Aligning Your Work Unit

How does Ritz-Carlton help each employee—regardless of where they work—bring the Gold Standard to life every day? As Horst says, *"We don't just build a hotel and put a name 'Ritz-Carlton' on there and say, 'Now it's a Ritz Carlton.' We put the heart and the soul into that hotel in the form of people."*

This means employers first have to find people with heart and soul—proven character and competence—and further develop their talents. Ritz-Carlton's HR development system is built around four core processes. These four core processes are selection, orientation, training certification, and ongoing environment

The HR department and every department head are jointly accountable for the effectiveness of these core processes. The bottom line of the system is a culture in which everyone is deeply committed to the Gold Standard and then does whatever necessary to fulfill it. Here is a closer look at each of these processes:

1. Selection. Working with an outside specialist, Ritz-Carlton has developed a world-class selection process. It screens applicants according to 11 performance factors (work ethic, self-esteem, persuasion, teamwork, service, empathy, exactness, etc.) all of which have been validated as critical to success in the hotel industry. It is a tough hiring standard. The application-to-hire ratio typically exceeds 20:1. But those who make it through will thrive in the Ritz-Carlton culture. Interestingly enough, many who are hired have no previous hotel or restaurant experience. This doesn't alarm the Ritz-Carlton managers; they have found that such employees are more open to adapt their habits to Ritz-Carlton's nontraditional approach.

2. Orientation. Every new employee is oriented to the company's values, the Gold Standard, and trained for his/her specific work role. For a new hotel, this process can be from seven to ten days to get the culture just right before the doors officially open. Once a hotel is up and running, an abbreviated orientation (three days) is held for each new employee. In the latter schedule, two days cover the Gold Standard and corporate values; one day is for departmental training and review of the department's mission. What is important is how each of these sessions is conducted. Even in the departmental training sessions, the trainers refer constantly to the Credo, motto, three steps of service, and the 20 basics. In this way they simultaneously teach employees what the company stands for and their personal role in making Ritz-Carlton the best hotel in town. Thus, even making beds, washing dishes, and serving guests in the restaurant become mission-centered activities.

Horst Schulze always conducts the opening orientation session for a new hotel. During his 90-minute presentation he outlines each element of the Gold Standard and explains, "The training you will receive in the next ten days isn't really all that important. It's our philosophy that is important. That's why we are beginning with it." Among other things, he talks about the need for each employee to have a voice in how the hotel operates; how to handle problems with each other; how he learned that success precedes the reward; and the need for everyone to internalize the Credo and values.

As he concludes the opening session, Horst assures everyone, "You have the opportunity to impact our business and our work environment. . . . I know you are skeptical of all this. Do you want to be part of creating excellence? Do you want to create a good environment? Do you want to speak up? If you don't, please don't come back tomorrow. But if you do, you are committing yourself to become a part of us. And I promise you this: by opening day, we'll be the best hotel in town!"

• • •

A good example of how Ritz-Carlton uses every opportunity to reinforce the Gold Standard came during the uniform issue portion of the orientation training in Barcelona, Spain. During the hiring process, a tailor fitted each new employee for his/her own uniform; now it was time to pick them up. As the first group entered the room, all the trainers on the service side of the desk (from a variety of Ritz-Carlton hotels worldwide) stood, applauded, and cheered! The new employees were intimidated by this outburst and stopped in their tracks. They looked around to see what all the commotion was about—perhaps they had come into the wrong room. They looked behind them—there was no one there. Finally, they comprehended what was going on—these leaders and trainers were standing and acknowledging them as the newest members of the family! They went home that afternoon with their new uniforms—and with a very different connection with their workplace. They had just experienced what it means to be treated as a lady or gentleman in a Ritz-Carlton hotel and were visibly committed to treat others the same way. Experiences like these in the first two days transformed these trainees from hopeful, but reticent employees into committed family members.

• • •

Another key component of orientation is the departmental mission statement. Start-up orientations provide employees the opportunity to create their own departmental mission statement with their supervisors. On-going orientations enable each new employee to become familiar with the departmental mission and see how they can contribute to it on the job. Here is one department's mission statement:

Employee Restaurant

The employee restaurant serves employees with genuine care and comfort, using the Three Steps of Service, striving to provide fresh, balanced meals. We provide a warm, clean atmosphere so that every employee has a chance to relax and re-charge so that they are able to serve the guests better.

3. Training Certification. This is orientation's bottom line, signifying the employee is committed to live the Gold Standard, fulfill the department's mission, and is able to meet the performance standards. Certification also takes place whenever an employee transfers into a new department.

4. Ongoing Environment. Three days, seven days, or ten days of training do not guarantee you'll stay at the top of the lifecycle. So Ritz-Carlton focuses on recommitting everyone to the values and continuously improving the work processes. Once a year every employee attends a four-hour refresher on the values. And periodic training programs equip associates to take part in quality improvements, better serve guests, or improve other job skills. Cross training in other departments is also common.

Even more critical is the daily lineup meeting in each work group. An old tradition in the hotel business, the lineup originally resembled a military inspection (*"Line up! Show me your hands! Let's see those shoes!"*). Ritz-Carlton has adapted this practice to include more than just a grooming and appearance review. All lineups are conducted with everyone standing (this is sure to limit the meeting's duration to less than 20 minutes!). Pertinent information for the day is reviewed, process improvement ideas may be documented, and one element of the Gold Standard is discussed: What does it mean? What do we do well? Where do we fall short? How can we improve? The Gold Standard agenda item is scheduled from the corporate office so that on any given day the same topic is being discussed in every hotel.

When the right person has been selected, oriented, certified, and becomes immersed in the on-going environment, some remarkable things happen. Here are just a few of the thousands of moments that define Ritz-Carlton's excellence:

• • •

Nick Canale of the Amelia Island staff was transporting several guests who had to be relocated to other hotels because Ritz-Carlton was sold out. One passenger told Nick how badly he wanted to stay at the Ritz-Carlton because of the service and facilities. He said he would particularly miss not being able to sit, relax, and enjoy a glass of fresh-squeezed "Ritz-Carlton" orange juice. After dropping this gentleman off at his hotel, Nick returned to home base and had a container of orange juice prepared and delivered to this man's doorstep along with a note apologizing that Ritz-Carlton was unable to offer him a room.

Bellman Jean-Baptiste Prunetti passed a gentleman coming from the restroom in the Palm Beach hotel. The man seemed quite flustered. Jean asked if everything was all right, only to learn the man had just broken the zipper in his trousers and was due back for a luncheon with four women! The quick-thinking Jean ushered the gentleman back into the restroom, asked him to hand over his pants, and repaired the zipper right there with a pair of pliers. The guest was greatly relieved thanks to a bellman turned tailor.

One family came to the Boston Ritz-Carlton to celebrate several events at Sunday brunch: it was the 25th wedding anniversary for one couple, their sister-in-law had just completed a half-marathon that morning, and Grandma and Grandpa were about to return to their winter home after an extended visit with their family. After helping the family pile out of the large van, doorman Kenny Young noticed a large pool of oil spreading from underneath the vehicle. Inspecting things more closely, Kenny determined the oil plug had recently fallen out. Getting a colleague to cover his spot, he retraced the van's path with the driver until he found the oil plug. Returning to the hotel, he made arrangements to have the plug replaced and fresh oil installed. "It will be taken care of," he told the guest. "Enjoy your brunch!"

• • •

These ladies and gentlemen serve everyone as ladies and gentlemen. And they have created a dynamic organization that is just beginning to hit the first peak on its lifecycle. They, too, share the dishwasher's dream.

Conclusion

Trust is a priceless ingredient in your organization. It binds people to a common cause and reduces friction as the work gets done. Trust with all stakeholders is one of the hallmarks of Leadership for the Ages. Trust comes from a combination of character (what you are) and competence (what you do). A personal mission, reflecting your deepest personal values, can shape and guide how you interact with others. When you allow another factor to drive your behavior, it distorts everything else and undermines your trustworthiness.

The evidence of your real mission is found in your habits. As the Monitor Corporation's Mark Fuller likes to say, "If you want to know what truly counts, watch management's feet, not their mouth!" Through the case example of the Ritz-Carlton Hotel Company we have seen how individuals living consistent with their Credo continuously earn trust.

In the next chapter I will examine some invisible strands of trust's spider web. Effective leaders have very different paradigms than others of their organizations, their stakeholders, and themselves. These paradigms are a crucial part of Leadership for the Ages. I will explore some of these paradigms to show how they naturally produce different behaviors and better results.

Applying what you have learned:

Here are some suggestions to put into action what you have learned in this chapter:

1. If you haven't drafted a personal mission statement, consider doing so now. (Contact me at www.confluenceconsulting.com for some materials to help you in this process.)

2. For each major stakeholder group, list two or three recent interactions in your work group that demonstrated (a) you were mission centered or (b) you were centered on something else. For any of the (b) responses, describe what a mission-centered antidote would have been.

4

From Subordinate to Steward

"He, who does his duty, has character; he, who does only his duty, has none."
—Hellmut Walters

"Leaders are the caretakers of the interests and well-being of their subordinates and the purposes they serve."
—Wess Roberts

"There is a loftier ambition than merely to stand high in the world. It is to stoop down and lift mankind a little higher."
—Henry Van Dyke

YEARS AGO A RENOWNED DOCTOR AND PROFESSOR used to tell his young medical students, "You can only see what is behind your eyes!" Looking into their puzzled faces, he then explained what he meant. "When you diagnose a patient's illness or prescribe treatment, you can only see the possibilities your training has placed in your head. You can only see what is behind your eyes."

Such is the power of a paradigm! The way you see the world strongly influences how you will respond to any given situation.

In this chapter I will examine typical paradigms of organizations, stakeholders, and leaders. These are the invisible threads that govern our behaviors—and the amount of trust we are able to earn.

Let's begin by looking at organizational paradigms. Why does your organization exist? Let the following experiences provoke your thinking about this question:

• • •

Mary was a college student working her way through school. When she got an unexpected low grade on an exam, she went to her professor to discuss the matter.

"Your teaching assistant didn't give me credit for these answers," Mary told the professor. "But I'm sure they are correct."

The professor studied the answers for a moment and then replied, "You're right. There's nothing wrong with these answers." Then, just as Mary breathed a sigh of relief, the professor added, "But I have a long-standing policy of never overriding my graduate assistants. I can't change your grade. I will talk to him about this so he doesn't make the same error in the future."

A disillusioned Mary shook her head and walked away.

• • •

In October 1993, forest fires raged out of control near Laguna Beach, California. Though the National Guard had airplanes capable of dropping water on the blaze, none were mobilized until 19 hours after the first alert. Why? The head of the National Guard said, "We still do not know for sure who is in charge." Elsewhere, the Marine Corps was willing to send volunteers, bulldozers, and water-dropping helicopters, but the local fire officials wouldn't take them because, "We have never drilled with them and they don't know our way of fighting fires." Meanwhile, 310 homes were being destroyed as the fire moved across the mountain.

• • •

I was sitting in a rental car shuttle late one Friday afternoon at the Kansas City airport, having finished a busy week on the road and looking forward to getting home. Just as the van was about to depart for the airline terminals, a man came running up and pounded on the door. The driver opened the door and in came the man, panting heavily and looking desperate. "Thanks so much," he said to the driver, "I've been stuck on the interstate for the past hour because of an accident. My plane is supposed to leave in seven minutes. Can you get me to the gate in time to catch it?"

"What airline are you on, sir?" the driver asked.

"United."

"That's in terminal C, sir. We have to stop at A and B before we go to C."

"Please! This is the last flight to my home tonight!" the man begged.

At this point the one other passenger in the van glanced at me and our nods answered the passenger's unspoken question—neither of us was in a hurry. "Ma'am," the other passenger said, "it's all right with us if you take this gentleman to his terminal first. Our flights are a little later."

The driver replied firmly, "I'm sorry, sir, but just two weeks ago our management sent out a bulletin stressing that under no circumstances are we to deviate from going to A, then B, then C."

The van dutifully stopped at terminal A, then at B where I got off, then headed for C.

• • •

These experiences are more than illustrations of bureaucracy and a slavish devotion to rules. I'm intrigued by a deeper issue: *what could possess intelligent, ethical people to respond as they did to these situations?* What's the underlying paradigm that explains their behavior?

Let's look at the common threads in these three examples. In each case customers/taxpayers had a desperate need and had paid for certain services. But each organization had policies that overrode the instincts of the professor, the National Guard and fire department leaders, and the shuttle driver. Why would they turn down such urgent requests? There are many possible reasons:

• The policies might serve to correct past problems, confusion, and inefficiencies. You have to think of all stakeholders—not just the few involved in these situations.

• Employees could get fired for violating the organization's policies.

• If you make an exception for one person, everyone else might expect the same treatment.

Now, if you were Mary the student, the California homeowners, or the distressed passenger on the airport shuttle, would any of these reasons mean anything to you? Certainly not! But rules and procedures controlled organizational responses in each case. We all face similar dilemmas whenever organizational policies come face to face with unique personal needs. Too often, organizations do things that prove they have something other than our interests at heart. Why don't leaders naturally make better choices? *They can only see what is behind their eyes.*

The Forgotten Trust

To get in touch with the relevant paradigms, let's start where all organizational transactions begin. Why do you deposit your money into one bank over another? As an employee, why did you choose to work in your current organization? Why do you stay? Why did you select certain schools for your children? Or, why didn't you seek out alternative schools as many others are doing? Why do you as a customer choose one automobile over another? Or a hotel? Or a brand of clothing? Why do you listen to certain radio programs or stay away from some movies? Why do you vote for one political candidate over another?

The answer to all these questions reveals what the true purpose of any organization is. As a stakeholder, you make your choices (you "vote") based on trust—a trust or expectation that those you have chosen will meet your needs. In our three case examples, what trusts were placed?

• Mary trusted that her professor would give her the grade she had earned once he saw her exam answers.

• In the California fire, homeowners trusted the National Guard, Marine Corps, and local fire departments to put out the fire and save their homes!

• The customer trusted the shuttle driver to help him get home that Friday night!

Indeed, we all share a universal trust whenever we interact with any organization: *make my life better!* But, how many people in your organization make the connection between what they do and improving their stakeholders' quality of life? Probably very few. This creates the dynamic I refer to as the *Forgotten Trust. We forget that our organizations (and our jobs) exist only as long as we honor the trust of our many stakeholders.*

Thus, the bottom line of any "business" is meeting needs—the physical, social, mental, and spiritual needs of its many stakeholders. The penalty for forgetting their trusts is severe—it may cause stakeholders to "vote" for someone else. What prevents people from remembering these basic dynamics, that their work really is a series of Emotional Bank Account deposits and withdrawals? I believe it is another paradigm that leads to the Forgotten Trust.

The Subordinate Paradigm

If people in organizations have forgotten the trusts placed in them, what are they thinking about instead? What is behind their eyes as they go about their daily tasks?

Especially in larger organizations, *people tend to think of themselves only as subordinates—that is, someone else is really in charge and responsible for what happens.* This is the subordinate paradigm. Technically speaking, everyone is a subordinate because everyone has a boss. In typical hierarchical organizations, however, this subordinate paradigm leads to the breakdown of trusting transactions. It tells individuals they are dependent on others for direction; that others are to blame for inefficiencies and poor policies; that *"theirs is not to reason why, theirs is but to do."* The subordinate paradigm breeds passivity, not proactivity. Here are some of its telltale expressions:

- "I only work here."
- "You'll have to ask someone else."
- "My supervisor said we couldn't do that."
- "That's against our policy."
- "Management made that decision."
- "We're not authorized to do this."
- "If it were my business, I wouldn't do it this way, but . . ."
- "It's good enough for government work."

Look again at our three case examples: the professor was *bound by his own delegation rule with his assistant.* The commanders of the National Guard and Marine Corps *waited for orders* before acting—even though the delay meant more houses burned to the ground. The shuttle driver *did not help* her passenger go directly to terminal C. As long as we think of ourselves as subordinates, our decisions and actions will be governed by supervisory approval, policies, and habits. But these make poor leaders. They can't provide the right answers to every situation. And, as we have seen, blindly following them may actually undermine our stakeholders' trust in us.

The subordinate paradigm is the nerve center of our bureaucratic world. It controls many daily behaviors. But, thankfully, as the members of the Ritz-Carlton organization have shown us, this mental model does not cripple every organization. What goes on behind the eyes of those who see beyond being a subordinate?

The Steward Paradigm

Just when you've had a frustrating confrontation with the subordinate paradigm, you go into another organization and encounter the following:

• • •

Our family was shopping at Wal-Mart for a bicycle for our son Scott's birthday. Once Scott had made his choice, we realized we had done our shopping in the wrong sequence. We had more things to buy, but needed to load the bicycle into our car. "No problem," said the clerk. "You just leave this bike here with me. I'll look after it while you shop. You can pick it up on your way out."

• • •

Once, while I was traveling with some colleagues, our flight was delayed five hours in Dallas due to incredible thunderstorms. Arriving in Houston at 2 a.m., the three of us wearily tried to get our rental car. After no response from the telephone hot line in the terminal, we went outside to see if any shuttles were running. They were! But after waiting a long time (long enough for other rental car shuttles to come around twice), our shuttle failed to appear. Finally, my colleague approached the Avis bus driver and asked, "Is (Company X) still open?" "Yes," the Avis driver replied. "I saw people in their office as I came over." Then, recognizing these non-customers' plight, the driver volunteered to drop us off at his competitor's gate!

• • •

The subordinate paradigm certainly doesn't explain why the clerk and bus driver went beyond the call of duty in these two situations. They both built trust, and in the bus driver's case even with those who weren't his customers. (We did become loyal Avis customers!) What helped these individuals remember their trusts? I call it the steward paradigm. Through its eyes, we see ourselves as stewards, or caretakers, for some portion of society's resources and needs. We recognize we have been entrusted with something of great value to someone else. This sense of stewardship is best illustrated in a Walt Disney movie based on the true story of "Buddy," a female German Shepherd and the first seeing-eye dog in the United States.

• • •

Trained in Switzerland and brought over to the U.S. in the 1930s, Buddy had great difficulty changing people's stereotypes about dogs. Restaurants, department stores, post offices—virtually every public place outlawed dogs in the 1930s, thereby excluding Buddy's owner, Morris Frank, as well.

The Seeing Eye, an institute to train other dogs like Buddy, was organized. Then a bill was initiated and sent to the state legislature, seeking to legalize seeing-eye dogs in public places. As part of the legislative review process, Morris and Buddy were invited to the state capital to demonstrate the dog was not a public menace, but a gifted partner who could do wonderful things for the blind.

One state senator had arranged a test to see how good Buddy really was. Meeting in the assembly chamber of the state legislature, Morris and Buddy were greeted by the senator who said, "Make your way to the Speaker's rostrum." Unknown to Morris, there were some obstacles in their path. The senator wanted to see how well Buddy could handle tight situations.

Morris gave the command, "Buddy, forward!" The dog froze. "Forward! Forward!" Morris repeated. Buddy still didn't move. Finally, very hesitantly, she led him forward like this:

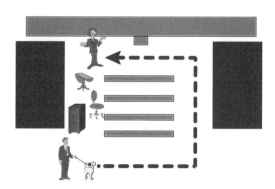

The senator was furious. "That's not fair!" he bellowed.

Of course, Morris wasn't aware of what was going on. He said, "Gentlemen, apparently you set up some obstacles for us. We have just witnessed a demonstration of what we call Intelligent Disobedience."

• • •

Intelligent disobedience was behind Buddy's eyes as she helped Morris walk through life. If he gave her any command that she knew would put him in peril, she was trained to find an alternative path to get him where he wanted to go. Buddy gave us a wonderful example of the natural law of adaptation: alter the process as necessary when environmental conditions threaten survival and well-being.

What a valuable lesson for every member of an organization to learn! *Intelligent disobedience*—don't blindly follow policies or procedures if they will actually defeat the greater purpose. Keep the whole picture in front of you. Be mission-centered. Choose responses that will safeguard your trusts. Be a faithful steward.

The steward paradigm is the antidote for the Forgotten Trust. It elevates our thinking from the details of the moment and keeps our focus on keeping our stakeholders' trusts. If situations arise that weren't envisioned when procedures or policies were defined, intelligent disobedience adapts to fulfill our mission, to serve the customer, to cut costs, and to eliminate bottlenecks.

Someone once said the difference between a politician and a patriot is that *a politician looks ahead to the next election; a patriot looks ahead to the next generation.* Haven't societies in all ages benefited from the legacy of great patriots—those men and women who moved beyond being politicians? In organizations we need to see ourselves not as someone's subordinate, but as society's steward.

Mission-centered leaders and organizations consistently produce evidence of this steward paradigm. At Ritz-Carlton it shows up throughout the Gold Standard, specifically in the motto, "We are ladies and gentlemen serving ladies and gentlemen." Nordstrom Department Stores call their steward paradigm Rule #1: "Use your good judgment in all situations." (There are no other rules!) Stewards believe that whoever sees the problem is responsible to resolve it. A Japanese-American client related a wonderful example of what this looks like:

• • •

While vacationing in Tokyo, my wife and I went to the Shihatsu department store to look at the new Sony Discman CD players. After looking at several models, I finally selected one to purchase. We were delayed slightly when the clerk misspelled my name on the credit card form. He tore up the form, filled in my name correctly on the new one, and finished the transaction.

After arriving at our relatives' home where we were staying, I pulled out the CD player and tried to demonstrate it for them, but the machine wouldn't play! I checked all the buttons and power cord. But it still wouldn't play. We finally determined this player had nothing inside its shell! Noting it was past closing time for the department store, I told my wife, "No problem. This is Japan. We'll take it back in the morning and exchange it."

The next morning before we had a chance to call the department store, there was a knock at the door. We were told some visitors were there for us. In the living room waiting for us were a distinguished-looking man with white hair and the clerk who had sold us the CD player! They had some packages in their arms.

The older man introduced himself as a vice president of the Shihatsu department store. He explained to us that after we had left the electronics counter, the clerk realized he had put the CD demo shell in our box by mistake. He immediately alerted security to watch all exits for us, but apparently we had already slipped out.

They first contacted every hotel in Tokyo where American business people typically stayed, with no luck finding us. Then they approached American Express because of the credit card receipt they had. In the early hours of the morning, they persuaded American Express to give them our home phone number in the United States. They rang the number and spoke with my in-laws who were babysitting our children. They gave them the phone number and address of our relatives in Tokyo.

"We have had some difficulty finding you," the vice president smiled. "But we want to correct our mistake." He then pulled out another CD player, showed me this one worked, and traded it for the demo model. "Because of the inconvenience we have caused you, we hope you will accept these gifts." They handed us the packages containing lovely bathroom towels and some CDs. Shaking our hands, they excused themselves again for any inconvenience they might have caused us and left.

Upon reaching their car, the older gentleman suddenly returned to our door. "I forgot one thing," he said. "I must also apologize for the inconvenience our associate caused you by misspelling your name on the credit card form. I hope you will forgive him—it was his first day on the job. He will do better next time!" With a polite bow, he returned to the car and they drove away.

• • •

How did the vice president know the clerk had misspelled the customer's name? The clerk had to volunteer that information. And how comfortable would a clerk feel, on his first day as a Shihatsu employee, to volunteer such information to a vice president if he couldn't trust how it would be handled? Trust is the real foundation of the Shihatsu culture.

The Saturn Corporation's Stewards

Whenever I discuss the steward paradigm, I immediately think of the Saturn Corporation. There isn't a better example of the lifecycle's ups and downs than the U.S. automobile industry. American cars shot to worldwide market dominance in their early years and stayed on top for decades before falling into recession as foreign competitors challenged them with better fuel economy, reliability, and luxury.

The biggest company in this scenario is General Motors. By the mid-1980s, many American consumers were doubtful that a GM car could provide the same value as a comparable Japanese or European model. Market shares and profits were plummeting. Within GM, managers privately acknowledged that the corporate culture often stifled creativity. So GM decided to create a new subsidiary—an organization that would have license to break with past traditions and prove an American car could compete with the best global competitors. Thus, the Saturn Corporation was born. Its challenge was expressed succinctly in a corporate film, "When you have been doing something longer than anyone else, how do you start over again?" And, how do you regain the trust of customers, suppliers, employees, and union leaders who have become suspicious, maybe even cynical, of company leadership?

An agreement with the United Auto Workers gave hiring preference to GM employees who were facing plant shutdowns in other locations. This meant the 9,000 people who would have to create the new paradigm were themselves products of the old one. Extensive consumer research was determining the car's features and state-of-the-art engineering was designing the technical specifications, but how would the Saturn production team ensure the final product was world class?

Saturn went about developing its new plant culture from the inside out. Everyone had to make GM's business (regain customers' trust) their business. The process began by clarifying Saturn's mission and philosophy with input from many members of the organization. The Saturn mission is:

Earn the loyalty of Saturn owners and grow our family by developing and marketing U.S. manufactured vehicles that are world leaders in quality, cost and customer enthusiasm through the integration of people, technology and business systems.

But, to bring this mission to life every Saturn member had to think about the many stakeholder needs he/she would have to fulfill. Notice how Saturn's philosophy specifies its sense of stewardship to its stakeholders:

Philosophy
We, the Saturn Team, in concert with the UAW and General Motors, believe that meeting the needs of Customers, Saturn Members, Suppliers, Retailers, Neighbors and Investors is fundamental to fulfilling our mission.

To meet our customers' needs:
• Our products and services must be world leaders in value and satisfaction.

To meet our members' needs:
• We will create a sense of belonging in an environment of mutual trust, respect and dignity.
• We believe that all people want to be involved in decisions that affect them, care about their jobs and each other, take pride in themselves and in their contributions and want to share in the success of their efforts.
• We will develop the tools, training and education for each member, recognizing individual skills and knowledge.
• We believe that creative, motivated, responsible team members who understand that change is critical to success are Saturn's most important assets.

To meet our suppliers' and retailers' needs:
• We will strive to create real partnerships with them.
• We will be open and fair in our dealings, reflecting trust, respect and their importance to Saturn.
• We want retailers and suppliers to feel ownership in Saturn's mission and philosophy as their own.

To meet the needs of our neighbors, the communities in which we live and operate:
• We will be good citizens, protect the environment and conserve natural resources.
• We will seek to cooperate with government at all levels and strive to be sensitive, open and candid in all our public statements.

To meet the needs of all Saturn investors:

• We will operate in a manner that promotes renewal and growth of the company and provides a competitive return for their investment and involvement in the business.

By continuously operating according to this philosophy, we will fulfill our mission.

Once crafted, this philosophy, along with Saturn's mission, was deeply communicated in all phases of organization building—selection, training, and team building. Labels such as "union" and "GM management" were subordinated to "Saturn team member." Whether the speaker was Saturn President Skip LeFauve or local union president Mike Bennett, the message of "Saturn team" was the same. The initial training program at Saturn was far more extensive than traditional GM approaches and had as a central focus the values and work systems innovations that would be needed to enable the Saturn team to restore the customer's faith in an American automobile.

The plant in Spring Hill, Tennessee began operation in 1990, and from the outset the Saturn car was well received by a curious public. In fact, customer enthusiasm presented its own test for Saturn's commitment to its mission, philosophy, and values. Sales took off far above predictions and many felt the pressure to speed up the production line to keep up with customer demand. As the production line speed increased, plant members responded by wearing armbands with a big "Q" (for quality). Why? Because they were concerned that a speed up would short-circuit their promise of world-class quality to their customers unless everyone stayed focused on quality!

In 1991, tests showed that antifreeze provided by a supplier was highly corrosive and could potentially damage the engine. Recall letters went out to 1,836 Saturn owners. The letters didn't promise to replace the antifreeze. They didn't promise to replace the radiator systems or even the engines. Saturn gave these owners brand new Saturns! Why do this? Because of the Saturn value that states: "We continually exceed the expectations of internal and external customers for products and services that are world leaders in cost, quality, and customer satisfaction. Our customers know that we really care about them."

Saturn President Skip LeFauve said, "The antifreeze decision (which cost $24 million) took about 20 minutes to finalize because it was based on our Mission, Philosophy, and Values. We discussed the potential loss of credibility with the public, but felt we either live our values or we don't. We've been fortunate that people have kept believing in us."

Saturn's resolve to live its values was tested before there was much evidence that it would win a place in the marketplace. What if the organization had responded in accordance with old habits? A skeptical public might have said, "Well, here they go again. They say Saturn's different, but this shows us that General Motors hasn't really changed anything!" Saturn's responses have been mission-centered from the beginning; Saturn has looked to its mission and values for guidance in tough times. And in so doing, Saturn's stewards won the trust of their customers. By its fifth year of production, Saturn had become the third best-selling model in America. J.D. Power consumer research consistently found Saturn among the top three in owner satisfaction and rated Saturn #1 in customer sales satisfaction.

As one indicator of its budding customer loyalty, on June 23-25, 1994, some 44,000 Saturn owners converged on Spring Hill to attend Homecoming. Patterned after the Harley-Davidson motorcycle company's family reunion, Saturn's Homecoming was a celebration and a thank you to all the car owners for helping make the first five years of business so successful. Committed owners came from all over. License plates from all 50 states and Canada were spotted in the parking lot. Even the first Saturn sold in Taiwan was there. The owner shipped his car to Los Angeles, then drove it to Tennessee.

Robin Millage from the small fishing village of Petersburg, Alaska was there. She bought her Saturn SL2 in 1990—sight unseen. Some time later, Saturn issued a recall on a seat part. Owners were instructed to go to their retailers, where they would replace the problem part. The closest retailer to Robin was more than 400 miles away. So Saturn sent the new seat and a retail consultant to her to make the switch! Now in 1994, Robin drove 3,000 miles to Spring Hill to show them she was still true blue.

A poster inside the plant best captured the moral of the Saturn story during the Homecoming tours. It read:

1985: If you build it they will come.

1994: We built it and they came.

As one Saturn's Ohio license plate at Homecoming put it, "Y BUY 4N." ("Why buy foreign?") And, all this has happened in an industry many were willing to concede to the Japanese just a few years ago!

Indeed, the company's first decade of production achieved some notable results. Saturn entered the twenty-first century as the fourth best selling car in its class. As of October 2000, Saturn had sold over 2.5 million cars since the first one rolled off "inspiration point" on July 30, 1990. The 2000 J.D. Power consumer research found Saturn's owner satisfaction to be second only to luxury model Lexus! The same study placed Saturn #1 in customer sales satisfaction in the U.S.—and Japan! Customer loyalty remained high as a second Homecoming celebration in 1999 drew even more than the 1994 event—over 60,000 owners. Saturn members have resisted numerous opportunities to subordinate their stewardship to other interests. The International UAW has twice called for a vote to abandon the Saturn partnership agreement and fall in line with the standard UAW-GM labor contract. Both times more than 70 percent of Saturn's members voted to maintain their unique partnership agreement.

But the path traveled to deliver these results has been anything but smooth. Competition has become more intense. A strong U.S. economy has drawn customers away from Saturn's low end to higher-priced models. As a result, both Saturn's sales and profitability have fallen in recent years. The organization is becoming more complex with the addition of a three-door coupe and mid-sized model in 1999 and a sport utility vehicle due out in late 2001. At the same time General Motors, in an effort to develop common product platforms for global competitiveness, has required Saturn to adapt some of its systems to fit within the global platform for each of its four models. Skip LeFauve and other Saturn pioneers retired or were moved to other parts of GM, leaving the corporation's fate in the hands of a new generation of leaders.

In the midst of all these changes, Saturn now faces a critical question: "As you blaze a new trail, how do you know when to change direction and when to stay the course?" Saturn's original mission, philosophy, and values set the direction for a very energized corporate culture and a successful business enterprise. But, the success formula of 1994 is not producing the same results today. Some things must change without eroding Saturn's original mission, philosophy, and values. Getting this right (what to change, what to keep the same) is what determines the future lifecycle of any organization. Get it right, and you will move to new heights. Fail to make the right changes, and you will follow in the declining footsteps of most companies.

One thing is certain: only adherence to natural laws will help Saturn "get it right" as it strategizes for the future. Saturn members must determine the ecological order for survival from the many (and often conflicting) stakeholder needs pressing down upon them. They must reaffirm their purpose and devise a new strategy that will keep many trusts. They must develop a new steady state that is consistent with their original purpose and with their strategy for handling the new complexities. They must mobilize every Saturn member to deliver this new steady state, increase the ways he/she can contribute to its success, and successfully partner with all others involved in the process to deliver new synergies and better results. In other words, they have to start over again and reapply the same principles that made them successful in the first place.

Adapting the organization to a changing environment is a formidable task. It is required at a time when many individuals would like to relax and enjoy their accomplishments of the first decade. Only stewards will pay the price to start over and align what they do with natural laws. Subordinates will begin the process, but cave in when some stakeholders start to give orders that contradict natural laws. Only stewards will keep the Saturn dream alive. Subordinates will tell us how others took over and ruined the company.

To Be Successful or To Leave a Legacy?

The examples cited in this chapter illustrate an important dynamic. Mission-centered leaders work from a steward paradigm instead of a subordinate paradigm. This brings each of them, sooner or later, to a fork in the road. They have to choose whether their primary mission is *to be successful or to leave a legacy.*

Think of these implications. As a steward, there may be occasions where you have to disregard your organization's rules, policies, and your boss's directives in order to keep your greater trusts. This is risky business. Cross the wrong people in your organization and you might get penalized! Careers have been derailed because of such "heresies." People usually succeed in organizations by playing by the rules, not breaking them.

On the other hand, how can you be a faithful steward if any one person or thing takes priority over mission, values, and stakeholder trust? Stewards, like patriots, look forward to the next generation. Certainly they want to be successful; but more importantly, they want to leave a legacy. These two targets are actually in different domains:

Being Successful:
- Defined by a few stakeholders
- Can be measured
- Plays by the rules
- Celebrated today

Leaving a Legacy:
- Defined by many stakeholders
- Hard to measure
- Subordinates rules to mission when necessary
- Celebrated today and tomorrow

As you can see, leaving a legacy requires a high level of proactivity. The rewards come largely from inside yourself. The rewards of success come largely from others.

Abraham Lincoln aptly summed up the credo of those who seek to leave a legacy when he said, "I do the very best I know how—the very best I can; and I mean to keep doing so until the end. If the end brings me out all right, what is said against me won't amount to anything. If the end brings me out wrong, ten angels swearing I was right would make no difference." Lincoln's "best" didn't please the Southern states at the time, but our generation looks back in gratitude to a patriot who kept America's principles above social rules of the day!

Let's consider another leader, and ask if he was successful. Here's a thumbnail chronology of his career:

• Age 19—withdrawn from college prep school because of a "conspicuous lack of success at his studies."

• Age 25—lost his first political election.

• Age 27—experienced great difficulty in mastering the skills of legislative debate.

• Age 32—rejected by his constituency due to his reputation for "radicalism."

• Age 34—lost an election after being labeled a traitor to his party.

• Age 41—removed from the executive cabinet because of disapproval of his policies.

• Age 48—lost election after speaking out on foreign affairs.

• Age 49—lost election.

• Age 50—lost election.

• Age 56—his views on Indians force his resignation.

• Age 57—exiled from power as both political parties thought him to lack "judgment, stability and discipline."

• Age 64—ignored by his fellow-citizens as he spoke out against the menace of Nazism.

Then at age 66, he pondered another try at public office.

What advice would you give this beleaguered politician? Why does he keep running? What should he do next? Let him tell you in his own words what he actually did:

"A call came from the king, summoning me to the palace. Upon entering, the king asked if I knew why he had called for me. I said, 'Your majesty, I have no idea.' . . . He said he wanted me to form a government . . . I felt as though I were walking with destiny! All that I had done up to that time was but a preparing for the task now before me. I thought I knew a great deal about it all and hadn't the slightest doubt we would succeed!"

Yes, this politician was Winston Churchill! He took office at an age most people are in retirement. But he rallied his country during its bleakest hours in World War II and kept its aim on victory.

Ironically, Churchill was defeated in the next election following the war! But this latest setback didn't dishearten him. He knew he had made a difference in the history of his people! Indeed, Churchill's unsuccessful politics failed to dim his legacy. His legacy is just as significant to his country as Lincoln's was to his. When the British government planned to lay a special brass plaque in the floor of Westminster Abbey to commemorate the valor of the Battle of Britain, they sought a slogan or phrase that would instantly rekindle each citizen's appreciation for the miraculous effort. Today, in that great hall you can read the simple words they chose: "Remember Winston Churchill."

When the aged statesman made his last appearance before Parliament, everyone was eager to hear his farewell message. Churchill tottered to the podium and said, "Never give up! Never, never give up!" Then he sat down! Those who knew Winston Churchill recognized these words embodied everything he stood for. There simply was no need for him to say anything more.

Conclusion

One of the curses of large organizations occurs when everyone feels like a subordinate. As soon as we begin to think, "I'm not in charge," we tend to act out of compliance rather than using our best judgment and doing our best in all situations. We stop thinking about the purpose of our work, being content to merely do our job. Such actions lead to the Forgotten Trust—people in organizations forgetting that they have been entrusted to make someone's life better. Only a paradigm shift from seeing ourselves as subordinates to seeing ourselves as stewards can overcome this Forgotten Trust.

Stewards naturally model mission-centered leadership. They clarify their most important values personally and organizationally and rely on these as their source of direction. Stewards also make a conscious choice about whether their ultimate aim is to be successful or to leave a legacy. Like Lincoln and Churchill, mission-centered leaders may not always be successful in the short term. But they are the ones who leave a legacy. Whenever the two paths (success/legacy) divide, stewards take the higher road! In the words of poet Robert Frost:

Two roads diverged in a wood, and I—
I took the one less traveled by,
And that has made all the difference.

In the next section, I will explore how mission-centered leaders earn enthusiastic followers by establishing a compelling, common purpose.

• • •

Applying what you have learned:

Here are some suggestions to put into action what you have learned in this chapter:

1. For each of your major stakeholders, list the fundamental trusts they place in your organization. Then give examples of how the subordinate paradigm or steward paradigm would respond to these trusts.

2. Discuss with your work group how the concept of "intelligent disobedience" could improve how well you safeguard stakeholder trusts.

Section

3

Shaping a Compelling, Common Purpose

5
Make Their Business
Your Business

"Profit is like oxygen. If you don't have enough, you won't be around for long; but if you think life is about breathing, you're missing something."
—Russell Ackoff

"We must love them both, those whose opinions we share and those whose opinions we reject. For both have labored in the search for truth and both have helped us in the finding of it."
—Thomas Aquinas

A MEMBER OF A VOLUNTEER GROUP CALLED one night to inform me he would not be able to take part in our project that evening. We were running short of people for this event as it was, and now this! I called a good friend, Pete, to see if he might be able to help me out.

"I'm sorry," he said, "but my daughter is flying in from out of town and my wife and I are going to meet her at the airport."

"Oh," I said with some disappointment in my voice.

"Wait a minute," Pete said. "You're in a tough spot, aren't you?"

"Well, yes," I replied.

"My wife can pick up our daughter," Pete said. "I will make it my business to be there tonight."

As soon as I heard the words, "I will make it my business to be there," I knew my problem was solved. I knew I could count on Pete.

• • •

Pete's choice of words got me thinking about the many organizations I associate with in a typical month. I invite you to do the same. How many employers, food stores, banks, schools, churches, temples, restaurants, government agencies, insurance companies, hospitals, physicians, repair specialists, builders, airlines, retailers, professional-service firms, amusement centers, and gas stations truly make our business their business? How many of them place as much value on our needs as we do? Our answers probably correlate with the number of individuals who have shifted from the subordinate paradigm to the steward paradigm. Yet, those few who do make our business their business earn our unwavering loyalty.

The ability to meet people's needs and honor their trust separates ageless organizations from those who eventually fade from the scene. You will recall one of the natural laws of living systems is ecological order—all elements of a natural ecosystem either fit into the order of things or they perish. Every organization exists in an ecosystem of stakeholder needs. A stakeholder is anyone who has a stake in the organization's well being—customers, suppliers, associates, communities, families. If your organization would endure, you must (1) identify which important stakeholder needs you intend to address, (2) commit all your organizational resources to meet those needs (make their business your business), and (3) consistently fulfill the needs.

The following three chapters will address numbers (1) and (2) in this overall process. In this chapter I will review some paradigms and practices for developing an information system that will enable you to identify your stakeholders' most important needs. Chapter 6 will examine how to go about shaping and committing to a compelling, common purpose. Chapter 7 will then look at how to align purposes at the team, department, and organizational levels. Let's begin by looking at how we think about stakeholders and their needs.

Shareholder Value or Stakeholder Value?

In recent years, it has been debated whether a company's focus should be to build shareholder value or stakeholder value. Public companies on the stock exchange feel intense pressure from their shareholders to improve results NOW. Yet, responding only to shareholder needs can lead to neglect of other needs, such as the environment, associate well being, and future innovation. And, the debate rages on: should you build shareholder value or stakeholder value? First, let's consider this debate from the legal world. What is the purpose of a U.S. corporation, *as defined by law?*

A) To maximize returns for shareholders *or*

B) To serve the interests of shareholders and other stakeholders

If you chose A, you are wrong! In most states (corporate law is decided at the state level), the answer is B. In the past decade 29 states have passed laws that explicitly permit (and even encourage) the corporate directors to consider the interests of a broad community of stakeholders when deciding what is best for the corporation.

Regardless of legal definitions, there is a compelling, pragmatic reason to see your organization as serving more people than just your shareholders and customers. In reality, you can't meet shareholder needs better than your competition without other stakeholders' deep commitment to "making their business our business." Even if all your associates were completely committed, it wouldn't be enough to guarantee a competitive advantage. What about those who supply your raw materials, or provide support services, or deliver your product to the customer? What if you did a 100 percent job and your stakeholders did a 50 percent job? You would eventually lose in the global market.

Consider this statement from Japan's Association of Corporate Executives: "Traditionally, the relationship of companies to their stakeholders has been expressed using such terms as 'putting the customer first,' 'putting the employees first,' or 'maintaining stable shareholders.' We, however, believe that the term 'stakeholder' should be defined to include any party that plays a role in supporting an organization's long-term success. Thus, every manager needs to be aware that the organization's survival is dependent not only on its customers, employees, shareholders, and distributors, but in a larger sense on the global community as a whole. Working to build mutual trust with all of these stakeholders is of vital importance and is in essence the definition of management."

Legally and pragmatically there should be no debate on whether to meet shareholder needs or stakeholder needs. The realities of your global ecosystem require you to address both. You might as well say to someone, "Which would you rather have, your heart or your brain?" One without the other is useless (and lifeless!).

The key in any ecosystem, even that of stakeholder needs, is balance. Natural ecosystems shape many disparate and conflicting forces into a balanced cycle that enhances each element's ability to survive and grow. This means you need an information system that continuously:

1. Identifies your key stakeholders (those who are critical to your survival and growth)

2. Determines their most important needs (what they hope to gain from their association with you)

3. Decides which of those needs your organization will meet and not meet

These three critical steps will allow your organization to fit into the order of things. Not all stakeholders are of equal importance to your organization. Not all of their needs are critical for your survival. You may not be in a position to meet all of their needs and expectations. And all of these needs certainly will evolve and change over time. So, Job #1 in any organization is to put in place a process that continually studies the global market-place and chooses how to fit in.

This choice is called defining your purpose. It may consist of such elements as a mission, vision, strategy, core values, objectives, goals, and other measures. Your purpose defines your business. And, if that purpose also addresses your stakeholders' important needs, then you have made their business your business.

Making their business your business is a high standard. You may be succeeding today at some lesser level, but that's only because competition hasn't caught on yet. The global market will educate them soon enough. Your challenge is to put these dynamics in place before they do.

To See Ourselves As Others See Us

The best way to understand the most important needs of your various stakeholders is to put yourself in their shoes and look at yourself as they see you. Unfortunately, we are all like the wealthy woman observed by the Scottish poet Robert Burns centuries ago:

• • •

Burns was sitting in his little community church one Sunday when the wealthiest woman in the county moved in front of him to sit down in her pew. She was elegantly dressed in her furs and finest clothing. But as she sat down right in front of Robert's face, he noticed something moving on her hat. It was a louse! Burns smiled, sat back and thought to himself, "She has all this money and a grand reputation. She has obviously taken great care to look her best—and if she could only see what I see right now, she would be mortified!" Reflecting on this episode later, Burns wrote an ode "To a Louse," which includes these lines:

O wad some Pow'r the giftie gie us
Tae see oorsels as ithers see us!
It wad frae monie a blunder free us
An' foolish notion.

(Translation: "Oh would some power the gift could give us,
to see ourselves as others see us!
It would from many a blunder free us
and foolish notion.")

• • •

Like Robert Burns' neighbor, we all have blind spots that make us vulnerable. Not only are we unaware of how some things impact our stakeholders, seldom do we examine the various stakeholder views as part of "the order of things" for our ecosystem. We tend to look at each stakeholder one at a time. Our fragmented view makes it more difficult to settle issues that are a function of the whole ecosystem's dynamics, things such as:

• How are stakeholder needs evolving over time and what changes should we make (if any) in response to them?

• What developments in one area are affecting the others?

• What are the patterns (similarities, differences) in these evolving stakeholder needs? Do these patterns require any changes in our purpose?

An effective strategic information system can help you answer such questions. This system enables you to see both inside and outside your organization; it can help you decide what needs to change and what needs to remain stable. Step one to making their business your business is to see your organization and its products and services through the eyes of your various stakeholders. Let's learn how one very successful CEO helped his entire organization do this.

The Moments of Truth

Some years ago, Jan Carlzon, then CEO of Scandinavian Air Lines (SAS), coined the phrase "the moments of truth." These moments determine whether or not your customers or other stakeholders stay with you. He estimated SAS's annual business was made up of 50 million such moments, each lasting an average of 15 seconds. For SAS customers, they include such things as:

- You get the seat you reserved.
- The magazines you like to read are available on board.
- You are served the special meal you ordered.
- The flight attendants are competent and cheerful.
- You take off and arrive on time.
- Your baggage arrives promptly and in good condition.
- Any problems are solved quickly and courteously.

These moments of truth define *what the customer wants to see.* This is a healthy paradigm to begin your pursuit of finding and fitting into the order of your stakeholders' needs. What are the moments of truth as seen by your organization's key stakeholders?

One good way to identify some moments of truth is to ask your shareholders, customers, suppliers, employees, and community agencies what they hope to gain from their relationship with you. Another valuable exercise is to look at your organization through the eyes of your customers (or any other stakeholder)—to interact with your organization purely as they would. For instance:

- Call your organization's main telephone number and ask a question that requires someone to return your call.
- Write a letter complaining about a product you bought or service you received.
- Take advantage of a free offer from one of your own advertisements.
- Make a request that falls outside of normal policy.

After a few interactions, it will become clear to you that the only thing you see as a customer or stakeholder is the end product or service. Everything else is hidden, as it should be. The second thing you'll observe is that your effectiveness isn't what you hoped it would be. Experiments like this will show you why many of the things that occupy your attention are of little interest to your customers. As a sign reminded me some years ago, "The fact that we are a multi-divisional, multi-functional, multi-cultural, multi-plant, multi-product company is not the customer's problem."

• • •

Fred was a vice president of a Fortune 500 company. As part of a major restructuring effort in his company, he was asked to interview three retail customers who sold his products. His assignment was to understand their moments of truth when dealing with his company. After the interviews, Fred made a most interesting statement to me. "I've been with this company 27 years, but had never actually spoken to a retail customer until last week. I was amazed at some of the things they want us to do for them. Many of the things that were important to them were administrative and service items. I had no idea they wanted these things from us. The wonderful part is that if we can deliver these things, they will help them, they will help our business, and it won't cost us a penny. We can do these things right away and strengthen our business."

• • •

The Stakeholder Ecosystem

If you look at your organization through the eyes of several stakeholders, a new picture will emerge. You will see how all your stakeholders form a field of "moments of truth" surrounding you. Your ability to fulfill their moments of truth is what props you up and prevents you from sliding down the lifecycle. And, you will recognize that each stakeholder only supports you as long as you fulfill his/her needs. Fulfill these moments of truth and your organization will prosper. But how do you know which few to fulfill? How do you handle all of these conflicting demands and expectations? To shape and maintain a healthy balance, remember three points:

• *You won't be able to meet all stakeholder needs.* Many will contradict each other. Trying to optimize all the pieces will suboptimize the whole—your organization! One of the critical leadership tasks is to choose which needs to fulfill and which to pass up. But, first you have to know what all the needs are before you can choose which ones to focus on.

• *The best way to serve any one stakeholder is to meet all critical stakeholder needs.* Not every one of their needs, but the critical few (e.g., moments of truth) that will make or break them, and you. As with any ecosystem, whenever you seek to maximize the interests of one element at the expense of another, you may end up hurting the very ones you are seeking to help. For example, what if you tried to maximize the interests of your customers at the expense of your associates' or community's needs? The result might be higher turnover and poor community relations to the point that you were no longer able to serve your customers well. Similarly, maximizing associates' needs for job security and income might place you in such an unprofitable position that you would have to close your doors—thereby destroying the very security and income you were trying to establish.

• *If you fail to satisfy the moments of truth for any stakeholder, you may lose their support, thus disrupting your delicate balance.* You might fall as they pull away! This is the frustrating but real paradox of an ecosystem. The best way to care for any one part of the system is to care for all parts. But, in the attempt to serve all, you can't afford to shortchange anyone.

Here is the really challenging part of the whole equation: these stakeholder needs are ever changing. You can't just determine today's moments of truth and organize yourself to meet them and then sit back. You have to develop a system to regularly take the pulse of all these stakeholders. You need a dynamic information system.

The Balanced Scorecard

Many organizations have started using a "balanced scorecard," a short list of key success targets representing all major stakeholder needs. Accompanying the balanced scorecard is a tracking system for monitoring the progress in each area. Such a balanced scorecard and tracking system are prerequisites to survival in the global market. But, all too often the balanced scorecard has been defined without adequate dialogue and analysis of the various stakeholder needs. How can you avoid some of the typical mistakes when creating a balanced scorecard?

The first step is to identify the moments of truth like Jan Carlzon did. Next, you must translate these moments of truth into concrete measures. What results must you achieve in order to satisfy each moment of truth? Once SAS took this step, its managers learned they were expected to deliver certain things, but were measuring others. Cargo shipments are a good example of this dynamic.

• • •

The SAS cargo division's primary success measure had always been shipment volume. This measure, of course, was meaningless to the customers. They wanted their cargo delivered promptly to the right location. SAS employees eventually designed a QualiCargo system to measure the moments of truth. The new measurement system tracked performance of things like:
- How quickly do we answer the telephone?
- Did we meet the promised deadline?
- Did the cargo arrive on the scheduled plane?
- How long was it before the package was ready to be picked up?

By measuring its performance against items like these and continuously improving what people did, SAS improved its on-time delivery rate from 80 percent to over 90 percent. They became the best air cargo shipper in Europe! (Coincidentally, their volume and revenues also grew steadily during this time.)

• • •

An effective balanced scorecard requires four kinds of information that are critical to your organization's survival:

1. Financial measures. All organizations have this, though many financial measures are not linked to other elements of the balanced scorecard. For example, one airline's volume and revenues were growing so fast that they overwhelmed the baggage handling system and staffing schedules. Thousands of bags were being lost each month and key employees were overworked until they finally quit. The airline soon went out of business. Part of the significance of the balanced scorecard lies in its ability to measure the parts and to see their impact on each other and on the whole.

2. Stakeholder feedback. This feedback should focus on the moments of truth: (a) What does this stakeholder hope to gain from your mutual relationship? (b) How well are you delivering against their hopes? (c) What could you do to improve?

3. Benchmarking. Staying atop the lifecycle also requires you to innovate, improve, and change more effectively than your competition as the world moves on. Only those who truly transcend the status quo can sustain "more with less" over time. *Benchmarking* is the practice of comparing what you are doing with *the best in the world* at that task, regardless of whether or not they are in your field.

4. Mission check. Those who are mission-centered need to know how well they are meeting the spirit of their chosen mission. The feedback in this area is a synthesis of the other three information systems and can only be processed from the inside out, from your *conscience.* This is perhaps the most rigorous feedback of all, for you can't fool yourself when someone asks you, "How are you *really* doing?"

If you are passionately committed to your organization staying on top of the lifecycle, you won't be satisfied until you have discovered what the moments of truth are for each stakeholder (from their viewpoint). Then you will use these moments of truth to draw up your measurements and monitoring processes. And, you will engage in measuring and monitoring with only one agenda: to truly understand yourself (your organization) as others see you.

Your organization probably already has a sound financial accounting system. In the next few pages, therefore, I would like to explore the other three information elements—stakeholder feedback, benchmarking, and the mission check.

Stakeholder Feedback

Stakeholder feedback helps you monitor the strength of your relationship with all those whose support is essential for you to fulfill your mission. Let me summarize the elements that make stakeholder feedback useful:

• It measures how well you are meeting the moments of truth for each major stakeholder.

• It's not a one-time event, but a process that is repeated periodically.

• It's used as part of a larger continuous improvement process to strengthen your ability to make their business your business.

• It provides input for both the diagnosis and prescription to improve what you do.

• It's most beneficial when coupled with organizational tools like the Organization Performance Model (to be discussed in chapter 8). This enables you to link stakeholder data with the root causes of your current performance. Stakeholder feedback should tell you as much about your own paradigms, assumptions, and values as it does about how stakeholders see your performance. This helps you get to the source rather than work only on symptoms.

Notice that I have said nothing about surveys, questionnaires, or performance appraisal instruments. Such appraisal instruments may play a part in gathering stakeholder feedback, but the end state is more than its components. Think of the process this way: You communicate periodically with your key stakeholders, you learn how others see you, you diagnose how their feedback relates to fulfilling your mission, and then you prescribe corrective action to improve your performance. As you engage in this process over time, everyone's economic well-being and quality of life are enhanced.

Watch for evidence of this process as a school administrator relates how he and his faculty interacted with one stakeholder group:

• • •

Over the past decade, as our schools began to look more broadly at all of our stakeholders—primarily by sending surveys out to the homes—we discovered that there was a large and growing "home school" movement in the area. Many families in our district needed schedule flexibility for their children that the schools were unable to give. In other cases, many felt they could provide a better education for their children at home.

Well, when the magnitude of this movement was discovered, a group got together and approached the customer through the state's home school organization. They said, in essence, "Look, we've really had an antagonistic relationship in the past, because we get funded by daily membership. Our position has been that any parent who took their kids out of school was hurting us financially. We've also believed that we can educate your children better because we are professionals. As a result, we've built up significant barriers over the years. We have not listened to your needs. But you are a significant tax-paying population. Let's see if we can create a win-win relationship."

Over the past five years, some remarkable things have occurred in all of our districts. First, they've stopped fighting with these home schoolers. They even take this approach: "You are taxpayers, this is your school, too. What parts of the school do you want to access? When do you want to use the gymnasium? What textbooks are you interested in using? Would any of your students like to participate in the athletic programs?" And in that process, the home schoolers have opened up and said, "Well, you know we really don't have enough activities for social studies, what do you recommend? How can we access your computers and educational software?" And so we've formed a working partnership by listening to that particular stakeholder group.

Stakeholder feedback is no magic elixir for solving your problems; it merely provides the forum from which to explore relevant issues. But, this forum's structure can help you see some of your blind spots, as a public accounting firm learned:

· · ·

Smith Accounting had seven partners and 40 employees engaged in normal audit and tax work. Smith Accounting made money by billing hours for its services. Each partner was responsible individually to bring new clients into the practice. As they did this, they would assign staff accountants to work on their projects. Staff accountants were recognized and compensated for the number of hours they billed. Consequently, they had incentive to accept the assignments from the partners and get as many billable hours as possible. Commonly, they would commit over 100 percent of their time to gain favor with partners.

After a few successful years, the partners recognized they were barely tapping into the synergy their organization might produce. So, they initiated a stakeholder feedback process and began to monitor their performance accordingly. The initial results showed clients were extremely satisfied with the services they received from Smith Accounting. However, staff accountants described several areas of difficulty they experienced at work, such as the way decisions were made, how planning was done, and how everyone was being rewarded.

These complaints surprised the partners, who wondered if the report could be accurate. Since there were only 40 employees, the Chief Operating Officer decided to interview all of them to verify the results of the report. He discovered the report was completely accurate. "Why didn't you ever say anything to us about these issues before now?" the bewildered COO asked. "Because we're all so busy getting our work done, there has never been any mechanism to talk about such things," several individuals responded. The partners carefully studied the feedback data and prescribed a few actions to improve their results. Smith Accounting continues to grow in both market competitiveness and profitability—and has built trust internally because they acted on their associates' feedback.

• • •

Let's consider the hidden contribution of trustworthy leadership. What kind of answers would this COO have gathered in his interviews if the employees felt threatened by his questioning? Or if the company had a history of shooting the bearer of bad news? Chances are, if the surveyor can't be trusted, neither can the survey responses!

The stakeholder feedback process can help you pinpoint emerging stakeholder needs, thus opening up new strategic avenues. Here's an example from the music industry:

• • •

Fletcher Music Centers in Clearwater, Florida sells organs. By conducting focus groups with senior citizens, its main clientele, the company found that what they wanted wasn't so much a musical instrument as companionship. Fletcher's whole sales approach was modified to meet this need, with free group lessons accompanying the purchase of every organ. Additionally, Fletcher organs are designed particularly for this group of buyers—large type on the keys and outsized knobs that are easier to manipulate for people with arthritis. Within a few years, Fletcher's revenues grew to $24 million.

• • •

These are only a few examples of effective stakeholder feedback playing a significant role in moving an organization up the lifecycle and helping it to stay on top.

Benchmarking

Another dimension of a balanced scorecard is the regular monitoring of how you compare with the global marketplace. This practice is known as benchmarking and has become popular in the age of downsizing. There is no natural law that says benchmarking must result in downsizing. The appropriate action must be defined by the context of the organization's environment and its alignment with its purpose. Many organizations benchmark their work processes, staffing levels, and financial measures against the best in their industry simply to understand where they stand in the global marketplace. This feedback helps them choose realistic, but challenging improvement targets.

The most dramatic breakthroughs have come, however, from those organizations that use a true global benchmark—not just the best in one industry, but the very best in the world at whatever is being studied. Here's an example of what I mean:

• • •

One manufacturing company had been struggling for years to increase the speed of its production changeovers. Typically, the production team needed 72 hours to readjust the equipment settings to run a different product. But, customer demand for product variations was driving the need for faster turnaround times and the company was beginning to lose business because of its slow changeovers. Finally, a team member, who was also a NASCAR driver, got the idea of treating the changeover process like a pit stop. His new paradigm of the situation led managers to ask the question, "How would we handle this changeover if we were a pit crew?" With this in mind, they made process changes that accomplished the same complicated adjustments in a mere three hours!

• • •

As this manufacturer learned, a paradigm shift could cause amazing changes in how the company functioned. Another example:

• • •

My neighbor and produce wholesaler Mike Bledsoe approached me one day after reading that Procter & Gamble and Wal-Mart hoped to reduce their inventory levels (amount of product stored in their warehouses) from 21 days to nine days through their new partnership. "I couldn't help but smile when I read that in the *Wall Street Journal,*" Mike said. "If I had even nine days of inventory in my warehouses, I'd have a lot of spoiled fruit and vegetables to unload. I'll bet if you treated Crest toothpaste as if it were perishable, you'd find a way to cut those nine days down to two."

• • •

What a way to shift a paradigm! Apply this global notion of benchmarking against some of your most critical processes:
• Who is the best in the world at transmitting information simultaneously to many geographically-dispersed locations?
• Who is the best teaching organization in the world?
• Who manufactures something with zero defects, with the lowest case costs, and with unparalleled flexibility?
• Who ships cases of product or materials better, faster, and cheaper than anyone else?
• Who is the best at serving their customers?
• Who makes sound decisions quickly, yet with real input and buy-in from many parties?
Think about how much better government laws and policies would be if governments treated them like a new product and benchmarked what they did against the world's best consumer products companies! Such "competition" could truly enrich the quality of life for all of us!

Mission Check

"When you're up to your neck in alligators, it's hard to remember that you originally started to drain the swamp." This popular saying is all too true in our organizational world. But, those who fail to take the time to consider how they are doing against their fundamental purpose, mission, or vision may be surprised and disappointed at how their actions have strayed from their original intentions. One of my clients tells of this traumatic experience:

• • •

I was talking with one of our vice presidents, a man with over 30 years in the business and someone who had written his "purpose and value statement" at the time he started working for us. In his statement, he described how people should and would be treated. Ironically, as we sat together, he was being kicked out, forced into early retirement ahead of his own schedule. And, we were both lamenting the company's upcoming massive reduction in force. At one point in the conversation, this man's voice broke and his eyes welled up, and he said, "You know, these people . . . we are really hurting them. These are our colleagues, these are our friends. These people, some of them, have been my friends for decades. And we are hurting them really bad!

"How did this happen," he asked. "How could we let this happen to them?" There was a long pause while we both considered what was happening and that we had no answer for it.

• • •

All the logical justifications in the world couldn't erase the profound question from this man's conscience, "How could we let this happen to them?" When leaders take the time to monitor what their conscience says to them, such questions are raised before regrettable, irreversible decisions have been made. The

Mission-Centered Models I introduced in chapter 3 summarize an effective way to use your conscience in leadership.

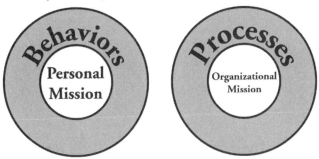

Whether the issue is how to treat your spouse, your supplier, or how to handle a reduction in force, use your personal and organizational missions to help you make decisions. Look to such principles for directing your behaviors and processes. These principles will be a better source of security than any special interest or short-term expediency. A wonderful example of this process comes from the Kenner Toy Corporation:

• • •

In the late 1970s and early 1980s, Kenner Toys was enjoying unparalleled success due to its top-selling "Star Wars" toys and games. Kenner executives were approached one day by the makers of "Rambo," a film about a Vietnam Special Forces veteran who wages a one-man war against local law enforcement officials. The filmmakers wanted to license Kenner to produce the Rambo line of toys.

As the Kenner executive team considered this invitation, their thoughts centered upon their corporate values, one of which was to only manufacture and market toys that would have a positive influence on the world's children. Because of the extreme violence and bloodshed associated with Rambo, the executive team felt its message crossed over the line prescribed by their values. Though they knew the Rambo toys would be a very lucrative deal for whoever produced them, Kenner graciously declined the filmmaker's offer.

Whether or not you agree with Kenner's decision is not the point. What is important is that they were in agreement about what to do. Their agreement was driven by their values. They felt they had been true to their conscience. And, Kenner's culture came out stronger because of the time they took to ponder the business offer after checking it against their mission and values.

Subordinate Everything Else to the Mission

Managing a balanced scorecard and the feedback associated with it is not always easy to absorb. You might be surprised, shocked, disappointed, and upset to learn what different stakeholders really think about your organization. But, if you allow your pride, ego, or your paradigm of reality to govern your response, then you are pushing your mission from your center and putting these other drivers in its place. And, all you've invested in the feedback system will now be at the mercy of your emotions or ego when it is time to take action. Here's a good example:

• • •

I once worked with a client who invited an executive of a large retail chain (a seller of my client's products) to address its general managers. The theme of the session was "Satisfying Customer Needs." The guest speaker had prior experience as an executive with one of my client's competitors. He had lived on both sides of the fence. At the outset of his presentation, this executive said, "I'd like to share with you how we look at your operation; how we tend to judge your company—and all of our suppliers—from our viewpoint."

Then he listed the following factors:

1. Are your products available at the time we need them?

2. Are your special promotions aligned with ours? (Do your "50¢ Off" coupons come at a time when we are prepared to give you maximum display space?)

3. What's the cycle time?

4. How flexible are your sales incentives? (Are they relevant?)

5. How compatible are your displays with our arrangements?

Continuing, he said, "We took the liberty of giving you a rating, either average, above average, or below average. And here is the report card we would fill out for you."

	−	Average	+
1. Product available on time		✔	
2. Alignment of promotions	✔		
3. Cycle time			✔
4. Incentive flexibility	✔		
5. Compatible displays	✔		

My clients, naturally, had great pride in their company. They felt they were the best. What happened when this customer told them they were average to below average in all five categories? People were suffering—silently—throughout the room.

Then the speaker said, "I told my associates when we did this rating, 'I can't go to this company and evaluate them like this without some kind of documentation or examples.'" He continued, "Your company announced a special promotion on a product. We advertised it in our flyers that go out to all the houses and the color supplements in the newspapers. We advertised it for the week of February 14 and we didn't get the product until February 28." In the back corner of the room, the general manager of this product's division suddenly went pale. Then the speaker gave further examples, item by item, which had led to these ratings.

How do you suppose these leaders responded to this message? They were very defensive. Of all the presenters in this three-day conference, this speaker received the lowest rating of all. Participants wrote down comments like, "Made sweeping generalizations from a few isolated incidents. Very opinionated with sketchy data. Hard to follow. Not logical."

• • •

This company espoused a deep commitment to serving its customers whether they were retailers or consumers. The speaker had been carefully chosen because of his experience and insights on both sides of the fence. And what was his message? "If you look at the business through our eyes, you are average to below average. Can we work together to improve things?" But, this executive's message was hard for my clients to hear. What amount of meaningful corrective action could come out of such a session? Very little, as long as pride and their own paradigm of their performance took priority over the mission. Ignoring such feedback only delays—and never eliminates—the results that will flow naturally from the current situation. Remember, True North doesn't move according to our perceptions or desires!

It is occasions like this that demonstrate the importance of becoming truly mission-centered—of subordinating everything else to your mission. What if the general manager of the late-shipping division, instead of sitting back in embarrassment, leaned forward to better understand what his customer was saying? What if, in the spirit of seeking better alignment and restoring trust, he sought out the speaker afterwards and asked for help to improve so that such things never happened again? Let your primary allegiance be to your mission rather than your ego and your own comfort zone. Missions aligned with natural laws will never lead you down the lifecycle; they can only move you up. Our own idiosyncrasies and emotions are what cause our downfall.

The following is a good bottom line to gauge the effectiveness of your information system: have you experienced any major surprises in the marketplace lately? I contend that any time you experience traumatic surprises like labor strikes, sudden marketplace swings, government regulations, competition's moves, etc., it can be traced to the lack of, or a poorly functioning, information system. The events themselves might not be prevented by such a system, but their surprise factor could be greatly reduced by timely feedback.

To sum up, using your stakeholders' moments of truth to shape your organizational mission and then acting in mission-driven ways is essential to making their business your business. In conclusion, let's see an example of how all the elements of the balanced scorecard can work together to help sustain you on your lifecycle.

Hillenbrand Industries: Balanced Scorecard and the Bottom Line

Hillenbrand Industries, located in Batesville, Indiana, has pioneered a new product that benefits society and has built its bottom line—all because it effectively utilized the elements of a balanced scorecard.

• • •

Through its subsidiary, The Batesville Casket Company, Hillenbrand Industries has earned a reputation as a supplier of choice in the funeral service industry. Until 1970, nearly all funerals were arranged within two or three days of a person's death. But, a steady change toward arranging funerals several years in advance of need has grown at a rate of 15 percent per year. In 1995, the number of pre-arranged funerals in the United States equaled the number of deaths; today, there are twice as many funerals pre-arranged as there are funerals held.

In view of these developments, funeral directors approached Batesville Casket Company, asking for guaranteed delivery and price of caskets for pre-arranged funerals. *(Stakeholder Feedback)* The requests were like asking a car dealer to guarantee delivery and price of a car at some unknown time in the future, even though the effects of price inflation and model changes are unknown. Batesville Casket executives wondered how to meet these requests responsibly. So they set out to understand the needs of all stakeholders in this emerging market and find a way to fulfill their moments of truth.

Most people paid for their pre-arranged funeral in one of two ways. Either they placed funds in a trust, or they bought an insurance policy. But, neither method of payment was completely satisfactory. Funds placed in trust incur taxes every year. Insurance policies typically require health questions that disqualify funeral planners, who average over 60 years of age. *(Benchmarking)*

Hillenbrand analysts compared funeral price increases with scores of inflation indices. They learned that funeral prices grew at the same rate as a common measure of inflation. *(Financial Measures)*

They also surveyed consumers and funeral directors to discover what they were seeking in pre-arranged funerals. They learned that consumers wanted to agree today on goods and services, pay today's price, and then be done. They wanted to tell their families, "Everything is taken care of. All you have to do is call the cemetery." Funeral directors wanted to be sure that inflation wouldn't erode the profitability of their services, and they wanted to be sure that they could deliver what they promised. *(Stakeholder Feedback)*

Though no solution was available to create such a win-win outcome, Hillenbrand executives knew their many customers really needed a new product. They made it their business to find a solution. No one would have blamed them if they hadn't found one. But, in their hearts, the Hillenbrand executives didn't feel they would really be serving their customers until they came up with a good solution. *(Mission Check)*

Eventually, a small group conceived of an insurance policy with no health questions, issued in the exact amount of today's funeral price, whose value was guaranteed to grow at that rate of inflation. But, they couldn't find an insurance company that would offer such a policy. So in 1985, Hillenbrand created what is now known as Forethought Financial Services (FFS) to satisfy the needs of consumers, funeral directors, and the Batesville Casket Company.

FFS is a special purpose insurance company that guarantees policies to consumers and inflation-adjusted payments to funeral directors. It provides funeral planning marketing services to funeral directors. Batesville Casket Company guarantees availability of a line of caskets and FFS guarantees prices. FFS has become the leader in the funeral planning industry. It had revenues of over $300 million in 1999 and is well positioned to meet the needs of an aging baby boom population.

• • •

Conclusion

The first step in "making their business your business" is to deeply understand what "their business" is. The balanced scorecard is a good tool to help you see the panorama of your world. It can reduce some potentially harmful blind spots. Once you understand what "their business" is, you must choose which of these needs will become "your business." This leads to the next step in establishing purpose—shaping a compelling mission that satisfies the critical moments of truth. In the next chapter we will see how timeless leaders have approached this challenging task.

• • •

Applying what you have learned:

Some exercises to put into action what you have learned in this chapter:

1. Talk with representatives of each of your major stakeholders to see how they define their moments of truth in your relationship.

2. For each moment of truth identified in #1, define a specific measurement (result) that will tell you whether or not you have met their needs.

119

3. Discuss with your work group how you might create your own ongoing stakeholder feedback process. Create a mechanism for people on the front line to get direct customer feedback.

4. Based on your stakeholder feedback, select one core process that needs to be better aligned. Go through the benchmarking exercise to expand your vision of how this process might be improved to deliver best-in-class results.

5. As part of #1, let your stakeholders read your mission statement and ask for their evaluation of where you are fulfilling it and where you are falling short. Ask for specific examples of each.

6
Shaping Compelling Missions

"Throughout the centuries there were men who took first steps down new roads armed with nothing but their own vision."

—Ayn Rand

"The greatest discovery of my generation is that human beings can alter their lives by altering their attitudes of mind."

—William James

THE RELATIONSHIP BETWEEN STAKEHOLDER feedback and the organization's mission is a great example of synergy. Stakeholder feedback, as we saw in the previous chapter, helps you shape the mission; the mission in turn helps you interpret new feedback and guides your responses to it. Each part enhances the other one's contribution in defining the organization's purpose.

Many organizations have started writing mission statements in recent years. Almost everywhere you go you see impressively framed statements hanging in corporate lobbies and conference rooms. They are referred to in annual reports and at shareholders meetings. Executives quote from them at management gatherings. But, how many of these carefully crafted statements really influence what goes on every day? The following experience made me wonder about this.

• • •

I had been on the road all day, it was getting late, and I was starving! Entering the restaurant's lobby, my eyes were drawn to the mission statement on the wall behind the cash register. The statement read something like this:

"Our mission is to provide our customers with a high quality dining experience in a home-like atmosphere."

This sounded awfully good to me! I was prepared to let the restaurant fulfill its mission. My eyes moved down from the mission statement. Sitting below it and behind the cash register was the cashier, reading a novel. She was completely immersed in her reading. After several seconds of standing around, I coughed to catch her attention.

"Oh, do you want to eat?" she asked, as she looked up from her reading.

"Yes, that's why I came in."

"Over there." She pointed to a doorway as her nose again disappeared into the book.

Moving to the doorway, I saw a sea of activity with people running back and forth. I stood there waiting for a while before trying to get someone's attention. "Excuse me, could I get a table?" I asked.

"Just a minute, I'm busy," a waitress said as she scurried off to the kitchen. Eventually a woman came and seated me, but didn't give me a menu. After several minutes I got a waitress' attention, "Pardon me, could I get a menu?"

"Just a second, I'm busy." At this point I began to understand what the restaurant meant by a "home-like atmosphere." In my own home this is the line my children have used when asked to help get dinner ready—"Hold on! I'm busy." I was beginning to comprehend the restaurant's mission statement!

The food was late, cold, and not very tasty, and I had to compete with the novel for the cashier's attention in order to pay my bill. I walked out of the restaurant vowing never to go there again. Yet, the mission statement had been so promising. My conclusion was no one took it seriously.

Interestingly enough, I was in another city sometime later and passed by another one of these restaurants. All the windows were boarded up. In my home community there used to be one of these same restaurants. It, too, has closed.

• • •

Could there be a connection between the owners, managers, and associates not taking their own mission statement seriously and all of the closed-down restaurants? If they had really developed a high quality dining experience and home-like atmosphere, would they have gone out of business?

Research tells us this restaurant's mission statement experience is typical of most organizations. Some years ago, a poll found that 85 percent of the Fortune 500 companies had a corporate mission statement, but only 15 percent of those companies used them when making daily business decisions. In other words, only 64 of the largest 500 companies were deriving any value from having a mission statement. Small wonder so many people around the world are cynical when the topic of mission statements arises. More disturbing than cynicism, however, is the misalignment between these organizations and natural laws. Any living system that does not have a compelling purpose is at the mercy of the environment's driving forces.

Failing to take a mission seriously can be devastating as this experience illustrates:

• • •

Carol was a new division manager whose supervisors advised that creating a division mission statement would help focus thousands of associates on achieving some challenging business targets. She initiated a process whereby the leadership team wrote a mission statement and then shared the statement with everyone in the division via video replays and large assemblies. The division redecorated its lobby to prominently display the new mission to all who entered the building.

The division began making good progress toward its ideals. But a few years later a new chairman entered the scene. He had little experience with mission statements and made it clear that he had no time for any "soft stuff." Shortly after, Carol began making decisions and acting in ways that were contrary to the division's mission. One senior manager became concerned and wrote to Carol to share his observations. Carol replied in a memo that it was no longer politically correct to speak about missions in this division!

In due course, Carol's "new" behaviors eroded her credibility with her associates. Sadly enough, the division's results began to falter. People everywhere were disillusioned. Within a couple of years, Carol left the company.

• • •

Failing to take a mission statement seriously can cause your leadership to evaporate into thin air. It's better to never begin such a process unless you are prepared to live by the outcome and sacrifice much for its ideals.

In this chapter I will review some principles and processes that can spell the difference between *compelling* and *meaningless* mission statements. My focus will be on the dynamics that are required to shape a common direction out of the many self-interests you and your stakeholders have.

What Makes a Mission Compelling?

In the examples of the restaurant and Carol's division, the attitudes of apathy contrast sharply with an episode from early American history. Inscribed today on the First Parish church (Unitarian Universalist) on the Lexington Common in

Lexington, Massachusetts is a pledge adopted in that township's second meetinghouse in 1773. It reads: "We shall be ready to sacrifice our estates and everything dear in life, yea, and life itself in support of the common cause."

On April 19, 1775, Lexington was the scene of the first battle of the Revolutionary War. The "shot heard 'round the world" was not fired in a moment of hot-tempered lawlessness; it was the natural consequence of the British army coming face to face with those who had taken the Lexington pledge. These words were very compelling to the people of Lexington!

The Lexington pledge contains two important ingredients: (1) "a common cause" and (2) the commitment to sacrifice everything for it. Today's organizations draft mission statements in the hope that, like Lexington, they will mobilize people to do the right thing in any situation. Unfortunately, we have seen how most of their efforts turn out. If your organization has a mission statement, pull it out now and look at it. Does it compel you to action? Are you mobilized to sacrifice other dear things for the common cause?

What is it about compelling mission statements that harnesses people's energies? What is it that, if missing, turns a mission statement into just one more mundane administrative process? Remember what Earl Nightengale called the strangest secret in the world? We become what we think about. This is a natural law of human behavior. Let's explore this premise.

What did the members of the restaurant staff think about? We know what was on the wall, but what was in their mind? If we could read their thoughts, their mission would look something like this:

Our Mission is to:
- Put in the time required to do the job.
- Do as we're told.
- Depend on the customer's good will.
- Go with the flow.
- Minimize our inconvenience.
- Endure until quitting time.

This statement is closer to what the restaurant associates thought about than the words on the wall. And the restaurant became what its people thought about—reactive, harried, and mediocre. It is ironic that as their life got easier (e.g., fewer customers), the company went out of business.

We become what we think about. Sometimes people think only about the moment. They react to each moment and the organization, in turn, reacts momentarily to situations. If this is the case in your organization, you will never be able to "make their business your business." The dynamics of a compelling mission look like this:

• You begin by focusing on the highest priority stakeholder moments of truth.

• Through an interactive process, all members choose these priorities as their own.

• Each person translates these priorities into personal responsibilities and actions.

• In daily work, you hold each other accountable to deliver on these priorities—subordinating everything else in the process.

This is precisely what the Lexington pledge accomplished. Now, suppose you took your mission statement seriously? What steps would you need to take as a leader to reach each person's heart and mind? Those who have followed this principle have given attention to three areas: Content, Process, and Practice.

Content: Tapping Into Stakeholders' Moments of Truth

Read enough mission statements and after a while you will see they all look very similar. There is an important reason for this: most people and organizations have the same fundamental desires and needs. An effective mission statement captures these desires and needs and commits the organization to fulfill them. Stephen Covey speaks of four basic needs that spark "the fire within" each of us:

• Physical/economic needs (the need to live)
• Social/ emotional needs (the need to love)
• Mental/intellectual needs (the need to learn)

• Spiritual/meaning needs (the need to leave a legacy)

Carefully examine the mission statement of your organization: either these four areas are included in the statement, or their absence explains why there is no fire within.

Some years ago professors John A. Pearce II and Fred David published a research study that affirmed the need for addressing all four needs. Pearce and David wrote to the Fortune 500 companies and asked for a copy of their mission statement. From the 61 mission statements they obtained to study, a content analysis revealed eight topics were generally covered. In other words, every point in the mission statements could be categorized under one of these eight headings:

1. Specifying target customers and markets (*Physical/Economic*)

2. Commitment to principal products or services (*Physical/Economic*)

3. Identifying the intended geographic domain (*Physical/Economic*)

4. Describing the core technologies (*Physical/Economic & Mental*)

5. Sharing plans for survival, growth, profitability (*Physical/Economic*)

6. Disclosing basic beliefs, values, philosophy (*Spiritual*)

7. Expressing the company's view of itself (*Spiritual and Social/Emotional*)

8. Stating the firm's desired public image (*Social/Emotional*)

Next, they broke down the performance of these 61 companies into four quadrants by profitability. Though the eight elements were found in many of the statements, Pearce and David identified three elements that were present in the top 25 percent profitable companies and significantly lacking in the other 75 percent. Which of these eight do you think correlate with high performance?

If you guessed #6, #7, and #8, you are right! Those organizations whose missions focused everyone's attention on the full list (and all four basic needs) outperformed those who neglected the spiritual and social/emotional needs.

Here are some mission statement examples whose contents address all four needs:

The Northwestern Mutual Way
The ambition of the Northwestern has been less to be large than to be safe; its aim is to rank first in benefits to policyowners rather than first in size. Valuing quality above quantity, it has preferred to secure its business under certain salutary restrictions and limitations rather than to write a much larger business at the possible sacrifice of those valuable points which have made The Northwestern pre-eminently the policyowner's company.
—Executive Committee, 1888

• • •

Matsushita
Basic Business Principles: to recognize our responsibilities as industrialists, to foster progress, to promote the general welfare of society and to devote ourselves to the further development of world culture.

Employees Creed: progress and development can be realized only through the combined efforts and cooperation of each member of our community. Each of us, therefore, shall keep this idea constantly in mind as we devote ourselves to the continuous improvement of our company.

The Seven Spiritual Values:
• National Service Through Industry
• Fairness
• Harmony and Cooperation
• Struggle for Betterment
• Courtesy and Humility
• Adjustment and Assimilation
• Gratitude

• • •

Broward County, Florida Schools

Our Mission

We, the School Board of Broward County, Florida, commit ourselves to a philosophy of respect and high expectations for all students (pre-kindergarten through adult), teachers and staff; and, with community participation and partnerships, we will provide the process and support which will give our diverse, multicultural student population equal access to a quality education.

Our Beliefs

We believe that all students should be taught how to learn.

We believe that all students should be prepared for a knowledge-based, technologically rich, and culturally diverse twenty-first century.

We believe that a safe and secure environment is requisite to teaching and learning.

We believe that learning should take place at home, in the school, and in the community.

We believe that student achievement is enhanced through partnerships with parents, businesses, governmental agencies and community representatives.

We believe that all individuals should be treated with dignity and respect.

We believe that schools should reflect the philosophy of participatory management.

We believe that each school should be accountable for improving student achievement and school effectiveness.

We believe that staff should be provided with professional development and training to improve student achievement and school effectiveness.

We believe that every level of the organization should make decisions based on students' needs and should reflect these beliefs and support school and district goals.

• • •

These are just a few examples. The next time you see a mission statement hanging on the wall, check to see if all four basic needs are addressed. Then watch to see if people "walk the talk." The ultimate test of your mission is whether or not it gives you meaningful criteria upon which to make any major decision facing your organization. Unless it can pass this test, your mission statement is not complete and you and others probably won't take it seriously.

Process: Involvement Brings Commitment

Many leaders are frequently shocked and disappointed by others' reactions to their carefully written mission statement. Senior managers proudly unveil the mission statement only to hear comments like:

- "It sounds like Motherhood and apple pie."
- "Sounds like every other statement I've seen recently."
- "It took you how long to write this little statement?"

Such expressions are your first clue that the mission is not compelling people to action! The process you use to create the mission will greatly affect the degree of commitment, cynicism, or apathy that may exist toward your mission. If a few leaders come back from an executive retreat and present a new mission to the organization, the chances are very slim that people will find the statement compelling. In contrast, the following steps will earn enthusiastic followers:

- *Process initiated by senior management:* One way to kill a mission statement is to develop it without senior management's deep conviction. Some organizations use an approach that begins with the grass-roots level in an attempt to get widespread commitment. Such approaches tend to be "politically correct," but often fail to make a difference in the culture because they don't capture the hearts and minds of the senior managers. I recommend *beginning* the process at the top to ensure the leadership, commitment, and involvement of senior managers. If the mission is to live, it must be compelling to them, too.

- *Significant and intense involvement of others:* the risk of beginning the mission development process at the top is that it may stop there. Remember the natural law: "We become what we think about." We *all* become what we think about—*every one of us.* Once you understand this, it becomes clear that you cannot write a mission only at the top or only at the grass roots. It is not *either-or*, but *and*. Top *and* bottom. Insiders *and* outsiders. Begin at the top, but make sure you get significant and intense involvement of others so that they own the mission. Involvement doesn't mean hearing about the mission in a mass meeting— involvement means contributing to it, shaping it, and deeply understanding it.

• *Stakeholder review and feedback:* one way of getting involvement is to open the process up for genuine review and feedback from all stakeholders. This process can get the mission into all the hearts and minds of those who must bring it to life.

• *Integrated sub-unit missions:* if you want people to take the mission seriously, have them translate the overall mission into a mission for their department or work team, like the Ritz-Carlton example. Doing this accomplishes two things: (1) it ensures individuals have understood the overall mission, and (2) it applies the mission to each person's specific responsibilities.

Let's examine two organizational case studies that illustrate how these guidelines can come together. First, we will look at a major division of the Shell Oil Company, then the city government in Mapleton, Utah.

Shell Shelf Division: From Despair to Rebirth

In late 1992, the Shell Oil Company was still in the middle of a major economic downturn that affected the entire oil industry. With sharply decreased revenues, Shell and many others were downsizing and reorganizing to be profitable and competitive in the new market. All of these changes had damaged the trust and commitment of those who remained in the division. Layoffs had taken a deep emotional toll on everyone. Employees feared that more layoffs might be needed. The Shelf Division was responsible for offshore production and the exploration for new oil sources in the shallow water ("shelf") of the Gulf of Mexico.

Past attempts to write a mission or vision were not compelling to those who ran the division day to day. There was apathy and even hostility toward these mission statements. Associates said cynically, "How can the company say it's committed to people and then lay off so many?" The contradiction between the mission and actual practice was confusing.

The Shelf Division leaders knew they needed to do something to restore everyone's faith and commitment to improve Shell's future. Following the guidelines on how to successfully create a mission statement, they embarked on the following process that lasted several months:

1. Initial communication. The leaders outlined the nine steps they intended to follow and asked everyone to get involved. In a letter to every member of the division, General Manager Jim Funk said, "Earlier this year I issued a Vision Statement developed by my management team. Since that time, it has become clear to me that the concept of a Vision Statement is not widely accepted in our Division. I also recognize that we missed a very important element in developing that Statement—we didn't get your ideas. I feel that it is important to develop a shared vision of what the Shelf Division will become and how we will work together as individuals, as teams, and as a Division."

2. Peer delegate training. A cornerstone of this approach was the selection of peer delegates, individuals who would represent approximately 30 of their colleagues in the feedback and writing processes. These delegates were chosen because they were natural leaders among their peers. Some were known as outspoken critics of management. The training in this step was intended to earn the delegates' enthusiasm for the integrity of the process. Jim Funk spoke with each peer delegate group, sharing why he felt this process was important, asking for their support, and answering any questions or concerns they had. One of these peer delegates, "Smitty," initiated the following e-mail message after his training session, encouraging people to attend the education meetings:

"Yes, I heard the shock waves going through Shelf Exploration. 'Now I've seen everything—Smitty is singing the Company Song.' The fact is that I am singing the same song I've been singing for years and those of you who know me have heard probably more than you care to. To those of you who don't know me, I have never been one to fly the [Shell] flag. However, I see the Shelf 'testing the water' when it comes to this vision stuff. . . . If we, as employees, can help make the water warm, there is a strong possibility that good things can happen. . . .

"I know, I know—that's a lot of soft talk and, yes, we've all heard how all these meetings aren't finding oil and gas. No one is forcing anyone to go to these things. It is merely an opportunity for us to get involved in charting the course for our company. Take advantage of it if you like—or don't if you think it's a waste of your time. I will ask you, though, that if you have something to offer, either seek out a 'Peer Delegate' and make sure they are representing you, or find some way to make yourself heard. Learn as much about this process as you can before you decide whether or not it's something you can support.

"Once again, those who know me know my motives. To those of you who think I'm just 'singing the Company Song,' I would suggest that perhaps the company is beginning to sing along with us."

3. Education meetings. Every employee in the division (~1600) was invited to attend one of two meetings or to view a video of the meeting to understand the overall process and its rationale. The turnout for the first session was somewhat light but reactions were extremely positive. The second session (which was after Smitty sent his e-mail message) was packed.

4. Questionnaire distribution. The peer delegates personally handed out the following questionnaire to each of their assigned colleagues and invited their thoughtful response:

"It's now the year 2000 and Shell is the most successful explorer and producer in the Gulf of Mexico. A reporter is interviewing you about the Shelf Division. How would you answer the following questions?

• How do we work differently than we did in 1992?

• What is it about Shelf Division that makes your work worthwhile and satisfying?

• What are the most important principles demonstrated by the Shelf Division?"

133

5. *Issues meeting.* After gathering all the completed questionnaires (~50 percent of the division members actually filled them out), the peer delegates met with the writing team to understand the themes and issues raised by the data and to agree on the core themes to be addressed in the vision.

6. *Writing team develops vision statement draft.* A small group of 15 took the core themes identified in the issues meeting and drafted the first vision statement. This team represented a demographic and diagonal slice of the division.

7. *Validate draft with peer delegates.* The writing team reconnected with the peer delegates to get their reactions to the first draft. Some minor modifications were made and the statement was supported by the entire group.

8. *Roll out vision to all staff.* The peer delegates handed the draft statement to each of their colleagues and invited their comments. The overall response was very positive; people felt like they had been heard. Here is the final, agreed-upon statement:

Mission: Our business is finding and producing oil and gas profitably in the Gulf of Mexico in water depths less than 1500 ft.

Shared Vision: We will be a thriving, competitive and respected business. We will succeed by seizing opportunity in our changing business environment through the innovation and commitment of each one of us.

Shared Values:
• We will treat each other, those with whom we conduct business, and the public with honesty, fairness, and respect.
• We will trust each other to do our jobs and help each other create an atmosphere of unity where we can enjoy our work and recognize the importance of each other's personal lives.
• We will all accept the opportunity, the authority, and the responsibility to question and correct all unsafe behavior and conditions. We will all encourage behavior that promotes being injury-free.
• The Gulf of Mexico is our backyard and we will treat it responsibly and with respect.
• Each of us will participate in developing challenging, clearly defined goals which are focused on corporate success through continuous improvement of our work.

• Each of us will freely, honestly and openly share information and ideas and value others' viewpoints.

• We will all recognize and acknowledge each other's contributions and results.

• We will recognize and capitalize on opportunities more effectively than our competition. We will seek simple, creative, and innovative solutions. We will learn from our mistakes, not dwell on them, and we will celebrate our successes.

• We will make decisions and accept responsibility at the lowest appropriate level.

• Leadership at all levels will be visible, accessible, responsible, and motivating.

• We will use teamwork, founded upon individual contributions, to achieve our goals.

Commitment: Commitment, as demonstrated through our actions, will make our shared vision a reality.

9. On-going feedback. The division committed to revisit the vision periodically to do two things: (1) to evaluate its performance against its standards, and (2) to see if any new developments called for modifying the vision.

Since the Division rolled the vision out, has it made any difference in the Division's results? Shell's 1994 annual report celebrated a resurgence in sales and profits, noting that for the first time since 1986 the decline in oil and gas production had been reversed. The main reason for this turnaround? New oil discoveries in the Gulf of Mexico. Who was responsible for many of the Gulf of Mexico discoveries? Those members of the Shelf Division who felt overwhelmed by insecurity and fear in 1992! The real test, of course, is what Shelf Division members would say has changed. They would tell you, "We're not perfect, but we are holding each other accountable—and we're trying to walk our talk." In one sense, Smitty was wrong. This "vision stuff" did help them find oil and gas.

The City of Mapleton: Governing by the Voice of the People

For decades, Mapleton has been a quiet farming community (population ~5,000) located 55 miles south of Salt Lake City,

Utah. The influx of new industry has brought thousands of new residents to the surrounding areas. Seeing how unmanaged growth had negatively affected some neighboring communities, many Mapleton citizens wanted to ensure the same didn't happen to them. Mayor Richard Maxfield and City Council member Marilyn Petersen were both elected on a platform committing themselves to listen to the voice of the people and to develop a vision statement to guide the city's actions. The process they used to fulfill their campaign promises was very similar to the Shell Shelf Division's process to create a vision:

1. Community survey. Volunteers delivered a citizens survey to each home and returned a few days later to collect the responses. The questionnaire asked citizens such things as:

• Why did you choose to live in Mapleton?

• What are the biggest problems facing our community today? In the future?

• If you were describing to someone ten years from now what it's like to live in Mapleton, what phrases would you hope to use?

• What phrases do you hope would not describe Mapleton ten years from now?

• What would you like to see unchanged?

• What would you like to see changed?

Despite the fact citizens had to write in their answers to each of these questions, over 70 percent of the 1,100 households responded thoughtfully to the questionnaire.

2. Survey data summary. Citizen volunteers (some of whom were experienced data gatherers) did a content analysis of all responses. The themes that emerged were:

• People came to Mapleton because of its rural, peaceful atmosphere.

• Overdevelopment and population growth were the biggest present and future concerns.

• Residents hoped to keep the city's peaceful, uncongested atmosphere from changing.

• Residents felt that growth and improvements needed to be controlled by the elected officials.

3. Draft a vision statement. A small group of the data gatherers put together the initial vision statement draft, using the key words from the survey themes as their guide. Council member Petersen was a member of this team.

4. "Constitutional Convention." A group of 43 citizens, chosen at random to represent the entire community, met to review and improve the vision draft. They were given the survey results to understand what were the community's wishes. After much discussion in small groups, they agreed with most of the draft, but made five significant improvements to it.

5. City Council ratification. The final statement was presented to the mayor and city council for their approval. Mayor Maxfield supported the statement by saying, "Our mandate should be the voice of the people as long as it doesn't go against the U.S. Constitution or the state laws." This is the statement the city council unanimously ratified:

We in Mapleton:
• Are a unique community retaining a peaceful, country atmosphere through rural master planning.
• Are citizens who participate in deciding matters that affect us; help our neighbors; and, when necessary, subordinate self-interests for the good of all.
• Preserve the beauty of our community and surroundings.
• Promote family values and community effort in order to maintain safe and friendly neighborhoods.
• Have well-planned, accessible, open areas.
• Encourage economic development as it harmonizes with our community lifestyle.
Because we hold true to these principles, our community offers a quality lifestyle for a family environment. In summary, We have controlled growth with community input.

We encourage:
• Family-oriented activities and facilities.
• Clean air and water.
• Preserving and planting trees.
• Gross density planning.
• Preserving animal rights.

• Pooling and sharing resources, facilities, and ideas with other communities.

• Maintaining our own police, fire, and emergency services.

• Aesthetic building and style codes for industrial and commercial areas.

• A general vote on issues with citywide impact (e.g., sewer, significant changes to the General Plan, etc.).

• Volunteerism.

• Preserving the beauty of Maple Mountain.

• Agriculture, parks, green spaces, trails and paths to accommodate walking, horseback riding and bicycling.

We discourage:

• Growth at the cost of open space, neighborhood privacy, health and safety, and ability to provide services.

• Dense road grids.

• High-density housing.

• Development on the mountainsides.

The vision statement has been tested in a number of council meetings since it was ratified in 1994. The vision statement has provided guidance in approving or rejecting some development proposals. For example, some proposed changes to residential areas were turned down when it became clear to everyone that animal rights were being restricted unnecessarily.

In the 1995 election to choose three of the five city council members, the vision statement became the major campaign issue. Voters wanted to know how many of the six candidates would really support the Vision. The election day turnout was the highest in recent history (about 67 percent), and the voters elected by a more than a 2:1 margin three candidates who had clearly demonstrated their commitment to the vision.

In the ensuing years, new mayors and city council members have been elected to office. Though the faces have changed, the voice of "We in Mapleton" has continued to set the direction into the new millennium as the new officials have followed the vision statement's lead.

Practice: The Mission as a Constitution

With the content of a mission statement igniting a fire within for all stakeholders and a process designed to create something compelling for all members, the mission statement should have great impact on the organization. It's important to remember, though, that a mission statement is only a statement of vision or good intentions—it can only make a difference when it is put to use in daily practice.

Those who take their mission seriously treat it like a constitution or other governmental code of law. In many nations a constitution is the supreme law of the land. Everything else is subordinated to the supreme law. If any other law, practice, system, or habit is found to be in contradiction with the constitution, it is the law, practice, or system that must change.

This constitutional metaphor illustrates how seriously you must take your mission statement. The mission should contain all the criteria for making any major decision. Now in practice, use the mission as the standard to evaluate everything else that goes on. Here are some practical ways to make the mission your constitution:

• *Introduce new associates to it* by sharing what it means and doesn't mean on a daily basis. This is the approach Ritz-Carlton uses. Some organizations even use the mission to shape hiring criteria and gauge potential associates' commitment to it in the interview process. Many use the mission statement to guide discussions of company values, standards, philosophy, and self-image.

• *Make it constantly visible to all stakeholders.* The mission is prominently displayed in halls, lobbies, conference rooms, eating/break areas. Furthermore, it is also referenced in contracts, agreements, and other forms of written communication with suppliers, contractors, customers, and other stakeholders. Most importantly, it is consulted frequently in daily conversation, especially when decisions need to be made.

• *Align all other organizational elements with the mission.* Shaping systems, structures, and habits to be aligned with the mission brings about the rare phenomenon of organizational integrity: what the organization says (the mission statement) and what it does (through systems, structure, and culture) are fully congruent.

• *Review the mission periodically* over the long term, revising it as appropriate to reflect changing conditions. In other words, treat it like a living document, not something that's written once and set in stone.

A great example of treating the mission like the supreme law of the land is the Johnson & Johnson Company. J&J's experience illustrates all three areas: content, process, and practice.

Johnson & Johnson: "Live By It or Tear It Off the Wall"

James Burke, taking over as Johnson & Johnson's CEO in 1976, was disturbed by the many signs that told him that people at all levels weren't taking the company Credo seriously. He said to his executive team, "Here's the Credo. If we're not going to live by it, let's tear it off the wall. If you want to change it, tell us how to change it. We either ought to commit to it or get rid of it."

Burke engaged in a process where he and company president David Clare discussed the Credo with every manager in the worldwide company in small discussion groups. It took two years to do this. The agenda was very simple: Here's the Credo. What do you agree with? What do you disagree with? What should come out? What should be added? What should be modified? Everything was open to question and input. Burke committed that he and the executives would do nothing until several discussions had been completed. Then they would start to draft a new Credo and get worldwide feedback from the J&J community.

Through these discussion meetings, they found phrases that bothered some people. But the Credo had been "undiscussable" since it had been crafted largely by the Johnson family. Through the years the Credo had come to mean less and less to the thousands of people who now worked at J&J. At the end of the two-year process the following Credo emerged:

"We believe our first responsibility is to the doctors, nurses, and patients, to the mothers, and all others who use our products and services. In meeting their needs, everything we do must be of high quality. We must constantly strive to reduce our costs in order to maintain reasonable prices. Customers' orders must be serviced promptly and accurately. Our suppliers and distributors must have an opportunity to make a fair profit.

We are responsible to our employees, the men and women who work with us throughout the world. Everyone must be considered as an individual. We must respect their dignity and recognize their merit. They must have a sense of security in their jobs. Compensation must be fair and adequate, and working conditions clean, orderly, and safe. Employees must feel free to make suggestions and complaints. There must be equal opportunity for employment, development, and advancement for those qualified. We must provide competent management, and their actions must be just and ethical.

We are responsible to the communities in which we live and work and to the world community as well. We must be good citizens—support good works and charities and bear our fair share of taxes. We must encourage civic improvements and better health and education. We must maintain in good order the property we are privileged to use, protecting the environment and natural resources.

Our final responsibility is to our stockholders. Business must make a sound profit. We must experiment with new ideas. Research must be carried on, innovative programs developed and mistakes paid for. New equipment must be purchased, new facilities provided and new products launched. Reserves must be created to provide for adverse times. When we operate according to these principles, the stockholders should realize a fair return."
—Johnson & Johnson

This statement exemplifies everything discussed in this chapter. The needs of all stakeholders are addressed. Top management is committed. Widespread review and feedback have earned the commitment of every J&J member. Now, what would happen if something unexpected were to hit Johnson & Johnson? You would find out what people were really thinking about.

J&J's big test came in 1982. After seven people died in Chicago, investigations determined they each had ingested Tylenol, Johnson & Johnson's flagship pain reliever. Someone had tampered with the bottles and laced the pills with cyanide. Now, suppose you are a J&J distribution manager in California. What do you do when you hear the news report? How do you know if the problem in Chicago is related to your product in Anaheim?

In the absence of factual information, members of the organization reverted to their values—their Credo—to decide what action to take. "Our first responsibility is to our customers." This suggested the right thing to do was to pull the product off the shelves until the facts were known. That would cost a lot of money, though, which might hurt J&J's profitability. Remember the hierarchy of priorities outlined in the Credo:

1. Our first responsibility is to our customers . . .

2. We are responsible to our employees . . .

3. We are responsible to the communities in which we live and work . . .

4. Our final responsibility is to our stockholders . . .

Because everybody at J&J understood and was committed to this hierarchy of priorities, the product was off the shelf across the nation in a matter of hours. Eventually, investigations proved that the problem was isolated to one store in Chicago. Only after it was clear that there were no problems elsewhere, Tylenol slowly made its way back onto the shelves—with a modified package. J&J invented the tamper-proof seal to ensure such an episode couldn't happen again.

James Burke made this observation after the Tylenol episode was over: "I do not think we could have done what we did with Tylenol if we hadn't all gone through the process of challenging ourselves and committing ourselves to the Credo. We had dozens of people making hundreds of decisions and all on the fly. And they had to make them as wisely as they knew how. The reason they made them as well as they did is they knew what the beliefs were of the institution they worked for. So they made them based on that set of beliefs and we made very, very few mistakes."

What was the ultimate consequence of using the J&J Credo as the constitution in times of uncertainty? Marketing experts will tell you that a high profile product recall is usually the kiss of death. Short term, the recall cost the company over $100 million, not counting the lost sales revenues. But after it returned, Tylenol's market share actually grew and is higher today than it was before the tampering incident. Can you measure the value of trust in the marketplace? Johnson & Johnson can.

As the final line of the Credo states, "When we operate according to these principles, the stockholders should realize a fair return." The Tylenol episode proved this statement to be true.

Mission Statements: Process or Product?

In conclusion, it is evident that there is more to a mission statement than the piece of paper (the product). The magic of mission statements is to be found in the processes used to create and nurture them. *The process is the product.*

The process is what gets everyone to focus on the same end. Focus is an important word. In the martial arts, a lot of attention is given to the concept of "Chi," one's life force. By focusing one's "Chi," mind and body can become aligned to break wooden boards or other amazing feats. Focusing "Chi" helps people become what they think about.

What was it that caused the members of Shell's Shelf division, citizens of Mapleton, and Johnson & Johnson to take their mission statement seriously? It was a process that created "Chi"—a common direction emerging from many individual values and self interests. The mission became a compelling cause to which personal preferences and many other factors were subordinated. And, the cause became compelling due to the leaders' unrelenting focus on content, process, and practice.

Once you understand that a mission's process is the product, you won't make the mistake of saying the mission is "done" when the piece of paper has been produced. If you have used quality stakeholder feedback to help shape the mission, and the mission truly represents timeless natural laws, then the content won't change very often. Any changes that are made, like at Johnson & Johnson, will come slowly and only after a thorough review. Like the U.S. Constitution, your mission will be a changeless core amidst all the other changes that surround you.

Your work isn't "done" just because the mission is hanging on the wall, however. You must keep the process alive for those who join the organization later, for those who may forget the mission in moments of crisis, and for those who don't seek its guidance when new situations arise.

Never forget a mission statement's process is the product. You may read other companies' mission statements and come away unimpressed, or fail to see the difference between them and dozens of similar statements. With mission statements, beauty is in the eye of the beholder. It's not important whether the Shell Vision, or the Mapleton Vision, or the Johnson & Johnson Credo moves you. What is important is that those who belong to these organizations were compelled to action—swift, aligned, consistent, targeted action that brought abundant results out of potentially catastrophic situations. Each person had something they knew was unalterable—their organization's changeless core of natural laws and values. Every employee had thought deeply about this changeless core because of the initiatives of their leaders. As a result, their aspirations have been realized and their organizations have prospered.

• • •

Applying what you have learned:

Here are some suggestions to put into action what you have learned in this chapter:

1. Analyze the content of your organization's mission statement. Place each element under one of the four basic needs:

- Physical/Economic: to live
- Social/Emotional: to love
- Mental: to learn
- Spiritual: to leave a legacy

Look at each of the four lists after you have finished. How balanced is your mission? Does its content need to be revised?

2. From the examples cited in this chapter, what process might you use to instill the mission in each individual's heart and mind?

7

Which Mission Do We Follow?

"It is more important to know where you are going than to get there quickly. Do not mistake activity for achievement."

—Mabel Newcomber

"Success is determined not only by knowing what to do ultimately, but by knowing what to do next."

—Winston Churchill

IN THE PREVIOUS CHAPTER, I ADVOCATED CREATING sub-unit missions to help everyone take the mission seriously. Many successful organizations have done this. However, there are individuals in these organizations who say things like:

• "We have a company mission, a division mission, a departmental mission, and a team mission. Just exactly which mission am I supposed to follow?"

• "My boss went to a program about visioning. Now she wants to write a vision statement. What are we supposed to do with our mission?"

• "We spend more time writing mission statements than we do getting our work done."

147

• "How do I resolve the conflicts between my personal mission statement and our organizational mission statement?"

Some of these statements are half joking, others are quite serious. All reflect an underlying issue that you, the leader, must address: How do you appropriately focus each level of your organization? We become what we think about, but people can get so confused by a plethora of missions that they stop thinking altogether.

In this chapter we'll see how some leaders have addressed having "too many missions."

A Case of Many Missions

Beta was a large multinational organization struggling to keep world-class products flowing from its research and development pipeline. Though it invested a hefty portion of its earnings each year in research and development activities, the rate of big product winners was slowing down. As part of an organizational effectiveness study, members at all levels of Beta's product development organization were asked a simple question, "What are your objectives as you do your work each day?" The interviewers hoped to learn from the responses what people really thought about each day. After hundreds of interviews were completed, the major themes (rank ordered) emerged for each organizational level:

Director	Group Head	Project Leader	Manager	Technician
1. Volume, profit, technical vision	1. Volume, profit, technical vision	1. Volume, profit, technical vision	1. Move projects ahead	1. Move projects ahead
2. Train, develop people.	2. Train, develop people	2. Train, develop people	2. Improve/apply technology	2. Competency, training, learning
3. Improve/apply technology	3. Improve/apply technology	3. Move projects ahead	3. Volume, profit, technical vision	3. Ranking, career
4. Help others w/ their job	4. Set priorities/ move projects	4. Improve/apply technology	4. Help others w/ their job	4. Volume, profit, technical vision

After a cursory review of the data, Beta's top management was delighted! All the important things were listed somewhere. People were focusing on their division's business objectives, sticking to their agreed-upon technology vision, developing people, and moving their projects forward.

Then a vice president noted the vast difference in the directors' list from the managers and technicians—those who actually brought forth the new products. The directors' list was more strategic. It focused on volume and profit targets and on developing a sound technology vision. But the directors were only 30 out of 4,000 in the organization! The focus of thousands of technicians was heavily weighted toward moving projects forward and improving their own competence and career status. "Developing people" had disappeared entirely from the lists at the bottom of the organization!

Another executive asked, "What about meeting customer needs?" A closer review of the data showed that only a few directors had even mentioned this point and the responses declined by level with ultimately no mention of it by the technicians! Another question was raised, "How many mentioned anything about 'product innovation' as an objective?" Answer: not one person!

Would you expect a product organization to struggle if few people consciously thought about meeting customer needs and product innovation? Or if the vast majority of people thought only of moving the authorized project along its timetable? Once Beta's managers got over the initial shock caused by this deeper understanding of the responses, they admitted the data perfectly described their culture. People were more internally focused on existing plans and projects than breakthrough innovation and customer needs. The strategic plans, created at the top of the organization, were being watered down as they moved to the bottom of the organization. Most people were thinking only of the "here and now" aspects of their work. Their thinking was producing the very product problems they were experiencing. Projects were moving forward on schedule, but not impressing enough customers.

This example reminds me of the rhyme someone wrote years ago: "As you ramble on through life; Whatever be your goal; Keep your eye upon the doughnut; And not upon the hole."

The Beta organization is hardly unique. I have seen countless missions and strategies slowly dissipate as they move through their organizations. Think for a moment about your own situation. What would you find if you asked people in your organization the simple question, "What are your objectives?" How many would you find keeping their eye on the doughnut?

The Beta experience highlights another important organizational dynamic. In a complicated organization of many layers and departments, every person figures out his/her own set of priorities for getting the work done. In other words, people are forming their own mission whether or not you do anything! But, as Beta learned, these individual missions are rarely revealed to management or aligned with other missions. In the absence of leadership, therefore, individuals establish their own sense of purpose and unintentionally create misalignments in the workflow.

Only leadership can transform misaligned multiple missions into a focused sense of purpose. It takes a great deal of effort to keep the overall mission clear and to align the specific, personalized translations of "who needs to do what." General Electric's Steven Kerr uses the term "line of sight" to describe this dynamic of keeping everyone's eye on the doughnut. As people work every day, they should have a direct line of sight between what they are doing and the overall mission of the organization. If not, your company may lose its focus like Beta did.

Why So Many Missions?

Effective leaders invest a lot of energy in seeing that the mission is clear, specific, and aligned at all levels. But, we have already seen that creating multiple missions sometimes adds to the confusion. One source of the confusion can be the terminology itself. Does your organization have a statement for:

❑ Mission   ❑ Strategy
❑ Credo   ❑ Objectives
❑ Purpose   ❑ Goals
❑ Vision   ❑ Strategic or Annual Plan
❑ Values   ❑ Operating Principles

If you checked even a few boxes, your organization may be experiencing some confusion. Let me try to decode what all these terms mean.

A *Mission* or *Credo* is usually defined as the organization's reason for being; its distinctive competency; the unique contribution it makes to stakeholders. In some organizations such a statement is called the *Purpose*.

A *Vision* is often described as a picture of what the future will look like if the *Mission* and *Values* are being fulfilled. It's a virtual reality image of the future. Yet I have read some mission statements that do this very same thing.

Values or *Operating Principles* are the code of conduct against which members hold themselves accountable as they work together. Some organizations define this code of conduct as part of their mission.

Strategy is typically more tactical, spelling out "how" the organization intends to compete in the marketplace. Strategies are often broken down into more specific units called *Objectives, Goals,* a *Strategic Plan,* or an *Annual Plan.* Some strategies, however, spill over and describe the organization's reason for being. Some visions are even time sequenced (Year 1, Year 3, Year 5, etc.) like objectives or annual plans.

Rather than get bogged down in a dictionary debate over what is the real definition of these terms, why not do the following:

• Examine what tools might help your company think about what you want to become: a clear reason for being, a living picture of the ideal future, a code of conduct, or a competitive action plan?

• Decide what you want to call each element and don't let other companies' terminology distract you.

• Teach people how to translate their terminology into your company's terms (e.g., what others call a *Vision* is the same as our *Mission*).

As you are defining your terminology, remember to keep your eye upon the doughnut and not upon the hole!

A great example of a company having multiple missions and not losing focus is the Ritz-Carlton Hotel Company. Let's return for another lesson from Horst Schulze.

Ritz-Carlton: One Purpose, Many Missions

In chapter 3 you were introduced to Horst Schulze and his remarkable associates at Ritz-Carlton. Their commitment to their Credo is a good example of an inside out commitment to purpose. Horst and others have spent many years in the hotel industry and are committed to serving their guests and growing personally in the process. In recent years, Ritz-Carlton has been sponsoring leadership programs in which participants have an opportunity to write their own personal mission statement. Their experience has shown that individuals who have thought deeply about their own personal mission are more likely to take the organizational mission seriously.

What causes this dynamic? If those who craft organizational missions have also thought seriously about their personal mission, you won't find any incompatibilities in the content of the different statements. Even when I come in contact with individuals who are cynical about their company's mission statement, I learn that most have no problem with the content of the statement, but rather are disillusioned by the daily practice. It is only when individuals do not take the mission seriously (they do not walk their talk) that people become cynical.

Recall the simple Ritz-Carlton Gold Standard (Credo, Motto: "We are ladies and gentlemen serving ladies and gentlemen," Three Steps of Service, and the 20 Basics) that focuses more than 18,000 people around a common purpose every day. With such a simple standard, why do anything more? At Ritz-Carlton, they want to make sure each person has a clear line of sight between his/her daily routine and the Credo. Therefore, they take the extra step of creating departmental missions.

Somewhere in the middle of countdown training, Horst conducts a mission session for the new hotel itself and each of its departments. The departmental mission statements serve two purposes: (1) to reaffirm that everyone understands the Credo, and (2) to translate the Gold Standard into their personal activities.

The structure of the session is simple; its implications are far reaching. Horst begins by pointing out that purpose is the difference between people and things. "People have purpose," he says, "a chair fills a function." Then he gets the group to answer three questions:

1. In your department, where do you want to be six months from now? (One group answered: the best restaurant in town, respected, famous, great service, good work environment, teamwork, clean, fun, professional, quality, profitable.)

2. What does it mean to be the best? (One group answered: hard work, willingness, teamwork, organized creativity, best service, best product, quality, punctuality, no conflicts, have fun working together.)

With this start, Horst turns the process over to the department head to finish writing the mission statement by combining (1) and (2) with: (3) How are you going to do what you said?

Here are some examples of hotel and departmental mission statements that have aligned employees' hopes and dreams with the Gold Standard:

The Ritz-Carlton, Naples Mission Statement

As The Ritz-Carlton Hotel Company grows, The Ritz-Carlton, Naples will continue to be the Company's "Graduate School" for Managers, and the leading practitioner of The Ritz-Carlton Philosophy of Service. As the consistent leader in guest Satisfaction, while helping employees achieve success, and producing impressive profit margins, we will be first at:
- Creating and implementing new strategies to strengthen the loyalty of current guests,
- Discovering and attracting new upscale market segments,
- Anticipating and responding to changing trends in Guest Wishes, and
- Developing new approaches to find, retain, and motivate employees.

• • •

Housekeeping

The Housekeeping Department will be recognized by all guests as well as employees throughout the hotel as a dynamic, committed and highly professional staff. The Housekeeping Department will be known for consistency in providing the highest quality in cleanliness in guest rooms as well as public areas, and for friendly, anticipated and efficient service. Guests will always enjoy the natural warm greeting and immaculately clean, comfortable ambiance of the Ritz-Carlton. Motivated, ambitious housekeeping employees will be a hallmark, providing a career path for growth of valuable team players, attracting only those special people who truly have a genuine care and concern for doing an outstanding job every day and building success for all. By practicing the 20 Basics and through two-way, open communication, employees will share the hotel's objectives and strive toward achievement of the highest industry awards such as the 5-Star and 5-Diamond recognition.

• • •

Remember, *with mission statements, the process is the product.* All the reinforcement around the Gold Standard simultaneously serves each hotel and department because they are so tightly integrated. And, there is no conflict between an individual's personal mission and their organizational mission because each Ritz-Carlton family member can see his/her values in their department's mission as well as the Gold Standard. Here is the full picture linking all of these missions together:

The Credo—our overall mission

↓

Hotel Mission—how my hotel adds value to the Credo

↓

Department Mission—how my group adds value to the hotel

↓

The 20 Basics—the code of conduct to fulfill all missions

↓

The Motto—our simplified mission

↓

Three Steps of Service—my line of sight to any mission

↓

Personal Mission—what's important to me

In contrast to the Beta organization, the Ritz-Carlton mission gains intensity as it moves through the organization. Each leadership team and department mentally creates a picture of how they will add value to the Credo. Each individual maintains a clear line of sight to the Credo by focusing on his/her department's mission, the Motto, and the Three Steps of Service. The attention paid to the 20 Basics reinforces all these. There is no confusion!

How does all this play out when a guest makes an unusual request?

• • •

One of the Naples, Florida employees, JoAnne Muenzer, was very proud of her five-star service pin, a coveted award for excellent service given to only a handful of employees at each hotel each year. JoAnne wore her pin constantly. One day a guest noticed it and asked, "Where can I buy one of those pins?" JoAnne replied, "We really don't sell these. They are just for the employees." The guest was really disappointed. She really wanted one of those pins! Seeing the guest's disappointment, JoAnne took off her pin and gave it to her. She never told anyone what she did. The only way management found out was from the letter the guest wrote thanking the hotel and JoAnne. Her colleagues were touched that she would do such a thing. Of course, she got another pin and went on to win the company's Five Star award for 1995, given to the employee who best exemplifies excellent service that year.

• • •

In such a moment, JoAnne only needed to remember that she was a lady serving another lady; that her job was to find some way to meet her guest's need. By focusing on those simple ideas, she kept her sight on Ritz-Carlton's Credo.

Employee commitment to the mission runs very deep at Ritz-Carlton. But it all starts with the president, Horst Schulze, who says, "It's immoral to ask people to work without purpose. We have to try to help them find a purpose. This is our obligation; it yields contented people and strong business results."

Aligning Multiple Missions

If all mission statements were tightly aligned like Ritz-Carlton's, individuals would not be confused about which mission to follow. Unfortunately, many missions are written in isolation and don't link well with others. Let's review a process that could help you check the alignment of multiple missions. Remember the Broward County School Board's Mission?

We commit ourselves to a philosophy of respect and high expectations for all students (pre-kindergarten through adult), teachers and staff; and, with community participation and partnerships, we will provide the process and support which will give our diverse, multicultural student population equal access to a quality education.

Let's assume for this example that you are a member of this school board. The first question on your mind is, "How can we ensure that each school, district staff group, and community stakeholder will be aligned to help fulfill this mission?" Consider these steps:

Step 1: break down the mission into its prime areas. In this example, these areas are:

1. Respect and high expectations for all
2. Community participation and partnerships
3. Provide process and support
4. Equal access for a diverse student body to a quality education

The main challenge is to align everyone to deliver against this bottom line.

Step 2: create a matrix—listing each stakeholder group that needs to be aligned with the mission. In the example below, let's assume you are trying to align the efforts of one school, a district staff group (media department), the Parent Teacher Association (PTA), and a local business alliance. (Please note the same analysis could be made for a strategy, fiscal targets, or any similar strategic plank. I will only illustrate the process for the district's mission.)

Step 3a: fill in statements from each group's mission in the appropriate matrix cell. An example might look like this:

Our Mission	School "A"	Media Dept.	PTA	Business Alliance
Respect and high expectations for all	✔		✔	
Community participation and partnerships	✔		✔	✔
Provide process and support	✔	✔		
Equal access to a quality education	✔			

Each check mark symbolizes one item from the stakeholder mission that aligns with the district mission.

Step 3b: Analyze the matrix. Ask yourself three questions:

• Does a blank cell mean the stakeholder is not aligned to give needed support? For example, what should the media department do to build a culture where "respect and high expectations for all" is typical? Would this department be more effective if it identified ways to use "community participation and partnerships"? How could media help provide "equal access to a quality education"? (Note: asking these questions doesn't automatically mean the media department has to put something in each cell. It's merely a good check-off process to see if an important potential contribution is being overlooked.)

• Are there redundancies in what different groups are trying to do? Take the "community participation and partnerships" row for instance. Are the intentions of the school, the PTA, and the business alliance aligned or redundant? If both school representatives and PTA members see themselves as primary fund-raisers with the business alliance, this redundancy could be wasteful—and perhaps annoying to local business leaders! Spotting this overlap might help the school decide to focus on federal grant money, leaving the PTA to work with the business alliance.

• Does each mission area appear to have sufficient resources to turn the goals into reality? Will "equal access to a quality education" be achieved if only School A is focusing on this? Could the other three groups add something to ensure our intention becomes reality? This step can help you see the forest as well as the trees.

Based on your analysis, revise the mission statements as appropriate.

Step 3c: if none of these groups currently has a mission statement, the task is simply to answer this question, "What unique contribution can we make in each of the four areas?"

This global view of the various missions can be very enlightening. For stakeholders who have heretofore looked at their role from a traditional viewpoint, they will find new, targeted ways they can add value to the mission. (How often is "equal access to a quality education" a conscious priority of a business alliance?) For organizations that think they are well aligned, they may be surprised by what they see once the matrix has been completed. Of course, the most important element in these three steps is the discussion of what it will take to translate your good intentions into reality.

Are We All on the Same Page?

As we end this section of the book, let me summarize what these three chapters mean to establishing purpose and trust inside and outside your organization.

First of all, you need to understand the most important needs of your key stakeholders and make their business your business. If every group knows that by helping you succeed, they help themselves succeed, their energy will flow naturally to your cause.

Next, you need to translate "make their business your business" into a statement of common purpose (mission, vision, strategy, etc.) that becomes a compelling driver of daily work behaviors. Remember that content, process, and practice make all the difference between compelling and meaningless missions.

Finally, you need to ensure that each individual has a clear line of sight between his/her daily work and the common cause. This calls for some sub-unit missions that are clear, focused, and aligned to add value to all levels of organizational effort.

If you do these three things well, you will fit into the ecological order of things and you will have a deeper sense of purpose that overrides all other concerns in times of prosperity or crisis. The organization will be poised for tremendous success.

The next big challenge is to sustain this energy and organizationally "walk your talk" as you do your daily work. This calls for structural integrity—processes, systems, and cultures that are aligned to purpose. We'll explore this important dynamic in the next section.

• • •

Applying what you have learned:

Here are some suggestions on how to put into action what you have learned in this chapter:

1. Survey a representative diagonal slice of your organization, asking the question, "What are your objectives as you do your work?" Record people's answers until their conscious respons-

es slow down and stop. Look at the patterns. What does this tell you?

2. Discuss with your colleagues which of these you already have and which would be worth defining:
 • Our reason for being
 • A vision of the ideal future
 • A code of conduct
 • A strategy that explains why we expect to compete successfully
    Then work to define these so that everyone is committed to make them happen.

3. Align team/departmental missions with the overall mission by following the example on pages 156 to 158.

Section

4

Building Systems That Never Rust

8
Mapping the Ecosystem

"Most ailing organizations have developed a functional blindness to their own defects. They are not suffering because they cannot resolve their problems but because they cannot see their problems."
—John Gardner

"All organizations are perfectly designed to get the results they get."
—Arthur W. Jones

I N THE PREVIOUS CHAPTERS I HAVE MADE FREQUENT references to ecosystems. You've had the opportunity to consider the ecosystem of stakeholder needs that surrounds your organization. Any enduring natural ecosystem must shape disparate and conflicting forces into a balanced cycle—and so must your organization. In this chapter I will elaborate on the nature of living ecosystems and introduce you to a model that can be used to map the elements and forces that are flowing within your organization.

Confluence in Nature

One of the most beautiful and historically significant areas in Europe is the region occupied by the Mosel and Rhine river valleys in Germany. The Moselle (as it is known at its source in the Vosges Mountains in eastern France) flows northeastward for

319 miles before emptying into the Rhine. The Rhine is the most important inland waterway in Europe. It rises in eastern Switzerland, flows 820 miles while forming part of the borders of Switzerland, Liechtenstein, Austria, France, and Germany and traverses the Netherlands before emptying into the North Sea. These two great rivers converge at Koblenz, Germany. The natural systems term for this convergence is *confluence—a flowing together of different elements to form a new entity.*

The Mosel and Rhine river valleys have partnered with other natural elements to produce some of the finest wines in the world. The weather and fertile soil attracted people who founded towns and villages and started cultivating grape vineyards. The wines produced in this region have been global players for centuries. The Saarland and Rhineland provinces where these two rivers flow have been frequent battlegrounds between France and Germany, most recently in the two World Wars. And this region remains a beautiful attraction to thousands of tourists every year. All this commerce, history, and culture from two rivers coming together!

The confluence of the Mosel and the Rhine is a good metaphor for looking at your organization. Like the vineyards in these river valleys, your organization is an ecosystem made up of natural resources, technology, and people that all flow together to produce goods and services. An organization that would live for ages needs a smooth coming together of all these elements. If there are barriers, bottlenecks, and friction along the way, the organization's longevity will be at risk. In order to keep things flowing smoothly in your organization, you need to understand its ecology and be able to cultivate its potential over time. This requires mastering "systems thinking."

Systems Thinking

The word *system* is a term that is frequently used, but seldom understood, in describing an organization. We talk about doing things systematically. Sometimes we complain, "You can't beat the system." And we often use metaphors like the following to describe our organizations:

- " A well-oiled machine."
- "Running like clockwork."
- "A high performance race car."
- "A small cog among all the big wheels."

Each of these metaphors compares the organization to a system. A system is an arrangement of interrelated elements. Being interrelated means:

- Each element can affect the whole and is affected by all other elements.
- The way each element affects the whole depends on at least one other element.
- The whole is greater than the sum of its parts.

Systems are characterized by a flow of *inputs* (people, materials, technology, knowledge, money) which are *transformed* by work processes into *outputs* (goods and services). Static systems (e.g., machines) are mechanical arrangements of interrelated parts operating in a stable environment. Living systems are "open systems," meaning they are "open" (and cannot close themselves off) to constantly changing environmental forces.

The fact that each element affects the whole and is affected by all other elements is what causes problems for leaders of organizations. In today's global market, the elements affecting your system are numerous, scattered across different continents, and often invisible. Nevertheless, you must find a way to see "the big picture" as you go about cultivating your organizational vineyard.

In his book, *The Fifth Discipline*, Peter Senge teaches the importance of *systems thinking*, or the ability to see the full pattern of relationships, interactions, and impacts the parts of a system have on each other. Systems thinking is not the same as thinking systematically about something. Thinking systematically is a sequential process, like making a list of all the things to do today. Systems thinking, or thinking *systemically*, is a synthetic process: it helps you see how the parts come together; how the individual items on your "To Do" list combine to help or hinder your effectiveness at work, or at home, or with an individual relationship. Thinking systemically is a vital skill when it comes to leading organizations. Leaders who can't see the patterned relationships of the parts will be surprised constantly by unexpected occurrences like Brian was in this experience:

• • •

Brian was in charge of maintaining high-speed production equipment for a modern manufacturing facility. The production lines ran 24 hours a day Monday through Friday, leaving only weekends to perform periodic maintenance tasks. These weekend crews were usually made up of Brian's maintenance specialists and selected production team members who worked a rotating shift schedule. The company was under tremendous cost pressures, so he found a way of reducing overtime expenses related to the Saturday maintenance shifts. By scheduling some team members to be off on Sunday and Monday, he could have them work on Saturday without paying overtime.

Monday following the first "low cost" maintenance shift, the Human Resources department was given an earful by some of the people who had worked on Saturday. They refused to ever work again under such unfair conditions! Brian was stunned when he heard this from the HR specialist. "What are they so upset about?" he asked.

"They said you were paying some people overtime for Saturday, but not them," The HR specialist reported.

"Yes," said Brian still not comprehending the problem, "I couldn't let my people take Monday off because of our other duties. I had to pay them overtime."

"So, you had people working side by side on Saturday, some getting overtime, some not," the HR person said. "Plus, those who had to take Monday off were angry because you disrupted their normal weekend activities."

• • •

Brian was caught in a trap that often ensnares someone who applies a purely systematic solution to a complex ecosystem. He had a bottom line problem to solve and he found a logical solution:

But this solution impacted far more than just the work problem. As is often the case, it isn't what we see that is the problem. It's what we *don't see* that causes our difficulties. Here's a more complete map of the ecosystem in which Brian had intervened:

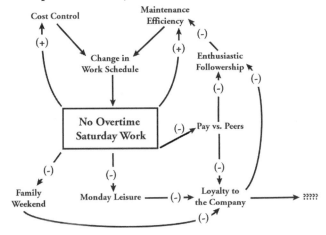

At first glance, his "no overtime" Saturday work plan appeared to be a big plus for both cost control and maintenance efficiency. But his intervention in one part of the system made a series of ripples that led to some unintended outcomes in other areas. Normal family weekend activities were disrupted. The day off on Monday was a poor substitute for those technicians whose children were in school and whose spouses worked. And working on Saturday with no overtime bonus (while their maintenance peers received theirs) only rubbed salt in the wound. The resentment accumulated over these issues damaged: (1) the technicians' loyalty to the company ("Do they think I'm just a little pawn to be moved around at their whim?") and (2) their enthusiastic followership. It wouldn't take long for these reactions to negatively affect maintenance efficiency. Some technicians were already refusing to do maintenance again. Longer term, the consequences would be more severe; some might even consider leaving the company, taking with them company-invested skills and experience.

The Nature of Organizational Ecosystems

Brian's dilemma illustrates why organizations are more complex than a sophisticated piece of equipment. An organization is a confluence of people, systems, and natural laws. People are the elements that make organizations so complex. When equipment breaks down, logical troubleshooting and prescribed action steps will correct the situation. (Notice that none of the production equipment was making a fuss about Brian's Saturday maintenance plan.) It isn't so easy with people. People are emotional, irrational, willful, self-centered and proud. They are also creative, charitable, cooperative and inventive. They can pose enormous obstacles to progress or can create solutions out of nowhere. Seldom can two people problems be solved exactly the same way.

Human organizational systems have characteristics that all successful leaders need to understand. The best summary of these characteristics is what Peter Senge calls the "Laws of the Fifth Discipline." Let me share Peter's 11 laws with you and show how each played out in Brian's maintenance plan:

1. Today's problems come from yesterday's solutions. Brian has a mutiny today as a result of yesterday's new work schedule. This is what happens when you change a part of the system without considering the whole.

2. The harder you push, the harder the system pushes back. The attempt to cut costs without losing efficiency led to technician backlash because it disrupted their weekend routine. Steady states don't like to be changed.

3. Behavior grows better before it grows worse. The first maintenance shift went well before the blowup occurred. It is usually the delayed reaction that tells you where the system is settling in after a change.

4. The easy way out usually leads back in. Brian solved the problem quickly and efficiently by himself. Now he and others will have to revisit the situation because some important human factors were ignored.

5. The cure can be worse than the disease. Once people lose trust in Brian and the company, it will affect far more than paying a few people for Saturday overtime.

6. Faster is slower. Brian's quick and easy solution will cost much more time to defuse the anger it has caused. Also friction has increased.

7. Cause and effect are not closely related in time and space. Brian had no idea his new shift schedule would disrupt family life, employee trust, and eventually threaten the very maintenance efficiency he sought to improve.

8. Small changes can produce big results—but the areas of highest leverage are often the least obvious. There are other less obvious solutions to Brian's problem. Some team members may not have family constraints and would actually volunteer for Sunday/Monday as their off days. There may be ways of handling the weekday maintenance work so all specialists aren't needed Monday through Friday and thus require overtime for Saturday work. The maintenance shift process itself could be organized differently to get the work done with fewer people.

9. You can have your cake and eat it too—but not at once. Both Brian and the technicians need to recognize that work schedules and family routines may need to be adjusted as market conditions fluctuate. Expecting to keep your situation totally constant as the rest of the world changes is unrealistic. Over time, however, you should expect some reasonable balance between company benefits and individual benefits.

10. Dividing an elephant in half does not produce two small elephants. Addressing a work issue in isolation didn't necessarily simplify things. Brian cut out some significant personal elements in his employees' quality of life. By doing so, he put the life, energy, and vitality of the whole organization at risk.

11. There is no blame. Organizational ecosystems are quite complex. It doesn't do any good to blame Brian for his plan backfiring. No one gets it right every time. That's why continuous improvement and openness to feedback are so important! You are only to blame if you give up or choose to ignore your ecosystem's dynamics.

These 11 statements may appear to be jibberish to non-systems thinkers. But these laws help us understand *why being efficient isn't always effective.* Violate the laws of Senge's "Fifth Discipline" and eventually you will suffer the consequences. Take a moment, reflect on each of the 11 statements, and think of some examples you've seen of each from your own work experience.

Brian's experience illustrates the need leaders have for a tool to help them see all of the human and technical elements in their ecosystem. You need a dynamic model that helps you think both *systemically* (to see all the parts, how they interact, and their impact on the whole), and *systematically* (to help you focus on the most critical interactions and the few action steps you might take to do the most good). Bottom line, you need a model that inspires your confidence that the actions you take to improve things will have the desired effect with no negative side effects.

Such a tool exists and has helped thousands of people better understand their ecosystem and skillfully plan ways to improve their effectiveness.

The Organization Performance Model

In my book *Designing Organizations for High Performance*, I first introduced the Organization Performance Model (OP Model)—a framework for thinking systemically about six key elements whose alignment critically impacts your organizational performance.

Recall Arthur Jones' quote at the beginning of this chapter: "All organizations are perfectly designed to get the results they get." Do you have any quarrel with this statement? It's not saying everything is perfect in your organization. It simply means that good or bad, strong or weak, your organization today is perfectly designed to get the results it's getting. I find this a very exciting phrase because it implies if we want to change our results, all we have to do is change the way things are designed. And as leaders, we can redesign what is not working well.

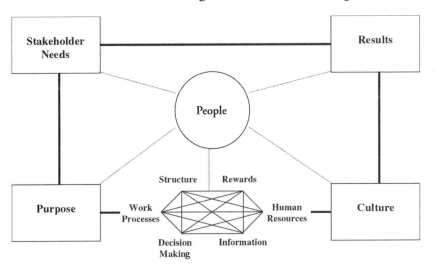

I've covered a number of the OP Model elements already, but think systemically now to see how they interact:

First, the Stakeholder Needs—the "moments of truth" for your organization. As we discussed earlier, they may consist of such things as:

1. Shareholder expectations

2. Customer expectations of product quality and service

3. Supplier expectations around product, cost, timing, flexibility and trust

4. Employee expectations of income, challenging work, job security and personal growth

5. Community expectations concerning corporate citizenship, environmental responsibility, and social standards

I call all these stakeholders your *"voters"* because this term clearly defines their relationship to your organization.

Stakeholders do have a choice in whether to support you or not. Each ultimately volunteers (votes) to support your cause with their money, approval, or work effort. Your survival depends ultimately on fulfilling their "moments of truth."

The second factor is the Purpose. This purpose sets the direction for what's important in the system. It may be expressed as a mission, vision, or strategy. It may also include more operational elements like operating principles, values, and goals. These define what things will be done and what things won't be done. They determine what the critical tasks of the organization will be. Any good mission or strategy will have to make some hard choices, saying "yes" to some stakeholder needs and "no" to others. But bottom line, your purpose must make your stakeholders' important business your business.

Third, Organization Design Elements. These are the organizational tools used to execute the purpose, such as work processes and technology, structure, rewards, information systems, decision-making processes and human resource systems. These tools provide structure to work tasks and reinforce patterns of behavior. They are the "glue" holding the culture in place.

Fourth, the Culture of the organization, or the work habits and norms that explain how the organization really operates. The way the system operates is what produces results—whether they are good or bad. Some examples of this include:

1. What people do every day in response to the stated mission and goals

2. Who makes what decisions

3. The tasks people do/don't do and how well they do them

4. How people otherwise spend their time—breaks, gossip, avoiding work, etc.

Those who have studied culture in depth will say it has an important "hidden" side—the underlying values and paradigms. The model includes these values and paradigms at the center in people because they are causal forces that "program" many of the other organizational dynamics. By separating these two: (1) the observable behaviors and work patterns and (2) the underlying values and paradigms, we focus on the core elements of culture and can see the dynamics of their cause-effect relationship.

Fifth, the Results being delivered currently. These results either fulfill or fall short of the stakeholder needs listed earlier.

Last, but not least, the People. They are like an invisible background—often overlooked, yet a vital part of the whole scenario. People are in the center because they are the programmers of everything else in the model. Mission, strategy, and design elements are all programs written, designed, and brought to life by people. Oftentimes people's paradigms set the direction for daily activities rather than the formal mission and strategy. They may follow the prescribed systems or find ways to get around them. Their paradigms, values, and assumptions influence how all the other elements are viewed and designed. These paradigms also tell the system when changes are needed or that the status quo is okay.

How the OP Model Adds Value

The OP Model's uniqueness isn't in its elements; many other models have them as well. What is unique is the OP Model's ability to show more of the "motion picture" dynamics of otherwise static elements. It can help you think systemically and fill in blind spots through two processes:

• *Diagnosis*—move clockwise on the model to diagnose why your organization is perfectly designed to get the results it gets. Meeting stakeholder needs depends on your results. Results come from culture shaped powerfully by the design elements. Purpose (or alternately people's paradigms) drives these results.

• *Design*—move counterclockwise to design all the elements to get the results you want. Stakeholder needs and natural laws should determine your mission and strategy. These should set the specifications for all design elements to shape new daily behaviors and lead to better results.

I will elaborate on each of these critical processes in chapters 9 and 10 respectively.

The OP Model can help you organize your own observations of organizational performance into an ecosystem map that will synthesize otherwise random viewpoints. Quality process analyses, HR demographic studies, employee attitude surveys, industry and market data, and technology data can likewise be plugged into the model to see how they fit in relation to everything else. One CEO said this about the OP Model: "We ought to require any group coming before the executive committee for capital appropriations to use this model. It will show us all how their request will improve the bottom line and it will spell out what else we will need to do with people to fully realize the return on our investment."

Leveraging the Ecosystem's Results

The OP Model can help you make order out of what appears to be a chaotic ecosystem. It can integrate into one systemic view the many information streams you currently have or need to have to understand your system's performance. But the model can also help you think systematically when choosing actions to take. Quality methodologies teach us to think of Pareto's Law, the principle that says 80 percent of the results come from only 20 percent of the related factors. This "80/20 rule" applies to improving ecosystems, too. Of all the data you uncover in a thorough diagnosis, 20 percent of it will leverage most of the improvements you need to make.

"I know that half of what we do is not essential," one executive told me after coming back from a Quality seminar. "But I'll be darned if I know which half it is!" This sums up nicely one of the leader's dilemmas. Which 20 percent of your diagnostic data could leverage the performance leap you need to make? How do you know the "critical few" items (as Dr. Joseph M. Juran calls them) against which to put your attention? Your ecosystem data, as mapped out on the OP Model, will help you tremendously in selecting the 20 percent.

Even with the OP Model as your framework, however, you will struggle to find the leverage points without systems thinking. Remember Senge's 11 laws? Two of them state, "cause and effect are not closely related in time and space" and "small changes can produce big results—but the areas of highest lever-age are often the least obvious." More often than not, today's poor results are rooted in systems or paradigms that seem total-ly unrelated. Understanding the real leverage points requires a careful systemic examination of the entire OP Model data map.

The Case of the Hired Hands

When you understand the complexity of living systems, you are not satisfied when you see or are informed about only the obvious factors associated with any result. You'll dig deeper to look for common threads between seemingly unrelated parts. And as you trace these threads, their confluence will reveal your ecosystem's leverage points. Here's an example of how the OP Model can help identify leverage points:

• • •

One day a corporate vice president asked me, "Would you come to my office, please? I want to show you something. It's the biggest problem we have, and you must help us with it."

Moving to his office window, the executive said, "Look at that. Just look down there. That is it—that is our biggest prob-lem." We looked down and saw hundreds of people going home. It was the end of the day. I said, "I don't understand."

The VP said, "Look at that. People streaming out of here. It's 4:30 right on the dot and everybody's gone." He added, "We have a lousy work ethic around here and you've got to help us fix it."

Because I had the OP Model imprinted in my mind, I began getting my client to help me fill in the boxes. I said, "Tell me more about the pressure you're feeling."

The executive replied, "Well, we've got competition in many different divisions. We're fighting world-class products and com-petitors in every one of them. I'm taking two briefcases home at night, trying to keep things moving and these people—look at them—they could care less. Four-thirty and they're out of here."

The cultural behavior the client was trying to understand was that people were leaving at 4:30. Mentally moving from the model's culture box to the design elements, I asked some additional questions, "Why are they leaving at 4:30?" The VP didn't know; that's why he needed help. I asked, "How are these people paid?"

"Well, they're hourlies," said the vice president, meaning they worked from 8 A.M. to 4:30 P.M.

"You think that has anything to do with the fact that they're leaving at 4:30?" I asked.

"Well, yes," the VP admitted, "but if they really cared . . ."

"Why don't they work overtime, then?" I asked.

"Oh, well, we've got to cut down on overtime," he said. "Our expenses are out of control and we're trying to cut costs, so there's absolutely no overtime."

"So they're paid from 8:00 to 4:30, and there's no overtime, and you're wondering why they're walking out the door at 4:30." The client paused. (This is what happens when you suddenly see into a blind spot.) Another question: "What happens at 4:20 to the photocopy machines in this building?" The VP didn't know, so I told him. "They turn them off and lock them up because the person responsible for them goes home at 4:30. If you're working on something and you've got to make copies past 4:20, you might as well go home."

Still another question: "What time does the air conditioning system shut off in this building?" The client again said he didn't know. (His office had a self-contained system.)

Answer: "Four twenty-five, because the person taking care of that system goes home at 4:30." On that hot, humid summer day, the vice president knew most people wouldn't want to stay after the air conditioning was off!

And yet another question: "What time does the escalator (that ran up and down the building's five floors) shut off?" Another blank stare from the client. (He had his own private elevator and seldom used the escalator.)

Answer: "Until about 4:40. So that means if you're working on the top floor, and you don't make it down on time, you walk down five flights of stairs. Most people make sure they're out between 4:30 and 4:35."

The conversation went on, but you get the picture. Notice how the different design elements contributed to the same behavior? The work process, how they were paid, information systems and some of the structures (escalators and air conditioning systems) all contributed to the problem.

At last I said, "You know, it seems to me, this whole system is perfectly designed to spit people out of this building at 4:30 every day." The vice president had to admit his problem went a little deeper than the work ethic.

Now let's follow this example all the way back to its roots. Where in the mission and strategy of this organization is it written to "have people leave punctually at 4:30 every day?" You won't find it anywhere. Then what is the root cause of all of the design element decisions? If it's not in the formal purpose, you have to go to the programmers, the people, to see what is driving everything else. Are there paradigms and values that aren't in the mission and strategy that explain what's happening? These two statements align well with the other dynamics:

• People are a cost factor. Limit their time to limit expenses.

• People are hired hands. They should only do as they are told.

For this single issue, then, the ecosystem looks like this:

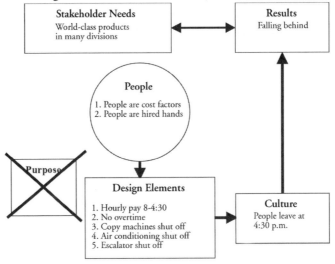

The "hired hand" paradigm has led to the creation of design elements that stop work at 4:30 every day. Yet, this company's results are falling behind its aggressive goals in several product divisions. The vice president lamented that the hired hands weren't behaving like owners. Yet, the entire organizational ecosystem was designed to produce hired hands. The root of the problem wasn't the work ethic; it was an outdated management paradigm about "hired hands."

Now, where's the leverage in this ecosystem to produce a drastic performance improvement? Put everyone on salary? Leave the utilities and equipment on later? Would these changes alone solve the vice president's frustration? Not hardly. These changes would help, but they are insufficient by themselves. The heart of the matter is the two paradigms "people are a cost factor" and merely "hired hands." As long as managers and associates think this way, nothing of significance will change for long.

Thus the leverage point emerges. What if this organization truly adopted the paradigm that "everyone is an owner"? If everyone's energy and potential were truly engaged against the company's product objectives, all other needed changes would be made naturally. And this company would get back on track. This is a good illustration of how critical paradigms are to any improvement within an organization. Getting people to change their behavior will lead to incremental improvements. But if you want transformational improvements, you've got to change their paradigms.

Having finished this example, I need to point out that every ecosystem is unique and will have unique leverage points as well. Combining systems thinking with the OP Model will enable you to spot true leverage points more consistently.

Conclusion

The OP Model is an effective tool to help you see the big picture of stakeholder needs, work processes, systems, relationships, and behaviors in their current ecological balance without getting lost in the tangle. Its sequential features enable you to trace multiple factors in the cause-and-effect streams that eventually deliver your results. And as you cultivate the ability to think systemically, it will help uncover your organization's leverage points, the 20 percent of the elements that could produce 80 percent of the results improvements you need.

There is bad news and good news associated with what we have covered in this chapter. The bad news is that the job of managing the ecosystem is never really finished. The environment is ever-changing, leading to ever-changing stakeholder needs and expectations. Designing your organization to meet these needs is an ongoing process. In addition, like Brian the maintenance manager, you'll find even your best analyses will have some blind spots and will have to be corrected after some experience.

The good news, however, is you can become ever more proficient at delivering what your stakeholders require in the Global Age and beyond.

In the remaining three chapters in this section, I will take you deeper into the core processes of reshaping what your organization delivers. Chapter 9 covers the process of organizational diagnosis, tracing your results back to their roots. Chapter 10 addresses how to design organizations consistent with natural laws. Chapter 11 examines what it takes to create a truly synergistic partnership with your stakeholders.

• • •

Applying what you have learned:

1. Think about an initiative or project in your organization that was extremely successful. Fill in a few factors in each box of the OP Model to explain the success. Identify 2 or 3 leverage points that explained why it was successful.

2. Repeat #1 for an initiative or project that failed.

9

Tracing Your Organizational Roots

"Our choicest plans have fallen through. Our airiest castles tumbled over, because of lines we neatly drew and later neatly stumbled over."
—Piet Hein

"It's a pity to shoot the pianist when the piano is out of tune."
—Rene Coty

A S A CHILD, I REMEMBER ENJOYING THE STORY of the *Emperor's New Clothes*. An emperor ordered his tailor to produce some elegant new clothes for an upcoming ball. The tailor was unable to meet the deadline but was able to convince the emperor that his new clothes were invisible to the eye. His staff dressed him in his new "clothes" and the emperor went out among the people. Not wanting to offend their monarch, all of the people played along with the illusion and complimented the emperor on his stylish outfit. But then the emperor passed by a small boy who didn't know any better than to react based on what he actually saw. When this boy declared, "the emperor isn't wearing any clothes," the whole charade came to an end.

There is absolutely no place for "the emperor's new clothes" syndrome in an organization that would last for ages. Emperors, empires, and organizations begin sliding downhill if self-deception and blind spots prevent them from seeing things as they really are. In this chapter I will explore specific ways the Organization Performance Model can help you see into your blind spots.

First of all, we need to be honest with ourselves about a few realities. Your organization today is perfectly designed to get every good and bad result it gets. Think of "designed" as the way your organization has chosen to accommodate, shape, and direct the various elements in its ecosystem. Some of this design you have inherited from your predecessors. Some of the current design is informal. But your organization is a confluence of activities and energy streams that explains the results you are getting. You need an effective diagnosis process to understand how all these streams really flow before you can make any constructive changes to the whole system.

The Diagnosis Process

How comfortable would you feel with a doctor's plan to remove one of your organs if he/she made absolutely no diagnosis beyond listening to your complaint of occasional abdominal pains? Without a good diagnosis there would be no confidence in the prescription. A thorough medical diagnosis examines all of the body's major subsystems to determine how fit each one is. Organizations require the same level of attention. When we diagnose them, we need to examine both the whole and the parts, see how everything works together, and then carefully correct the defective systems without damaging the healthy ones. I have seen too many organizations prescribe medication and even surgery based on very superficial or no diagnostic data. The OP Model has been proven to help anyone at any level of the organization understand what is causing the group's results to be what they are today. The diagnosis process begins by examining stakeholder needs and then proceeds clockwise around the OP Model to trace the cause-and-effect streams that are producing today's results:

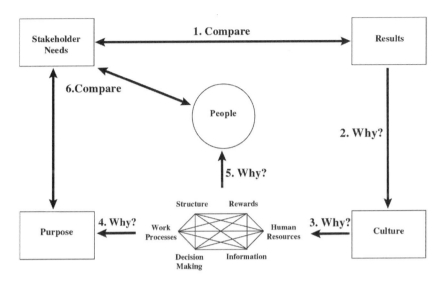

1. Compare current results with the most critical present and future stakeholder needs. This gives a reading of the organization's "vital signs."

2. Examine the culture to see the behavioral "symptoms" connected with the vital signs.

3. Analyze the design elements to understand how they have shaped the culture.

4. Identify those parts of the purpose that have influenced the design elements.

5. Deduce any people paradigms that are also "root causes" of the entire flow.

6. Compare the purpose and paradigms with stakeholder needs to check their alignment.

As I further describe this diagnostic process, I will use the actual case of a metropolitan public school system ("Metro Schools") to illustrate the real-life power of this examination.

• • •

The Metro Schools district was frustrated in its efforts to improve the education it delivered to its students. The superintendent had worked hard to instill the following vision into every staff member, teacher, principal, board member, and citizen:

Our Vision

We will work together to achieve:

1. Improved academic achievement levels
2. Reduced dropouts
3. Improved discipline
4. Better placement in the work force
5. Increased involvement and support of our parents and the community
6. An improved financial status

But all efforts to unite behind this vision had failed. While everyone voiced their support of its direction, their actions lacked. Confrontations between the administration and the teachers union became more heated. The public remained largely uninvolved. And the students still suffered as a result.

• • •

Step 1: Compare stakeholder needs with current results. We begin diagnosing by comparing the present and future stakeholder "moments of truth" with the results actually delivered at present. Given this comparison, we can determine which areas need to change and which need to be safeguarded. Here's what this comparison looked like for Metro Schools:

STAKEHOLDER NEEDS		RESULTS
1. Improve academic achievement levels 2. Reduce dropouts 3. Improve discipline 4. More effective placement in the work force 5. Increase involvement/support of parents & community 6. Improve financial status	**1. Compare** ◄────────►	1. Achievement levels up, but not high enough 2. Dropouts increasing 3. Discipline is eroding 4. ????? 5. Apathetic as before 6. Worse due to escalating health care costs

Comparing the vision (which represented the needs of many stakeholders) with the current results showed major discrepancies. The schools weren't delivering on a single expectation. Why was this so? We begin to answer this question by moving clockwise through the rest of the model.

Step 2: Examine the culture. The cultural examination is done by looking at each result (good or bad) currently produced and asking the question "Why?" For example: why haven't achievement levels climbed higher? Why are dropouts increasing? Why are parents and the community still apathetic? To answer each of these questions, we focus first on observable daily behaviors. I have found the "fly on the wall" test to be an effective way to do this. This test asks you, "If you were a fly on the wall, what would you see (or hear) happening in your work place?" Answering this question converts vague descriptions into something more meaningful:

- "Tunnel vision" is seen by the fly as "people work only on their own projects."
- "Poor motivation" is seen as "people wait to be told what to do."
- "Customer oriented" means "everyone goes the extra mile to help a customer."
- "Poor teamwork" shows up as people saying "That's not my job" when asked to help.

You see, the fly cannot judge anyone's motives (e.g., "poor motivation") or read minds. The fly can only describe what it sees or play back what it hears. All of the fly's observations above are specific behaviors that explain why some results are satisfactory or not.

Conflicting agendas and special interests characterized the Metro Schools' culture. Even though their educational results were not improving, the fly saw too many administrators, board members, and teachers focusing their attention on other concerns. Meetings were held and task forces appointed, but no concrete actions to improve things ever emerged. The Board had one agenda, administrators another, and teachers yet another. Each group claimed the right to be involved in major decisions, with conflicts escalating between administration and the teachers union. The superintendent was a frequent tie-breaker when others were unable to reach a decision. Finally, any proposed expenditures were scrutinized to death because of the public's demand to cut costs.

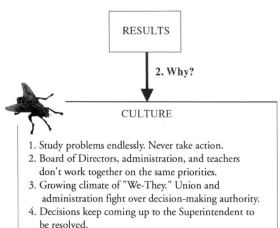

In this case, Metro's poor results were explained by what the fly did not see or hear. Instead of giving attention to tutoring programs, or work/study collaboratives with business, or reallocating staff resources to better support each school, the leaders were fighting each other for control or trying to avoid public criticism.

Why is it that these professionals were focused on agendas that didn't follow the vision? You have to go further upstream to find the source.

Step 3: Analyze the design elements. Having identified the cultural behaviors that influence results, the process now moves to the design elements. What is holding the current culture or operations in place? The organizational culture is determined by the quality of and alignment between six major design elements: the work processes, the structure within which people are organized, how decisions get made, how they are rewarded, what information they use, and the human resource systems that hire, train, and develop their abilities over time. As Deming and other quality experts have reminded us, 85 to 95 percent of the real causes for poor performance lie in these design elements!

This step in the process takes each culture behavior previously identified and asks why it exists. The answers are then sorted into each of the six design element categories.

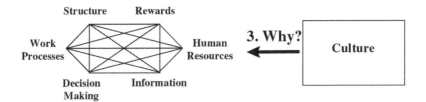

Examining Metro's design elements was most revealing! Through the years a number of practices had emerged that worked against delivering quality education to the students. Here are just a few examples:

Decision Making	Work Processes	Information Systems
• Most personnel moves are governed by collective bargaining—with little local discretion. • The superintendent's office decides instructional budgets. • Principals decide 1st year contract renewals; thereafter peer appraisals by teachers/administrators determine it.	• Most actions center on defending one's organization against budget attacks. • No action plan exists for developing people or systems.	• No measures exist of how well H.S. graduates are absorbed into the work force. • Much communication from the teachers union either has nothing to do with labor relations or seeks to gain a voice in other decisions.
Human Resource Systems	**Structure**	**Rewards**
• There is high mobility from school to school by principals and teachers. • There is high turnover among key staff members. • Most administrators come up through the ranks. • No formal successor planning. • Most teachers/staff come from different backgrounds than the students. • HR training was cut by the budget.	• All teachers have the right to transfer to another school. • Personnel, equal employment, Affirmative Action, labor relations report to three different depts. • There is a large planning research and evaluation staff. • Decentralizing staff would increase the headcount. • The newest staff goes to the hardest schools. • Several authorized positions are unfilled.	• Teachers are tenured at three years. Salaries are not based on performance. • Teachers feel threatened by the Board's attempt to put them on one year contracts (so downsizing would deliver immediate savings). • Principals are stressed out due to a 70+ hour work week and challenges to their salary level by the teachers union. • The more difficult schools to turn around are viewed as undesirable to work in by teachers.

This information made it easier to understand why the key players weren't working together on the same priorities. The least experienced teachers were assigned to the schools with the most problems, but had the right to transfer. They exercised this right routinely, keeping the experience levels lowest at the hardest schools. After three years, teachers were tenured and were fairly secure in the system. Principals felt burned out by their heavy load and also gravitated to the more enjoyable schools or district administration positions, so the very best educators moved steadily away from the students with the greatest needs.

The School Board, in response to heavy taxpayer pressure, was attempting to downsize and operate within the budget. This threatened teachers and led to deterioration in relations between the union and administration.

The structure didn't have the right people in the right place to improve the education delivered. Each school was supposed to operate autonomously on day-to-day matters (referred to as "site-based management"), but instructional budgets were decided by the superintendent. A teacher's right to transfer was part of the union's collective bargaining agreement and could not be challenged. The traditionally centralized district staff groups remained too far away to really help teachers. Decentralizing them would probably increase staff if each school got its fair share of resources.

On top of everything else, people development had been neglected for years. New teachers came from different backgrounds than the students they taught. Helping students and teachers relate well to one another was a real challenge. Because principals and teachers transferred frequently, any rapport that had been built was lost. And there was no organized way to help the successors take advantage of previous experience. Training for teachers was one of the first items cut in the budget crunch.

Thus Metro's performance was completely logical: everyone was focused primarily on preserving their self-interests in a system beset by economic problems. Very few had time to "work on the system"—to actually upgrade the quality of education. But the current system did not place the best resources in the best place to improve the educational process. As a result, Metro Schools was getting what it had been getting for years: poor results.

• • •

You may be asking yourself now, "But why would these educators write such a positive vision and then spend all their time focusing on their own best interests?" The answer comes in the next two steps.

Step 4: Identify those parts of the purpose that influence the design elements. Design elements are chosen based on purpose (mission, strategy) and/or paradigms (the deeper level of culture). To find out what is really driving everything else, we study the design elements and look for elements of the mission or strategy that are the logical drivers of the "spider's web." Look at the data in the design elements and ask yourself the question, "Is there a logical connection between any purpose statement and this data?" If yes, note the points in the purpose box. If purpose is not the logical driver, then you move on to step 5 and examine the paradigms the organization is actually following.

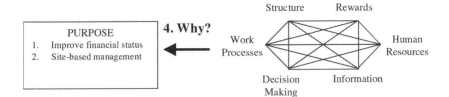

A review of Metro's strategy and mission yielded only two points that logically explained why some of the design elements had been programmed to do what they were doing. Site-based management explained why teachers were evaluated by their peers and principals. It also explained why each school and staff group was fighting the district's attempts to trim their budgets.

The move to cut budgets was driven from the vision statement "to achieve an improved financial status." Being torn between the teachers and the taxpayers, the Board and the super-intendent were intervening to cut costs. Instructional funds and staffing levels were their immediate areas of focus. But none of the other vision elements was driving how the district operated.

Notice what happens when only one aspect of the vision or strategy drives the organization. It disrupts the stakeholder ecosystem and eventually causes everyone to lose. Now the question is, "Why would these educators choose to focus only on one strategic plank and one vision element?"

Step 5: Deduce the paradigms that are root causes of the entire cycle. Given how people actually work every day in the organization and how they have shaped their design elements, it is very likely that some other "mission or strategies" are actually driving things in addition to or in place of the formal ones. Just as the organizational culture doesn't always match formal organization charts or job descriptions, the real driver isn't always the same as the formal strategy or mission.

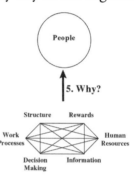

The OP Model helps you deduce the core paradigms by extrapolating them from the pattern of cultural behaviors and design element choices. Perhaps this math example will help you see how to do this: How many straight lines can you draw through a single point in space?

The answer, of course, is an infinite number. This is like trying to find the root cause of a problem by brainstorming a list of possible answers. Each answer is plausible, but which is the real root, the source from whence everything else springs? Let's go back to our math example. How many straight lines will connect two points?

There is only one straight line that can connect A and B. Think of these two points as "Culture" and "Design Elements" in your organization. As we have seen, there is a logic stream that connects cultural behaviors with the design element dynamics. Now, if we extrapolate this straight line into space, mathematically it can only intersect a given plane at point C as illustrated below:

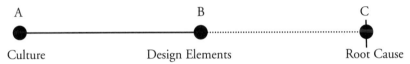

Point C is the root cause, the real driver of everything else in the connection. The Metro data show how this process works in real life. Here is one logic stream from what we have already learned:

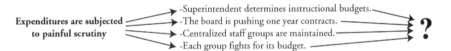

The fly on the wall observes that any expenditure is subject to painful scrutiny. The design elements explain why: the superintendent determines each school's instructional budget, the board is pushing one year contracts for all teachers to save money now from staffing reductions, centralized staff groups are maintained because they are smaller (though less effective in supporting teachers), and each department and school fights for its proposed budget.

Clearly, all school funds have multiple interests competing for them. Deciding who gets them is a painful process. Now what is the logical extension of this stream? To improve academic achievement levels? Reduce dropout rates? Improve discipline? This logic doesn't connect, does it? How about these two possibilities:

- "Show the community we can spend less than last year."
- "Students must temporarily take a back seat."

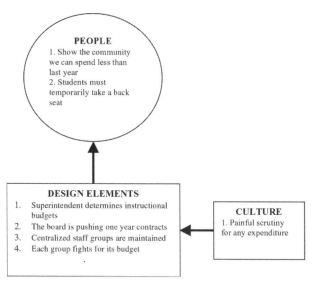

You may quibble with the wording of these two "missions," but don't they connect better with the rest of the stream than the formal vision? This is one of the unique strengths of using the OP Model for your diagnosis. The real root causes are typically very difficult to see. Following the logic stream enables you to see into your blind spots!

Step 6: Compare the purpose and paradigms with the stakeholder requirements. This comparison provides a timely warning as the Metro Schools example shows. Currently the paradigms (from People) are overriding all of the formal purpose with two exceptions. How people see things (paradigms) shapes what they do (design elements and culture), leading them to get what they don't want! Obviously their paradigms (and some of their stakeholders' paradigms) must change before any significant educational progress will be possible.

Metro Schools is suffering from a lack of structural integrity; few of the elements are designed to deliver the vision. One insight emerging from this scenario is that the stakeholders themselves are seriously misaligned. Until they develop a truly common, compelling purpose, self-interests will continue to fragment the school system.

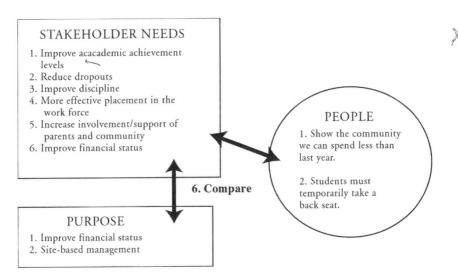

Finding Metro Schools' Leverage Points

The bottom line for any diagnosis is deciding specifically what to change and what to maintain to improve your results. The question to consider is, "If I could only change four or five things to improve the results, what would they be?" But remember, you are trying to change a living ecosystem, not a machine. Elevating your performance is more like caring for a vineyard than replacing your computer's hard drive. Here are some suggestions to help you identify the leverage points to better balance the ecology:

• Are there a few paradigms that drive many design elements and behaviors? The earlier examples have illustrated how paradigms are frequently sources of high leverage because they drive so many other reactions downstream.

• Does the purpose have a positive influence on the present dynamics? Is the purpose a strong driving force? Has the purpose been displaced by other values and paradigms? If the direction is off course or has little influence on daily work, correcting this situation will have high leverage.

• Do some design element boxes have more data in them than others? If you address one element, it will influence several cultural behaviors and therefore increase your leverage.

Understanding the Leverage Points' Ecology

As a final step before leaving the diagnosis process, I recommend using Kurt Lewin's "Force Field Analysis" to better understand your leverage points. A force field is made up of driving forces (propelling you towards your vision) and restraining forces (barriers to progress; drivers of the status quo). Your present design (the status quo) reflects a balancing of these two forces. In the diagram below, notice that each force has its root (like the weeds or vines in your vineyard). If the restraining roots aren't eliminated, their weeds will grow back. If the driving roots aren't nourished, they may wither and die. Also note how the different arrow widths symbolize different strengths. Here's how I would summarize Metro Schools' Force Field:

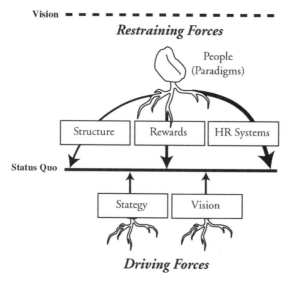

The current drivers are strategy and vision, but these are much weaker than the resisting forces. That's why the schools are struggling to improve. The major resistors are:

(1) the poor human resources development systems that keep inexperienced teachers in the most difficult situations,

(2) the rewards system that provides no negative consequences (to teachers and principals) for delivering mediocre edu-

cation, and provides no positive consequences for those who excel at educating students,

(3) a structure that locates the most experienced resources too far away from each site.

There is another dimension to the rewards system: because of multiple agendas, working on the system itself is a punishing experience! The root structure feeding all three resistors lies in people's paradigms of "showing we can spend less than last year," "students must temporarily take a back seat," "things must change—but not in my area," and "you can't trust the system— power allows me to determine my own destiny." Without extracting these roots, new resistors will grow to take the place of any old ones removed. This organization is perfectly designed to get what it gets. It won't get anything better until the vineyard is skillfully reworked.

As you think about your strategy for improving this situation, picture this force field as though you were driving down the street in your car with one foot on the brake, the other on the gas pedal. How would you make the fastest progress on your journey? By removing your foot from the brake, or in other words, eliminating the resistors. This is usually true for organizational force fields as well. However, in Metro's case, you can't afford to neglect the importance of also pressing harder on the gas—strengthening the forces of strategy and vision.

In summary, Metro Schools would improve its educational process if everyone would recommit themselves to their total vision and strategy and then realign their design elements to help them deliver. The most critical design elements to begin improving would be the human resource systems, rewards, and structure. In this process of recommitment and realigning, they would have to make sure harmful paradigms are rooted out and replaced by the vision.

In actuality, Metro Schools did nothing to address any of these critical forces. The splintered Board united around only one issue—to terminate the superintendent's contract. A new superintendent was hired. Some small steps forward have been made, but Metro continues to get what it always has been getting.

This is a classic example of blaming an individual for what a faulty system is delivering. True North doesn't budge for human organizations any more than you might expect the weather to selectively care for some vineyards. The OP Model diagnosis can only show you how everything in the organization is really operating. It can't make the tough decision for you or finalize your actions to rebalance the ecosystem's force field.

Conclusion

Before moving on, let me summarize two key points:

First, diagnose before you prescribe. You probably don't have the time or money to waste on blindly tinkering with your organization's elements. The diagnosis process described here takes much of the guesswork out of designing. And if you use the OP Model as your process guide, a high quality diagnosis can be done in a relatively short time.

Second, the real competitive advantage lies in being able to distinguish critical drivers/resistors from extraneous ones. Shaping an improvement strategy to weaken or eliminate key resistors (and their roots!) while strengthening the driving forces (by feeding their roots!) is a sound prescription.

As complex as the diagnosis process is, it is but the first step (and I might add, the easier step) toward better alignment and better results. Despite all the work done in recent years to restructure, downsize, and reshape the way work is done, the number of highly effective organizations is still relatively small. Too many are controlled by the roots of bureaucracy rather than by natural laws. In the next chapter I will describe the design process and review high performance design principles to help you put natural laws to work in your organization.

• • •

Applying what you have learned:

Here are some suggestions to put into action what you have learned in this chapter:

1. Practice looking at what goes on through the eyes of a "fly on the wall." Write down some one-word descriptions of your organization's culture. Then, for each word, write down 2 or 3 descriptive phrases of what the fly would see or hear to justify the word.

2. Diagnose one good or poor result by going through the process summarized on page 183 and illustrated by the Metro Schools case.

3. Do a Force Field Analysis to reveal the most critical drivers, resistors, and roots in your diagnosis.

10

Putting Natural Laws to Work

"The neglected leadership role is the designer of the ship. No one has a more sweeping influence than the designer. What good does it do for the captain to say, 'Turn starboard thirty degrees,' when the designer has built a rudder that will turn only to port, or which takes six hours to turn to starboard? It's fruitless to be the leader in an organization that is poorly designed."

—Peter Senge

"If to do were as easy as to know what were good to do, chapels had been churches, and poor men's cottages princes' palaces."

—William Shakespeare

WE ARE AT A CRUCIAL POINT IN ESTABLISHING Leadership for the Ages. You are developing your leadership from the inside out; you have started by living consistently with your personal mission and by increasing your technical competence. This earns you enthusiastic followers. You have been able to shape a compelling, common mission, so you and your key stakeholders have the same aims. Through your balanced scorecard and dynamic information system you are keeping in touch with how well you are fitting into the ecological order of stake-

199

holder needs. And through the diagnosis process you have learned how well you are aligned to fulfill the moments of truth.

Now it's time to engage in the design process—shaping or reshaping the organization's design elements to get the results you want. Your organization will not deliver sustained perform-ance improvements *until* it has been redesigned. Mahatma Gandhi once said, "There are 99 people who believe in honesty for every honest man." Similarly, there are 99 organizations that desire structural integrity for every one that has it. This chapter aims to help you be "the one."

Natural Laws Govern

Begin thinking about the design process with your organiza-tion's lifecycle. The objective of the design process is to become perfectly designed to meet your stakeholders' moments of truth. Do this consistently and you will stay on top of the lifecycle through the ages. Remember, in chapter 2, we determined that the following natural laws explain why organizations either sur-vive or become obsolete:

1. Ecological order—each element of the ecosystem must fit into the order of things.

2. Purpose—everything else is subordinated to the highest purpose: survival for self, group and species.

3. Steady state—survival is maintained via steady processes that follow a proven, functional routine.

4. Mobilization—threats to survival and the steady state are sensed and met.

5. Complexity—systems develop more complex, specialized functions.

6. Synergy—the whole is greater than the sum of its parts; synergy comes from new relationships.

7. Adaptation—processes change as necessary when environ-mental changes threaten survival.

Take a moment and compare the performance standard of these natural laws with the actual performance you uncovered in the diagnosis process. Aren't the remedies to your major diagnosis problems contained in these seven natural laws? Would your relationship with any stakeholder be in jeopardy if you fit into the order of things? Would you have any motivation problems if the mission were compelling for everyone? Would any customers be disappointed if your steady state consistently delivered more than they expected? Would your cycle time be shorter if the system mobilized those closest to every process deviation to correct it promptly and skillfully? Would you deliver more with less if everyone's skills continually expanded? Would team synergy be able to overcome individual weaknesses? And if you could remain focused on purpose and adapt in countless ways to a changing environment, would you ever slide down from the life-cycle peak? These natural laws govern our effectiveness. Make them come alive in your organization and they will sustain your survival and growth through endless changes and transformations in your environment. They are the formula for enduring through the ages.

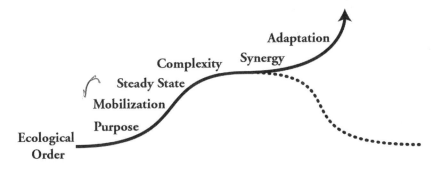

The Design Process

The natural laws of living systems are an important foundation for the work of designing your organization. The process itself is very straightforward. But if the process does not align how you work every day with these natural laws, it will have been a waste of time. Your aim for every step of this process should be to put natural laws to work for your benefit. As you can see in the following diagram, the design process goes in the opposite direction we used for diagnosis. The process begins with stakeholder needs and moves counterclockwise:

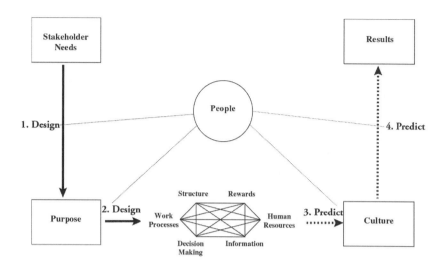

The four steps in the design process are:

1. Create the purpose (mission, strategy, etc.) to be aligned with stakeholder needs.

2. Create the six design elements to be aligned with the purpose.

3. Predict the positive and negative impacts the new design will have on the culture.

4. Predict the results that will be produced by the new culture. If the predicted results will still fall short of the stakeholder needs, then revisit steps 1, 2, and 3.

If the designing appears to be simpler and more straightforward than diagnosing, don't be fooled! Designing is far more complicated (and time consuming) than diagnosing. The OP Model is a good road map for the journey you will take, but there are many stops to be made along the way. This book is not the place to give you all the answers for each stop. You may find it necessary to consult other experts and use additional methodologies to truly design things properly. Let's turn up the microscope on this design process and examine it more closely.

Step 1. Design the purpose to be aligned with stakeholder needs. This is the same process addressed in chapters 5-7. A mission, a balanced scorecard, and their aligned feedback systems are invaluable for accurately pegging how you are performing

versus the stakeholders' moments
of truth. One important element
of purpose not addressed is strategy. This, too, is an area that covers volumes. I won't try to go into
the details of strategic planning,
other than to say that the process

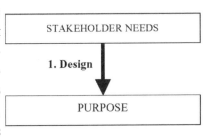

should help you answer three crucial questions:

• What "business" are we in? (What hard choices have we made
about which stakeholder needs to fulfill and which to leave alone?)

• What are our basic technologies (tangible or intangible)?
(What are our core competencies?)

• How do we choose to compete in our "businesses"? (What
are our core products and services? Our plan of attack? Our
sources of competitive advantage?)

The bottom line of a strategic planning process is found in
your ability to answer this question, "Why should we legiti-
mately expect to compete and succeed in our market place?" The
references for this chapter will point you to some approaches that
I have seen answer these questions. If this step is successfully executed, your organization will fit into the ecological order of
things and have a compelling purpose.

*Step 2. Fashion the six design elements to be aligned with the
purpose.* With the new direction clarified, we now move to shape
(or reshape) the various organization design elements to be perfectly aligned with it.

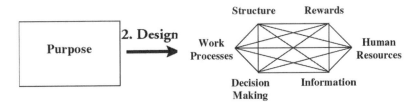

This is another complicated step, one that deserves deep study
in its own right. There are scores of approaches and consulting

firms who specialize in each of these six systems. The fundamental logic stream, however, is quite simple:

• Mission and strategy are the roots for determining your core tasks and work processes. Every major process should help bring the mission and strategy to life.

• Work processes become the basis for designing the other five design elements. These should work synergistically so that the work processes operate flawlessly.

• The aligned design elements produce the cultural behaviors that enable you to get the desired results.

It's the ability to design these elements synergistically that makes the difference. Too often, managers have designed one or a few of them in isolation from each other. The improvements that have emerged are small compared to the potential of true synergy. This chapter focuses on describing high performance design principles that can guide your efforts in step two.

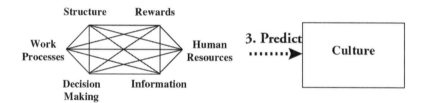

Step 3. Predict the positive and negative impacts the new design will have on the culture. This step is frequently overlooked. It means taking the time to test your reshaped design elements from the viewpoint of the fly on the wall. What will the fly really see if your new systems operate as designed? Answering this question is not blind guesswork if you have done a comprehensive diagnosis. You can refer back to your diagnosis Force Field Analysis to see if the new systems are strong enough to eliminate the critical resistors and drive the organization to higher performance levels. Here are some questions to ask in this step of the process:

• How have the restraining forces' roots been cut out?

- How do your new elements eliminate or weaken the restraining forces?
- Will the new design elements be strong enough to drive performance upward?
- Are the drivers' roots aligned with natural laws?

When your new design elements are aligned with natural laws, you will have a culture characterized by a dependable steady state, mobilization, natural complexity, synergy, and adaptation.

Step 4. Predict the results that will be produced by the new culture. Here again, if you have done a thorough diagnosis first, this prediction will be far more accurate than mere guesswork. This is a reversal of the diagnosis step #2 that identifies the behaviors causing each current result. This time we analyze the behaviors from step three to see if they connect logically with the desired results.

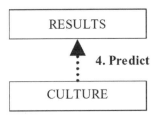

How Ritz-Carlton Is Designed

The Ritz-Carlton Hotel Company is a good example of an organization design yielding a high performance culture. I have already shared how much Ritz-Carlton invests in getting its credo into everyone's heart and mind. Now let's look at the other half of their success formula—how they align everything to fulfill the credo.

"People always ask me why we spend so much time on the credo and our values," President Horst Schulze says. "Some of our employees still ask me this from time to time. I want to show them how living our credo contributes to our bottom-line success." What follows is the diagram Horst uses to illustrate Ritz-Carlton's ecosystem. Think of it as their flow chart for success.

Let me explain some of this flow chart's "logic streams." The ecosystem's bottom line is to have a profitable business where three main stakeholders are happy: the guests, the owners, and the employees. Attending to all three sets of needs will ensure

Ritz-Carlton fits into the order of things and remains atop the lifecycle.

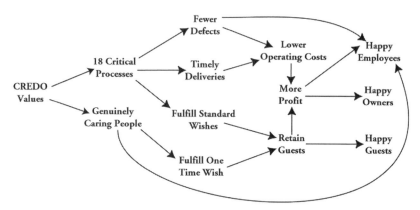

The credo and values are the source of everything good that flows from left to right in the diagram. The hotels' distinctive products are (1) impeccable service and (2) a memorable experience. Service is broken into 18 critical work processes that aim to fulfill the guests' "standard" wishes. (Examples: reservations, reception, housekeeping, guest room preventative maintenance, valet parking, room service, concierge, etc.) By perfecting these 18 processes, the hotel will have fewer defects and more on-time deliveries. This lowers costs and creates a more exciting work climate for employees.

But each guest also has that "one time wish," some unusual request that no system can ever be prepared to handle. Like black ink instead of blue in the room's ballpoint pen. Or a special shoe rack. Even letting the family chef use Ritz-Carlton's kitchen. How does an organization equip itself to handle such one-time wishes? Only through genuinely caring people—people who sincerely want to help their guests, who won't be second guessed for exercising "intelligent disobedience" to solve unique problems. Such genuine care only comes from a deep commitment to the credo and values; it is always voluntary.

Once everything is aligned, success flows naturally through the system. Guests who find their standard wishes and their one-time wishes fulfilled will come back again and again. Happy guests mean more revenue. Because the critical systems are in place, costs go down and profits go up. This makes the owners happy. With a good profit situation, more money can be given to employees for salary increases (even in tough times). Couple this with a defect-free working environment and colleagues who genuinely care for one another, and you get happy employees as well. As long as moments of truth are fulfilled like this, Ritz-Carlton will stay on top.

Compared to what goes on in your own organization, you can appreciate how deceptively simple this flow chart is. Unlike Metro Schools, Ritz-Carlton has used its credo as a constitution. The 18 critical processes are derived from the credo and integrate all other elements to shape a culture that fulfills the stakeholder moments of truth better than the competition. But notice that it is the programmers, the "genuinely caring people," who must align everything else in the ecosystem amidst changing conditions and new guest requests. This is a good illustration of the hard work and holistic thinking it takes to create structural integrity in an organization.

Why is this degree of alignment so hard for others to achieve? The answer lies in their paradigm of structural integrity.

The Bureaucratic Paradigm

For decades, the world has viewed organizations as machine-like systems comprised of lifeless components. Alignment, order, and control have been based on the bureaucratic paradigm articulated years ago by theorists such as Frederick W. Taylor and Max Weber. Because it is so widespread, one of my experiences should remind you of your own encounters with it:

• • •

While living in Germany, I needed to get new license plates for our cars at the local bureau of motor vehicles. I arrived 10 minutes before the office opened at 9 A.M. and was the second person to be served at the window. The official handed me some forms to fill out. I completed the forms and within a few minutes was back at the window and handed them over. "That will be 50 Deutsche Marks for each car," the official said. I began to pull out my wallet when he said, "No, you don't pay here. You must go to the next department around the corner."

As I rounded the corner, I was astonished to see a long line of people in front of the second window. "Where did you all come from?" I asked. "We started yesterday," said the woman in front of me. This was my first clue that things weren't going to be as easy as I had imagined. After some 45 minutes I finally made it to the window, paid my fee, and held out my hand for my new plates. "You don't get your plates here," said the official after stamping my paperwork with the famous German seal of approval, "you get them at the next department."

"Is that around the next corner?" I asked.

"No," came the reply, "it's across the street in the basement of the white building."

Crossing the street, my eye was drawn to a very long line at the curb that eventually disappeared down the steps into the basement of a white building. This line was incredibly slow. We inched forward and by 11:25 I could see why the line's progress had been so slow: one man was methodically setting out the metal numbers and letters and stamping out each individual license plate on the spot! As my turn came, the man informed me that he was going to lunch and would be back at 1:00. "But I've been at this all morning!" I pleaded with him. "What am I supposed to do while you go eat?" He shrugged his shoulders and left me to answer my own question. I didn't dare leave and lose my hard-earned place in line! So I sat and waited while he ate.

Punctually, at 1:00 he reopened the window and began to process my plates. In due time they were finished. Again I held out my hand to get them. "Not so fast," said the man, "you must first give me your old plates."

"But my old plates are on my cars," I said, remembering the family station wagon sitting in my garage 20 miles away.

"There are no exceptions. This way we ensure that no plates are used illegally," said the man. With a large knot now churning inside my stomach, I gave up my place in line and drove home to remove the old plates from the station wagon. Returning to the parking lot, I then removed the plates from my other car and returned—apprehensively—to the basement window line. It hadn't shrunk much during my absence; I took my place at the rear. Another eternity passed before I was at the front again and handed in my old plates. Upon receiving the new ones, I thanked the man and began to depart.

"Wait a minute!" he said. "You must return to the other building and obtain the final stamp." Ironically, the final stop was at the same window where I had started in the morning. After one final line to wade through, and at a few minutes past 4 P.M., I had my final stamp, my four new license plates, and one lost day's work to catch up on.

· · ·

This is what happens when an inexperienced customer comes face to face with a bureaucratic system! You've probably had similar experiences in organizations large and small. The universality of these dynamics illustrates the power of a paradigm. Whether we are in Germany or Hong Kong, whether dealing with a government or private agency, a service or product enterprise, most organizations we encounter are rooted in this bureaucratic paradigm.

Just exactly what is the bureaucratic paradigm? It's the assumption that an organization is like a machine: a collection of parts driven by a single control mechanism. Flowing from this paradigm are six basic rules:

1. Task Specialization—"job fragmentation." Tasks are specialized and reduced to the smallest possible work cycle. In the license plate example, remember that each task in the process was separated organizationally and physically from all others.

2. Performance Standardization—"find the one best way." Work is specified to be performed the same way every time. The technical monument to this thinking is the assembly line. But even administrative processes can be organized like an assembly line. The German license bureau procedures, characterized by forms, rubber stamps, and metal plates, were always followed. No exceptions!

3. Central Decision Making—"unity of command." Decision making is exclusive to those in authority. Without the license bureau official's final stamp of approval, the entire process was invalid.

4. Uniform policies—"that's what the book says." All parts of the system are treated alike. Like a well-oiled machine, the license plate process handled everything according to policy, but made no provision for specific customer or employee needs.

5. No duplication of functions—"that's not my job!" Tasks are handled exclusively by those assigned. The license bureau organization made it impossible for anyone to help outside their assigned area. When one person went to lunch, the entire process stopped.

6. Reward physical activity—"the hired hand." A person is paid for physical labor and skills. There was no incentive for anyone in the license bureau to do anything other than the assigned task. Innovation, customer service, and process improvements were someone else's responsibility.

How have these six rules affected our society? Without question they have outperformed the agrarian society from whence they sprang. They have enabled us to mass-produce goods, thereby contributing to a higher standard of living for everyone. They do delineate job responsibilities across departments and up and down the hierarchy. And they drive out ambiguity.

But the rapidly changing needs of customers, suppliers, and associates have made bureaucracy an out-of-balance model for the Global Age. The very root of bureaucracy's problems lies in the paradigm itself: an organization is like a machine. Customers, suppliers, and associates are not machines! In ages past these stakeholders have complied with the organizational work rules. But individuals today are resisting them more and more. And these rules are failing to meet the global market needs as well as they met the industrial market's needs.

Most people have a love-hate relationship with bureaucracies. Some may love bureaucracy's order, sense of control, and efficiency when they work inside one. Yet most of them hate dealing with a bureaucracy as customers! It's not hard to see how these six policies naturally lead to the subordinate paradigm discussed in chapter 4. Once tasks are specialized, standardized, and isolated and decisions are made in advance (as policies) or only by hierarchy, then all the hired hand has to do (or can do) is follow along.

Bureaucracy's Counterfeit Core

Chapter 3 discussed the importance of centering our lives and our organizations around our missions. We all need a stable center, a changeless core that won't flip flop around in the midst of all the other changes occurring around us. Missions based on natural laws should be this stable center for each of us. They don't move with societal trends as we have seen in the lifecycle research. Our own deepest values don't shift from day to day. Your organization's fundamental reason for being, your values toward all stakeholders, your commitment to improving quality of life—these shouldn't change dramatically. It is this changeless core that gives us a sense of security and enables each of us to exercise intelligent disobedience. As Friedrich Nietsche once said, "He who has a why can endure any what."

The dynamic of organizational centers brings us to an important aspect of the bureaucratic paradigm. As time moves on, the rules of bureaucracy can become a counterfeit imitation of the mission's changeless core. The bureaucratic counterfeit stabilizes procedures, systems, and structures and moves them to the organization's center. This provides the illusion of stability, but eventually leads to even bigger problems. It is like the painkillers that athletes use to momentarily numb the senses so they can compete in an important game. Once the drugs' effects wear off, the ailment remains and the pain may be even greater than before. The drug can only hide the effect of the physical punishment for so long. Then reality sets in. Here's an example of a potential counterfeit core—a fast food restaurant supervisor's checklist:

	Yes	No

Greeting the customer
  1. There is a smile
  2. It is a sincere greeting
  3. There is eye contact.		

Taking the order
  1. The counter person is thoroughly familiar with the menu
ticket. (No hunting for items)
  2. The customer has to give the order only once.
  3. Small orders (four items or less) are memorized rather than writing them
down.
  4. There is suggestive selling.		

Assembling the order
  1. The order is assembled in the proper sequence.
  2. Grill slips are handed in first.
  3. Drinks are poured in the proper sequence.
  4. Proper amount of ice.
  5. Cups slanted and finger used to activate.
  6. Drinks are filled to the proper level.
  7. Drinks are capped.
  8. Clean cups.
  9. Holding times are observed on coffee.
  10. Cups are filled to the proper level on coffee.		

Presenting the order
  1. It is properly packaged.
  2. The bag is double folded.
  3. Plastic trays are used if eating inside.
  4. A tray liner is used.
  5. The food is handled in a proper manner.		

Asking for and receiving payment
  1. The amount of the order is stated clearly and loud enough to hear.
  2. The denomination received is clearly stated.
  3. The change is counted out loud.
  4. Changed is counted efficiently.
  5. Large bills are laid on the till until the change is given.		

Thanking the customer and asking for repeat business
  1. There is always a thank you.
  2. The thank you is sincere.
  3. There is eye contact.
  4. Return business was asked for.		

Notice how this checklist breaks down the basic customer interaction process into a number of discrete steps. It can be very helpful as a performance standard. Once trained and accustomed to such a system, you would expect team members to deliver consistent performance every day . . . and provide a sense of stability. But such a checklist can also be misused. We all know that no day is totally predictable, no matter how well organized we are. So, in the unpredictable moments, what do people focus on? This is the critical question that defines what the changeless core really is. The best way to answer this question is to observe the culture as a fly on the wall and see how people respond when something doesn't go according to the book. If they focus only on procedures like this checklist, the results could be self-defeating. For example:

• • •

A mother waited in the drive-through line of a fast food restaurant with her 18-month-old child. When she got to the speaker, she said, "I'd like an orange juice and a vanilla milkshake."

The voice at the other end of the speaker replied, "We're not allowed to serve milkshakes before 10:30 A.M."

The mother looked at her watch and said, "It's 10:25."

Answer: "I'm sorry ma'am, but we are not allowed to serve milkshakes before 10:30."

The mother considered the situation: her 18-month-old daughter wanted a milkshake; she needed to keep her pacified while they were underway; there were cars behind them; there were cars in front of them; there was nowhere to go. Finally she said, "I'll wait for five minutes."

The voice on the speaker said, "Okay." So she sat there for five minutes to get what she needed.

• • •

Certainly, this was one situation that called for "intelligent disobedience." Why didn't the employee serve the customer? Because he had been conditioned to blindly follow policies and checklists! As you can see, without maintaining a line of sight to the mission, bureaucracy's rules could actually drive away customers. I shared the fast food checklist with one of America's leading health centers some time ago and one of the professors had a very insightful comment. He said:

"I have just lived the very thing you're talking about. In recent years we have developed a patient care checklist for our medical students just like the fast food one. We found the new medical students were following the checklist, but they were no longer diagnosing the patients' real needs. They were becoming lousy doctors because all they were doing was following the checklist. Those of us who created the checklist realize this is just a framework from which to start. You also have to develop rapport with the patient. You must interact with them and examine beyond the symptoms to understand what is really going on. But those things are hard to put on a checklist."

Beware of counterfeit centers! Their false sense of security only reinforces the bureaucratic cultures that customers loathe. These cultures, as seen by the fly on the wall, include such things as:

1. Individuals simply going through the motions without regard to the mission.

2. Poor quality of service or product; in some cases even sabotage.

3. Uneven performance from person to person or group to group.

4. Delays in action, primarily waiting for management approval or for an indispensable specialist to make time for you.

5. Mistrust of others—this mistrust is rooted in a lack of confidence in others' decisions as evidenced by managers closely supervising those below them, workers withholding important information from management for fear of reprisal or increased workloads, and all members of the organization dealing with their customers on the basis of formal policy only.

6. Responses like, "I just work here," "Ask the boss," "That's what the book says," and "That's not my job."

7. Poor customer orientation: people focus on minimizing their own inconvenience rather than fully satisfying the customer.

8. Special crafts, technologies, and skills are valued over results; one's job title is more important than what one can do.

9. An emphasis on time spent, units produced, or sales volume.

10. Little renewal of technology or experimentation with new ways of operating.

How might you go about uprooting the negative aspects of bureaucracy in your own organization? The bureaucratic paradigm's roots are so deeply entrenched! Freeing ourselves from them is what makes designing more complicated than diagnosing. What driving forces would be strong enough to keep order and efficiency while becoming more innovative and focused on everyone's moments of truth? We need to balance the structure and predictability of the bureaucratic paradigm with the flexibility and adaptability of natural laws.

High Performance Design Principles

Over the past five decades some organizational design principles have emerged that have outperformed bureaucracies in many different cultures around the world. Despite volumes being written about these principles and the organizations who have pioneered them, they remain largely misunderstood and underutilized today. On the following pages I will give an overview of some of these principles under the headings of the six organization design elements.

Work Processes

High performance design begins by aligning the daily work activities with the purpose. Three design principles accomplish this:

1. Work processes are derived from mission and strategy. The major streams of activity are taken from the imperatives flowing from mission and strategy. Activities that are not directly tied to fulfilling the mission and strategy are challenged and eliminated. Here's an example of this principle derived from a European company:

Our mission is
• Superior value in our products and services to our customers. Our customers are the consumers, trade and export clients
• A level of profitability which is competitive with other investment alternatives the mother company has world-wide
• A working environment which helps employees to develop their full potential
Excellence in achieving our mission will be measured by our ability to reach in our current lines of business the following within the next three years:
• A 33 percent volume increase
• A profit margin increase to three times the level achieved to date
Fundamental to achieving this objective will be generating an adequate level of profit on our established and recently introduced brands
Our strategy to achieve the mission will be to build an organization that is always "one step ahead" of our competitors. This will be possible when each member of the organization contributes a measurable extra value to our business progress (volume, productivity, and cost effectiveness). This will be influenced by:

Innovation
• Promote a culture of learning, creativity, change, and action. Everybody's business is identifying opportunities and problems, and developing solutions.
• Excellence in Execution towards Results
• Develop commitment to and pride in executional excellence. This will achieve results which allow us to feel proud and enthusiastic about ourselves, our work, and our company.

Teamwork
• Strengthen the joint effectiveness between departments, across organizational boundaries and hierarchical levels, and within the European company. This also includes the relationship between the company and employee representative groups. "We're in this together" is the attitude pervading the organization.

From the content of this mission and strategy flow the following primary work processes:

1. Product creation and delivery
2. Customer service
3. Profit management
4. Work environment
5. Volume growth
6. Innovation
7. Excellence in execution
8. Teamwork

Note that none of the traditional departmental labels appear in this list. This is intentional.

Structural integrity comes from aligning all organizational resources to primary work processes, not from rearranging current departments. It is healthy to temporarily ignore current departmental structures and focus instead on what has to happen functionally to bring the mission and strategy to life. In this example, the company will achieve its mission and strategy if it can create structural integrity around these eight work processes.

2. Work processes are connected in a quality process flow. Quality methods are used to map out each work process identified in principle #1 and ensure a free-flowing delivery of the product or service by eliminating artificial barriers, redundancy, rework, or delays. This process mapping can functionally connect the tasks of the work processes with the support systems of structure, information, decision-making, and training. In this example, asking a few basic questions can connect all design elements with the work process.

Supply	Task 1	Repair	Support	Decide	Task 2	PRODUCT OR SERVICE

• How will Supply people, Task 1 & 2 people, Repair people, Support people, and Decide people best work together on the tasks? This is a question of structure.

• How will we reward the right behaviors and discourage the wrong behaviors? This defines what the rewards will be.

• Who has the right knowledge and experience to make decisions at each step? This becomes the decision-making system.

• Who needs what information to perform efficiently and effectively? This is a user-based approach to building the information system.

• What skills and behaviors does this process require? The answers should shape the backbone of the Human Resources systems, from hiring to training, to advancement.

3. Work processes are not over-designed. The bureaucratic paradigm has taught managers to try to specify everything about the system. The Tavistock Institute in England has identified the principle of "minimal critical specification" and has used it to find the balance between structure and flexibility in organizations. This principle simply states that you should specify no more (rules, policies, procedures) than is absolutely essential, but you should specify those few things that are essential. Voluminous policy books are thereby replaced by a few critical guidelines managed in a culture of committed, informed, and skilled members who use their best judgment to manage daily operations (like Ritz-Carlton). For instance, as part of Sears' corporate turnaround in the mid 1990s, new CEO Arthur Martinez replaced 29,000 pages of policies and procedures with two simple booklets. "We call them 'freedoms' and 'obligations,'" he said. "We're trying to tell our managers what they're responsible for, what freedoms they have to make decisions, and where to turn if they need help. But we don't want to codify every possible situation." Sears has been making a turn around. It lost $3.9 billion in 1992 but has bounced back to earn $ 901 million on revenues of $28.6 billion in 2000.

Structure

Structure is an important part of keeping a work process free-flowing that permits people to come together to complete the tasks without delay, redundancy, or rework. The most important structural characteristic is self-sufficiency (e.g., enabling individuals to handle the problems in front of them without being dependent on resources or skills that others have). Self-sufficiency is achieved through the following principles:

1. Control errors at the source: errors, or deviations from the ideal process, are controlled where they originate. No one would argue with this principle, but very few organizations measure up to its standard. In order to control errors at the source, the people closest to the problem must have the knowledge and skills to make the corrections. In a production setting, this means the machine operator would have the wherewithal to make minor adjustments and repairs to the machine so that it keeps running. If a maintenance specialist must be called constantly to adjust and repair, efficiencies go down and costs go up. In an administrative or managerial setting, the deviations usually require judgment and decision-making to correct. Structurally, the best person to handle such issues is the person closest to them. Going up the hierarchy for a decision is just as costly as waiting for a maintenance specialist on the production line.

A unit of the IBM Corporation in Rochester, New York researched the effect of violating this principle. IBM reported its findings in terms of units of time required to fix a problem at various stages. If the problem was corrected in the design stage, it took one unit of time. If it wasn't caught until the production stage, 13 units were required to fix it. If it went undetected until it got to the customer, the effort required 92 units. Think of all the organizational resources that are linked to each unit of time: people, wages, facilities, equipment/supplies, levels of supervision. If problems aren't stopped at their source, they usually are moved up the hierarchy or to distant staff groups, leading to delays, rework, extra expense, and an end result that is often not fit for use by the customer.

Some organizations have tried to implement this principle without developing people to handle the increased responsibility. In order to abide by this principle and improve results, organizations have to develop in every associate a greater commitment to the mission, a greater range of skills, and greater discernment.

2. Self-sufficient teams: this extends the principle of error control to the primary work teams in the organization. Work teams are organized to be self-sufficient in daily operations and decision making. This requires staffing the team with sufficient numbers and skills to handle all the functions related to fulfilling its mission. In the illustration here, there are nine functions that are critical to team performance. A self-sufficient team has the necessary skills and is responsible individually and/or collectively for fulfilling each of them on a daily basis.

3. Self-sufficient units: the self-sufficient team model is extrapolated to the larger organizational unit. A self-sufficient unit (department, division, etc.) produces a tangible product or service. Such a product or service represents a change of state in the order of things. For example, raw materials are transformed through various stages into a finished product. Information is updated, analyzed, and synthesized to yield more value to customers. Such changes of state, therefore, hold the keys to determining self-sufficiency. An objective way of drawing boundaries between self-sufficient units is to determine where there is an actual change of state in the process flow. Take the following production process for example:

Supply	Task 1	Repair	Support	Decide	Task 2	PRODUCT OR SERVICE

Some operations have separate departments for each of the functions listed above. But the material that flows from supply to product only undergoes two changes of state: (1) when Task 1 transforms it into a product form and (2) when Task 2 converts it into the final product. Three self-sufficient units, therefore, would be possible:

1. Supply
2. Task 1 (including all repairs, support, and decision making)
3. Task 2 (organized similar to Task 1).

Depending on the factors of technology (how complex is each unit?), territory (how distant are they from each other?), or time (how long does it take to complete each?), these three could be combined into one self-sufficient unit, be divided between Supply and Production (combining Tasks 1 and 2), or remain as three separate entities. Once these boundaries have been clarified, all interdependent functions should be grouped within the same unit, especially if they need to interact frequently.

A good litmus test for this principle is to examine the steps in the process and ask two questions: "How interdependent is each function?" and "How frequently do people need to work together to complete the process?" If the organization is highly interdependent (e.g., engineering skill to complete a construction project) and needs to work together frequently (several projects always underway), then it makes sense to organize the resources together.

You can test the pragmatism of the self-sufficiency principle for yourself. What happens in your organization when you have to go to another department for needed resources?

• Do you have to "get in line," meaning your priority must be evaluated against others?

• Do you have to wait for someone else's attention?

• Do you find your desired outcome being modified because the other department isn't quite prepared to do everything you need?

Add up the impact of the delays from each of these answers and you will have quantified your own "IBM factor." You will see how expensive it is to control errors downstream instead of at the source. As a final word on this point, let me say that organizing in this way usually creates a system with more people close to the heart of the organization's mission and fewer in central staff groups.

4. Multi-functional teams: the self-sufficient team concept also applies to the management of an integrated product or service line. All interdependent functions are represented on the core team, whose major tasks are to compare the results vs. stakeholder needs, shape the purpose, and coordinate all departments' execution to reach the targeted results. The work of the team is mostly analytical and conceptual. The execution is handled daily by the individual departmental units. But the multifunctional team adds value by aligning all the pieces for greater synergy. I will give some specific examples of this structure in the next chapter.

5. Networks and virtual organizations: multifunctional team processes also enable different entities in different locations to "come together" as needed. It is another application of the "petal" diagram. Because these teams add value at the strategic and conceptual

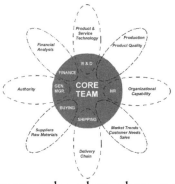

level, physical location is important only when they come together. Modern video conferencing technology even permits people in different locations to "attend" the same meeting.

6. Boundary Management: as individuals control errors at their source, as work teams become more self-sufficient, and as multifunctional networks become more critical in delivering results, the manager's role in each unit shifts from supervision to boundary management. This means managers add value not by supervising what goes on inside the team/unit, but by working on performance issues between the team/unit and its various interfaces (e.g., poor quality materials from suppliers, installation of new equip-

ment, aligning production with marketing promotions, etc.). These issues often "fall through the cracks," adding enormous waste, rework and cost to the system. W. Edwards Deming used to sum up this principle this way, "Managers work on the system, not in the system."

Decision-Making

This element must balance two opposite forces, the unity of command and immediate response. Unity of command seeks to align decisions with purpose and the ecological order of things. Immediate response seeks to align decisions in real time with the events that transpire as the work is done. Bureaucracies entrust decisions to a few officers and managers. But, as any customer or associate can attest, this often precludes an immediate response. Some organizations have empowered people at the lowest level to make key decisions. If the "empowered" ones are not committed and skillful in what they do, however, their decisions may not be aligned with purpose. Out of this polarity emerges one design principle:

1. Empower the experts: decisions are made at the level of most appropriate knowledge and experience. This has less to do with one's position in the hierarchy than with one's position in the work process. Typically the person with the most knowledge and experience is the one closest to the issue to be decided. This may be the CEO for a marketplace issue and a front-line person for an operational issue. Under this principle, decision-making would be pushed down to lower levels only after these levels had developed the appropriate knowledge and experience.

The practicality of applying this principle depends on the design of the other support systems.

Rewards

This is a subject that has been researched and experimented with for centuries. And it is still one of the least understood of all the design elements. The source of most misunderstanding is in our paradigm of "rewards." People equate rewards typically only with such items as pay, promotion, and formal evaluations. A true reward is anything that motivates you to do one thing and not another. Some of the strongest rewards don't cost the organization anything. For instance, peer pressure is a reward that costs nothing. So are the things a manager pays attention to and follows up on. Another way to describe rewards is "consequences." Because each reward is perceived by us humans in our own idiosyncratic, personal ways, very few generalizations can be made about effective reward systems. These design principles are among those few:

1. Reward what you truly want. Research shows you get what you reward. Most of the time reward systems are designed around one or a few key outcomes (e.g., production, meeting deadlines, seniority). Here are two examples:

• Professors and teachers who are tenured have been rewarded for years of service. So you get people to stay with the organization for many years. But do you always get top teaching and research?

• One large automotive repair chain paid its mechanics for the volume of repairs they made. Result? In 1992 the attorneys general in 41 states alleged that mechanics were repairing things that weren't broken. The company paid just under $15 million to settle the charges and eliminated commission for mechanics.

Such one-dimensional reward systems explain why bureaucracies produce "hired hands." World-class organizations need much more than just hands. They need mind and spirit as well. They need what the Ritz-Carlton has—the systems and genuinely caring and capable individuals to meet any customer's need (anticipated or unanticipated). And effective rewards reinforce all of the organization's needed behaviors.

Flowing from this principle is a key design point. Formal and informal rewards should be aligned with stakeholder needs, mission, vision, values, and strategy—because you get what you reward.

2. Pay for contribution: the overall pay system is linked to actual work performance and overall contribution to fulfilling the organization's purpose. This more balanced standard replaces what is often rewarded: seniority, job title, productivity, volume growth, or customer service. The survival instinct is blunted when anything other than contribution to overall results and mission is the basis for rewards.

3. Balance extrinsic and intrinsic rewards. Extrinsic rewards are things like pay, promotions, bonus incentives, job titles, and fringe benefits. They are formal and bestowed on someone by the organization. Intrinsic rewards, on the other hand, are informal and are available to everyone through the nature of how work gets done. Examples would be a learning environment, interesting and challenging work, team identity, a sense of contribution, and personal growth. Of the two, intrinsic rewards are the more enduring.

Alfie Kohn (author of *Punished By Rewards* referenced at the end of the book) summarizes years of little-known research that reveals a disturbing fact: the more you tie extrinsic rewards to intrinsically motivating work, the less motivating the work itself becomes. This explains why professional athletes would suddenly refuse to play the game they have loved for years, why some people would turn down challenging and exciting (but risky) assignments, and why some people just can't avoid overtime even when the company's cost picture is in critical condition. Emphasis on extrinsic rewards can diminish the intrinsic rewards of work. It is necessary to strike a balance between the two. Designers who follow this principle identify what is intrinsically rewarding about their organization's work processes and avoid tying excessive extrinsic rewards to these elements.

Information

In our Information Age, there has never been so much information available to so many so instantly! Yet many organizations are "data rich and information poor" because they do a relatively poor job of shaping and managing the information they give to people to do their work. Too many lack the information they need to self-correct what they are doing. And too many are distracted by information that adds little or no value. The following three principles can help you determine "who needs to know what to do what" in the organization:

1. Stakeholder Feedback System. As covered in chapter 5, this means you regularly gather high quality feedback from all key stakeholders to understand how the organization is doing against the moments of truth.

2. Point of Action. This principle states that information should be designed primarily to go to the point of action and problem solving. How do you know who needs what information? The balanced scorecard should tell you what the most important results are and how well you are delivering against them. The work process quality analysis should have identified who needs what information to complete their tasks. Your structure should identify who needs to control deviations at their source. Flowing from these three design elements are the information needs that must be shaped into an effective system. The principle here is a paradigm shift from the way most information systems are approached. Rather than "design information to go first to the top," design it to go primarily to the point of action.

Many organizations have a "need to know" information system—only give people the information they need to know to do their job. There is nothing wrong, conceptually, with such a system. Problems can arise, however, when an individual's "need to know" has been transformed by restructuring, reengineering, and new competitive demands. Think about the principle of "information to the point of action" in relation to these systems in your organization:

- Financial performance
- Sharing of best practices
- Changes in procedures
- Customer feedback
- Safety performance
- Government regulation

In each case, is the flow of information designed so it goes first to the point of action? What would it take to revamp any of these systems to be in line with this principle?

3. Targeted. This principle merely states that information should be targeted to those who need it. This goes against the grain of our e-mail culture in which one push of the button sends one message to the entire population. Non-targeted information becomes noise in the channel, requiring time, attention, and energy to wade through. Applying this principle merely requires one to think through who needs what information and to design the system to deliver information to the right targets.

Human Resource Systems

As we saw in the OP Model, people are the programmers of everything else in the organization; they are the keepers of the flame that must shine through the ages. The organization's results over time rise and fall with the abilities of its human resources to work and adapt in an ever-changing environment. The human resource systems handle all phases of hiring, orienting, training, developing, coaching, and separating people from the work processes. These principles are the cornerstones for effectively aligning people with work processes:

1. Key factor selection. Members are selected based on key performance factors drawn from the purpose and work process requirements, especially those factors that are hard to train for.

2. Key factor training. Training is provided to help members continuously improve their performance in the key factor areas.

3. Roles organized around whole tasks. This applies the principle of self-sufficiency to each individual work role. Each role is shaped around a whole task as measured by a tangible output or service. An example of this would be forming automobile assembly line workers into a self-sufficient team that would produce transmissions, brake systems, or complete the final assembly of the car. Another example would be bringing together insurance associates responsible for receiving insurance claims, determining benefits to be paid, processing the checks, customer correspondence, and reimbursement distribution into a customer team responsible for a product line (life insurance, accident insurance, etc.) or a geographical base of customers (western region). Such organizations provide a "line of sight" between each individual and the organization's purpose.

4. Multi-skilled work roles. Remember, in nature, complexity is tied to ever-increasing functionality and ability to adapt to changes in the environment. This principle develops natural complexity by having each member develop skills in more than one function. This enables the work system to become more flexible and adaptive over time. In the assembly line and insurance team examples, this means each team member eventually would have the opportunity to become skilled in all work roles within the team. The "Multi-Skill Wheel" diagrammed here illustrates some typical skills that could be incorporated into an individual's career path over time.

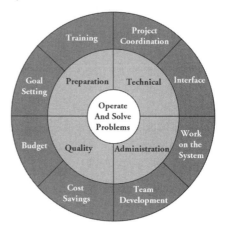

5. Cross-functional career paths. Over time, each member also has the opportunity to work in different functions to increase expertise and better understand the total organization. Thus assembly line associates could also work in the accounting department, or supply, or distribution. Typically subunits that interface with each other have a hard time appreciating each other's situation. Working for a time on the other side of the line not only creates natural empathy for each other, it also develops the knowledge and perspective for solving interface misalignments that steal time and money from the bottom line.

How Design Principles Align with Natural Laws

The design principles just outlined are a powerful formula for organizing in the Global Age—or any age for that matter—because they embody the natural laws of living systems.

These high performance design principles can provide you with a deeper understanding of many of the so-called management fads that bid for your attention from time to time. The next time you read about a new approach that seems to be getting good results somewhere else, ask yourself, "How does that line up with these design principles?" Or do the same if someone recommends a new information system to you. Ask yourself, "Will this enable me to get information faster to the point of action?" In this way you can avoid blindly applying new approaches without being clear on what they are intended to accomplish. Merely moving to a team system or reengineering your work processes won't guarantee success any more than writing a mission statement in isolation will motivate all employees. By the same token, focusing on principles early may help you incorporate something you might have dismissed out of hand just because it appeared to be only a fad.

Natural Law	High Performance Design Principles
1. Ecological Order	• Balanced Scorecard • Stakeholder Feedback System
2. Purpose	• Compelling purpose • Key factor selection • Roles organized around whole tasks • Reward what you truly want
3. Steady State	• Work processes derived from strategy • Quality process flow • Minimal critical specification • Targeted information
4. Mobilization	• Control errors at the source • Information to the point of action • Empower the experts
5. Complexity	• Self-sufficient units • Self-sufficient teams • Boundary management • Design informal rewards
6. Synergy	• Multi-functional teams • Networks and virtual organizations • Balance intrinsic and extrinsic rewards • Pay for contribution
7. Adaptation	• Multi-skilled work roles • Key factor training • Cross-functional career paths

Those organizations that have built themselves around these design principles are characterized by:

• Everyone acts like an owner.

• There are no artificial barriers. People don't say, "That's not my job."

• Continual improvement is sought: no one gets complacent with today's success.

• People do whatever it takes to get the job done.

• The right individuals are assembled to solve problems.

• Strong leaders are found at all levels of the organization.

• "Pushing back" on top management is a norm. One's ability to contribute to a problem or opportunity is more important than one's rank or status in the organization.

Conclusion

Collectively, the high performance design principles represent some profound paradigm shifts from bureaucracy's rules. Some of the major paradigm shifts include:

• Moving from "performance standardization" to being mission driven

• Moving from "task specialization" to thinking of all tasks as part of a process

• Moving from efficiency to self-sufficiency

• Moving from thinking hierarchically to thinking functionally

• Moving from narrow spans of control to wider skill sets

This chapter has only touched on the core principles that can help your organization become aligned to get the results you want. Take seriously the readings on the reference page to familiarize yourself more deeply with possible applications of these principles.

All organizations are perfectly designed to get the results they get. Designing around high performance principles creates a structural integrity among purpose, each of the six design elements, and culture that enables high performance to be natural, free flowing and exhilarating!

• • •

Applying what you have learned:

Here are some suggestions to put into action what you have learned in this chapter:

1. Analyze the strengths and weaknesses the six bureaucracy rules have contributed to your organization. Pay particular attention to the cultural behaviors that flow from them.

2. Study your organizational/departmental mission and strategy. List the primary work processes that should naturally flow from the content of the mission/strategy.

3. Use the high performance principles discussed in this chapter to brainstorm changes in the six design elements that could improve the organization's functioning.

4. Do a Force Field Analysis to test whether or not your proposed design element changes would actually change your current behaviors to be mission/strategy driven.

11
When Partnerships Are Synergistic

"Some people seek to get. They seek money, power, or prestige. With persistence and luck they might obtain what they seek. Some people seek to give. They want to provide opportunities, growth, and independence for others. Whether they are lucky or not, they will be able to obtain what they seek. They will find opportunities to help people grow . . .

"When 'getters' get what they want, it is usually at others' expense. The human costs are almost always heavy. When 'givers' get what they want, others prosper with them . . . Only to them does allegiance flow without expense of energy on their part. People want to work with them and for them."
—C. Terry Warner

"An institution is like a tune, it is not constituted by individual sounds but by the relations between them."
—Peter Drucker

S OME TIME AGO A LARGE COMPANY (LET'S CALL it Alpha) took out a full-page advertisement in the newspaper. It opened with this sentence: "We'd like to thank our best suppliers worldwide." Then 152 suppliers were recognized as Alpha's Suppliers of the Year. At the bottom of the page, the final sentence read: "Working together to achieve customer enthusiasm with exciting Alpha products."

The casual reader might have been impressed with this company's recognition of its best suppliers. But those who had worked with Alpha smiled at the advertisement's irony. Just two years before this recognition, Alpha had torn up its contracts with many of these suppliers and demanded the terms be renegotiated with significant across-the-board price reductions. During this episode, one of Alpha's suppliers asked me, "How do we know they won't do the same thing six months from now? They tore up a legal contract and made us bid lower. They could do it again. They've destroyed our trust in them."

Despite their resentment, this company and most of Alpha's other suppliers swallowed hard and lowered their prices. However, the suppliers compensated in their own way, as one of them explained, "I can tell you how we and everyone else will make up some of the loss. We'll lower the quality of our materials." My ears perked up at this statement because Alpha's biggest problem at the time was declining sales due to consumer perceptions that its products were of inferior quality. Later I read where an industry observer stated, "I don't know of any major supplier who will take a new design to Alpha today, because, in the end, they will give it to the lowest bidder."

Notice how committed these "partners" were to "working together to achieve customer enthusiasm with exciting Alpha products." What was the bottom line of this situation? Did the cost savings from supplier contracts and the full-page advertisement actually help Alpha's business? In the short term, Alpha did save millions of dollars. But its position in today's marketplace continues to decline because customer perceptions of its poor product quality are unchanged. And Alpha's senior management is still trying desperately to squeeze out more profits.

Such will be the fate of those who try to use Industrial Age intimidation tactics in the Global Age. The Industrial Age was characterized by big organizations bringing together people and materials and leveraging their size to outperform their competitors. Bigger was better. But in the Global Age, organizations must:

• Develop a familiarity with customer needs in many different cultures.

• Be competitive with the best in class in every step of their work processes.

• Tap into many local labor markets and supply chains to be better, faster, and cheaper.

• Expand and contract their resources as required by fluctuations in multiple markets.

No single organization can do all of this. This is why strategic partnerships have replaced mega corporations as the organizational vehicle of choice in the Global Age. As Dartmouth professor James Brian Quinn likes to say, "If you aren't the best in the world at something, you are giving up competitive advantage by doing it yourself." So you partner with others who can add value to your product/service ecosystem. But, strategic partnerships present new dilemmas, namely:

• How do you disperse people across organizations and locations while keeping their hearts and minds unified?

• How do you give sufficient rein to the front lines without losing accountability and commitment to the overall purpose?

• How do you develop a work culture in which many diverse ideas and ways of doing things can be respected, tested, and leveraged to discover new, leading-edge solutions?

Competing in the Global Age requires you to partner with many other organizations to stay aligned with the market. Regardless of how self-sufficient you are internally, you will always have to work across boundaries with individuals who have somewhat different allegiances. The instrument to harmonize yourself with these outsiders is a network of synergistic partnerships. This is not the same as an association of retaliating groups who have been squeezed, outsourced, reengineered, and downsized. Neither is it a monolithic organization divided into dozens of subsidiaries held together by bureaucracy's glue. The rules of bureaucracy don't have the bonding power or flexibility to meet global performance requirements.

This chapter will explore what a network of synergistic partnerships really looks like. As with everything else in the world of organizations, these partnerships must be developed from the inside out. Accordingly, I will examine first the paradigms that are the heart of a true partnership and then share some organizational practices that have made a difference.

The End Justifies the Means?

A win-lose paradigm can no more lead to synergistic partnerships than the rules of bureaucracy can produce self-sufficient organizations. The Alpha company is a good example of one traditional paradigm of stakeholders. This paradigm tells managers that suppliers, employees, governments, and even customers are simply a means to an end—the end of winning a profit for shareholders. According to this paradigm, winning for the shareholders justifies doing what must be done to any of the other stakeholders. Squeezing suppliers, exploiting employees, outmaneuvering government officials, and charging the customer more for minimal benefits are all just good management practices if these actions are in the best interest of the shareholders. A manager once made a piercing observation of this paradigm: "I wonder about the ethics of business—'charge as much as possible for a product which was made by someone else who was paid as little as possible.' You live on the difference."

The "end-justifies-the-means" paradigm misses an important aspect of living systems. No living entity can remain in a losing relationship very long without withering away. Animals eventually migrate out of hostile environments. Seeds take up root only in those areas that will sustain them. People change jobs or dissolve marriages if they are constantly losing in the relationship. Thus, anyone employing this paradigm will become misaligned with the order of things—especially in a global market that offers people a wide variety of options. So what are today's paradigms that can help us do better than "the end justifies the means"?

Paradigms of Synergy and Partnerships

The natural law of synergy says, "The whole is greater than the sum of its parts." A corollary to this law states that trying to optimize each part singularly will suboptimize the whole. Through tracing the roots of the related word synergism, we find these elements:

Syn—similar, alike, aligned

Erg—a unit of work or energy

Ism—bound together by a common factor

From this definition, we understand synergy isn't created by *adding* things together, it comes from *bonding* things together *differently*. Synergy isn't necessarily the number of resources you have, or the cost of each individual item, but the way in which everything comes together. This explains why one organization reduces its employee enrollment and sees no gains in productivity or profitability while another does the same and not only increases profitability, but actually builds trust as well. The key point for competing in the global network is to change the nature of your relationships—how you work together with your stakeholders. Let's explore two paradigms that can help you accomplish this:

Paradigm #1: "We are just scratching the synergy surface." In the competitive race for market share and profitability, companies frequently develop a comparative standard of excellence. You are doing well if you are beating the competition. Since the competition often has the same foibles you have, you only have to be incrementally better to be on top. This is a poor measure of your organization's potential synergy. Your paradigm of your own synergy will shift dramatically if you will consider this question: If every group does its job 95 percent correct and "on time," what is the likelihood of getting the right product in the consumer's hands "on time?"

Product Development defines concept (.95)

Engineering tests equipment   (.95)

Production teams are trained   (.95)

Advertising releases copy	(.95)
Sales writes the order	(.95)
Purchasing orders materials	(.95)
Supplier delivers materials	(.95)
Plant inspects materials	(.95)
Plant produces product	(.95)
Plant inspects product quality	(.95)
Distribution ships product	(.95)
Sales promotes with Retailers	(.95)
Customer need is fulfilled	(.95)

Answer: $(.95)13 = .49$, or you have a *49 percent* chance of satisfying your customer!

This example, based on one used by Dr. Myron Tribus, retired professor of engineering at MIT, is thought provoking—and a little disturbing. First, the 49 percent itself is disturbing. Second, you are aware that some of these groups in your organization aren't performing at 95 percent today, meaning your actual percentage is probably *less than* 49 percent.

What can you do about this situation? Your organization is probably already doing exactly what every other organization has been doing for years. Since everyone doesn't do their part exactly right the first time, you have built in buffers to fortify the 49 percent process to look like something much better than it is. Examples of these buffers include:

- Building higher inventories
- Paying more for rush orders
- Expecting longer start up curves
- Employing more people
- Tolerating more rework
- Compromising on quality
- Spending more advertising dollars

When you identify these buffers in the system, you uncover what I call the "Hidden Enterprise," the forgotten, underground activities that keep you in today's race, yet at the same time add time and expense to your efforts. They represent negative synergy because they drain the system without adding any new value. Here is an example of the Hidden Enterprise:

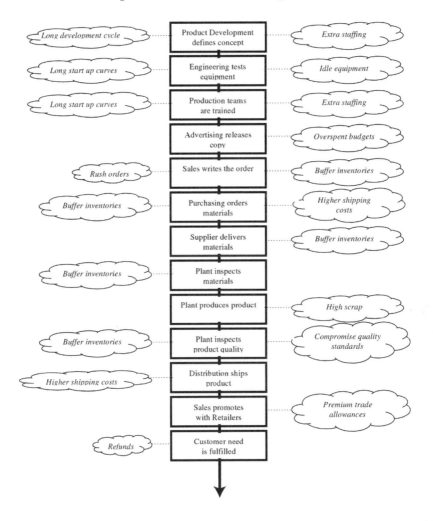

Once the reality of the Hidden Enterprise sinks in, you will echo Horst Schulze's sentiment about Ritz-Carlton's leadership position in the hotel industry: "We are the best of a bad lot!" This statement comes from one who recognizes his organization is just beginning to scratch the synergy surface. Look at your system in absolute quality terms, and you will have a healthy discomfort with today's organizational performance.

Before moving on, you must remember that your hidden enterprise is an ecosystem held in balance by all its stakeholders. To improve the 49 percent process in this example, product developers, engineers, purchasers, suppliers, production teams, quality people, distributors, advertisers, and sales people have to work for each other to get things right the first time and every time. This leads us to the second paradigm shift.

Paradigm #2: "Our stakeholders are literally our partners." Much of today's literature discusses the importance of strategic alliances and partnerships in competing globally. To move beyond a superficial understanding of the word "partner," think about the actual relationship you have with your stakeholders by following this mental exercise:

Imagine yourself as a fly on the wall observing your work processes. Where is the source of your work flow? Who specifically starts the ball rolling? Is this initiator a member of your organization or is it a stakeholder? Now follow the flow forward in as much detail as you can. Do you see the people from different organizations providing services or tangible goods that various people in your organization need to fulfill their mission? If you were unaware of the different organizations and departments involved (as any normal fly would be), you would conclude by simple observation that all these people were working together as part of some overall process.

The fly's view tells you that your stakeholders are literally your partners. Suppliers, customers, employees, government agencies, unions, families—they are all your partners in some way. You need them and they need you to fulfill your fundamental purposes. Any time either of you exercises your option to dissolve the "partnership," both sides feel the loss. And if all stakeholders *literally* were your equal partners, could you:

• Tell them to mind their own business?
• Pull rank on them?
• Ignore what they have to say?
• Treat them as adversaries?
• Force them to leave?

- Keep sensitive, but relevant information from them?
- Make decisions affecting them without consulting them?
- Intimidate them to comply with your demands?

You can't do these things with partners in any of life's arenas—not at work, not at home, and not in neighborhoods or communities. You, like Alpha, may be able to get away with such "win-lose" tactics for a while, but retaliations will occur.

What if, instead of retaliation, you had real partners who volunteered their best resources (finances, people, technical innovation, services, ideas) to help you when you really needed them? Here's an example of two leaders who developed a true partnership:

• • •

In the late 1980s, Wal-Mart chairman Sam Walton and Procter & Gamble CEO John Smale agreed to an innovative idea: they would better align their business systems with each other in the belief that it would improve the bottom line for both organizations. To initiate the improvements, P&G managers from advertising, information services, logistics, sales, manufacturing, distribution, and finance moved their families from Cincinnati, Ohio (P&G's hometown) to Bentonville, Arkansas (Wal-Mart's headquarters). They formed a task force with their Wal-Mart counterparts. Their charge was simple: study how we each do business and develop totally aligned systems to better serve the consumers who buy P&G products in Wal-Mart stores.

Historically, manufacturers and retailers in the consumer products industry have competed with each other for profit margins. How could the unspoken competitive juices between P&G and Wal-Mart be eliminated in this critical project?

At 8:02 A.M. on the new team's first workday, "Mr. Sam" Walton himself came through the door—unannounced and unexpected! He greeted the receptionist and asked, "Where are the P&G folks? I want to welcome them to our team." He was told they weren't in yet; they were all at the bank trying to cut through red tape related to their home mortgages. Apparently, the local bank was hesitant to approve mortgage loans for so many out-of-towners.

Sam asked the receptionist, "Do you have a telephone I can use?" He called the bank and said, "Hello, this is Sam Walton. I understand some of our partners from Procter & Gamble are having trouble with their mortgages. These people are my business partners. Is there anything we can do to expedite their loans?" Not surprisingly, every loan was quickly approved.

Those who knew Sam Walton will tell you this episode was "typical Sam." He had a natural ability to win people's allegiance because he thought of their needs as well as his own. His behavior revealed how seriously he took this new partnership. As far as he was concerned, there were no boundaries separating Wal-Mart and P&G: their business was his business. Sam Walton's win-win thinking laid the groundwork for a win-win partnership.

From that day forward the managers from the two companies truly worked together for the same end. They made many changes that, though not ideal for either company's existing systems, did a better job of fulfilling the consumers' needs. Marketing plans and product promotions were tightly coordinated to present a timelier, unified message to consumers. Shipping systems were aligned to make it easier and safer to move products through the entire pipeline. Information systems were simplified to allow for faster tracking and reporting.

These improvements enabled the combined P&G/Wal-Mart organization to deliver a box of Tide or a tube of Crest toothpaste from the production plant to the store shelf with the highest quality, lowest cost, and in the fastest time ever. The more efficient pipeline cut warehouse inventories in half, freeing up capital for both partners. Part of the cost savings was passed on to the consumer, yielding a lower purchase price than competition could offer. Not surprisingly, the sales volume and profits of both P&G and Wal-Mart improved dramatically.

. . .

Before this experience, both Procter & Gamble and Wal-Mart would have told you their customer was the person who bought their products. Spending time, money, and resources to satisfy a retailer (Wal-Mart) or a product supplier (P&G) would have been a lower priority than satisfying the consumer. But everyone was better off after these two companies chose to become real partners.

A Synergistic Design Process

From your paradigms flow the processes and habits you employ to produce the results you get. If you believe you are only scratching the synergy surface and your stakeholders are literally your partners, and if you recognize that a synergistic network can be developed only from altered relationships, then your approach to designing your organization will be different than others. Procter & Gamble and Wal-Mart actually modeled this new design approach in establishing their partnership. They focused their attention "one level up" from their own organization to achieve new synergies, i.e., they addressed their *interdependent* work processes.

Historically most organizations have focused only on their own work process when they went about designing improvements. They have attempted to optimize only their piece of the whole. But designing a synergistic network requires altering the relationship among several members. This means, you must begin the design process by seeing how your organization fits into the larger order of things, as this diagram illustrates:

In *Designing Organizations for High Performance*—I call this the "outside in" design process—you start outside your own organization and then work your way into your core operation. This "outside in" approach can help you eliminate the hidden enterprise by designing flawless processes at each of your interfaces. The outside in design process follows the OP Model design steps with *the stakeholder partnership tasks* as the work process to be designed. A generic model of this design approach is as follows:

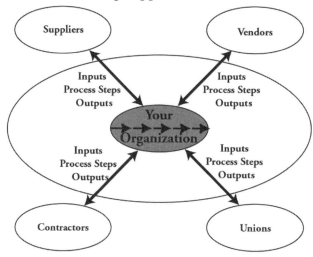

1. Reaffirm the critical needs of both parties (yours and the stakeholder's).

2. Lay out the key inputs, process steps, and expected outputs and design the flow to deliver high quality every time.

3. Design the support systems of structure, decision-making, rewards, information, and human resource systems to optimize the work flow. Use high performance design principles to build the self-sufficiency of those who work together in these processes.

4. Predict the new behaviors in both organizations as a result of the new design.

5. Predict the new results that will emerge from the new behaviors.

Once these processes have been designed, you move inside to your original core process and use the same tools to adjust it as needed to be compatible with the new stakeholder interfaces.

In chapter 10, I reviewed several high performance principles that require outside in designing "one level up" from your own role or unit: multi-skilled work roles, multifunctional business teams, and boundary management. This synergistic design process is one form of boundary management. In this chapter I will share some not-so-obvious applications of designing "one level up" that have produced synergy in many different settings:

• Ritz-Carlton's synergy between people and information technology
  • Saturn's synergistic technical center layout
  • Vizir laundry detergent's European business team
  • Broward County Schools multiple stakeholder partnerships
  • Procter & Gamble's global product network

Synergy between Technology and People

One example of designing "one level up" is to move your focus from your own individual tasks or departmental tasks to the overall work process. A good example of this is the guest registration process (one of the 18 core processes derived from the Credo) at Ritz-Carlton hotels. Nearly all hotel registration systems are computerized, but the Ritz-Carlton edge comes from a synergy created by the employees and the computers all focused on *the process* of outstanding guest registrations. "We introduced this concept in the United States in 1992," explained Laurie Lemmons-Murphy, Guest Recognition Program Manager at the Atlanta Buckhead Ritz-Carlton. "The system enables us to develop a profile of our guests and cater to their wishes when they return. It's been a big success since we expanded it to all our hotels." Here's how the process works to give each guest very personalized service:

Step 1: The travel agent or guest requests a reservation (including any special needs) and is confirmed by a Reservation Agent (either a Ritz-Carlton employee or an authorized representative).

Step 2: The guest's name and special needs are entered into the central reservation (COVIA) data bank. If it is a repeat guest, any preferences from past visits will also show up on the record.

Step 3: All the data from Step 2 are downloaded to the hotel where the guest will be staying.

Step 4: A Daily Guest Arrivals Report is generated at each hotel, summarizing all guests who will be checking in that day and what their needs/requests are.

Step 5: The hotel Guest Recognition Coordinator reviews the Guest Arrival Report and generates the Daily Guest Recognition and Preference Report, which breaks out the guest preferences functionally for each department (front desk, housekeeping, room service, bell stand, etc.).

Step 6: Each employee who plays a part in preparing for the guest's stay does whatever is needed to fulfill the requests.

Step 7: The renowned Ritz-Carlton service is delivered. In the spirit of continuous improvement, each employee carries a small note pad to record any new preferences they may observe during this stay.

Step 8: New guest preferences are passed along to the Reservation Agent to be entered into the data bank.

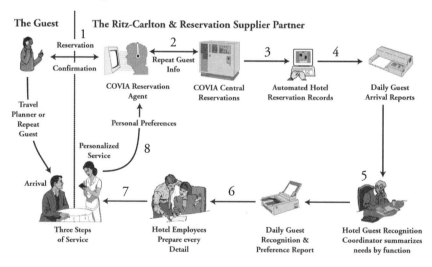

This system is incredibly effective. Here are some examples of this "effortless" process:

One guest checked into the Atlanta Buckhead hotel. Because he had stayed at the Ritz-Carlton in Phoenix many times in the past, the Buckhead staff knew he wanted *USA Today* instead of the *Wall Street Journal* and that he preferred down pillows to foam.

Another guest had the following comments from past visits noted on her Daily Guest Recognition and Preference Report: "Room not ready two times; messages missed." You can bet the staff was on its toes to avoid these same errors on this visit.

One very frequent guest's profile had the following comments: "Requests Evian in ice bucket and fruit bowl upon arrival. Also two laundry bags and extra stationary upon arrival (replenished daily). Requests *New York Times*, the *Wall Street Journal, Financial Times* (every morning), *London Times, Daily Telegraph* in the PM. Requests speaker phone. Prefers view with large windows. Drinks port; likes truffles; uses pepper mill."

• • •

Multiply the care and comfort delivered by this process to thousands of guests and you begin to see why Ritz-Carlton is a leader. But each system is only as good as the programmers who run it. How does the organization motivate its thousands of employees to actually use the note pads and follow up to put in down pillows instead of foam? The motivation comes from their intrinsic commitment to the Credo.

Co-locating Saturn Partners

Another way to foster synergy is to create the physical environment that enables interdependent partners to interact frequently and spontaneously. In the P&G/Wal-Mart example, relocating the P&G partners was a key to effectively achieving the mission. As the following example from the Saturn Corporation shows, changing the stakeholders' physical location can build a common perspective and self-sufficiency and make simultaneous actions almost effortless.

In the Saturn plant in Spring Hill, Tennessee the traditional assembly line has been improved by what Saturn calls a "synchronous design process." This is an application of "just in time" thinking to eliminate waste and stimulate continuous improvement. The bottom line of the Saturn plant's synchronous design is that Saturn can deliver a car to you 17 days after you order it from the retailer. The industry average for order-delivery is 80 days!

In today's competitive market, though, the advantages of synchronous design are needed in all aspects of the process, not just in manufacturing, if an organization is to reduce its total cycle time. Jay Wetzler, Saturn's first engineering vice president, applied the plant production line thinking to the layout of the technical center where the new Saturn models were designed and modified. "We found that the same principles that helped us eliminate non value-added work in the plant also saved us much time and rework in the design stages," explained Ron Rogers, who succeeded Jay Wetzler as Saturn's engineering head. "We began by asking ourselves what engineering's product is. It's not a car—that's the plant's product. Our product is drawings and specifications." Looking at the design process as an assembly line yielded the following flow:

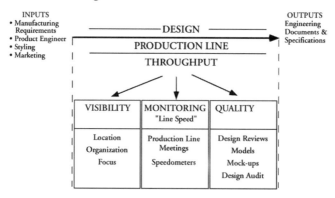

The design production line is fed by inputs from manufacturing, engineering, and marketing. Its output is engineering documents and specifications. The design process throughputs are shaped by three factors:

• Visibility—this comes from a common focus, organization, and location.

• Monitoring—measuring its "line speed" of drawings vs. schedules.

• Quality—reviews, models, and audits of design work.

When a push for improved profitability required "doing more with less" in 1993, Saturn engineering transferred several staff members to other divisions. Saturn took advantage of the office shuffling to lay out the offices and work spaces so that designers, engineers, and program managers, who previously were housed in three separate buildings several miles apart, would now all work in the same building.

"We laid out the new work spaces based on their functional relationship instead of by departments." Ron said. "Our complete design and engineering team was clustered together by vehicle compartments." Here's an example of the rear compartment's office layout:

REAR COMPARTMENT

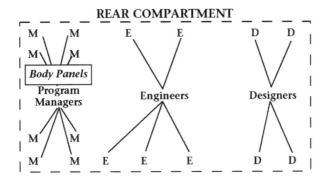

Within each cluster, the designers were seated at one end with the engineering in the middle and the program managers at the opposite end. This co-location allowed for ease of two-way communication about the program status, assistance needed, or problem resolution. The program managers literally could get a feel for how everything was going just by going to the water cooler. Thus everyone maintained a line of sight to the overall mission, problems were identified and resolved faster, and cycle time was reduced. "Instead of calling a meeting," Ron said, "people just turned to their neighbor and talked."

The overall technical center layout applied these same benefits to the entire design process. Just as each compartment integrated all team members, the office layout clustered all compartments around an open area where the latest Saturn vehicle mock-ups (made of wood, cardboard, and plastic) were kept. Those who directly touched the output (designers) worked in the inner circle next to the open design area. This arrangement helped everyone stay focused on the overall vehicle objectives. At one end of the open area stood the production status board that summarized where each group/project was versus its objectives and schedule. At the other end was the design review and quality audit area. Because of its location, this area was conducive to eliciting meaningful participation from all relevant departments for any review.

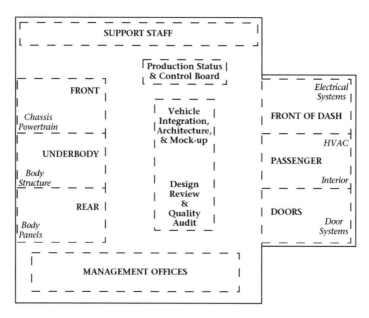

With this layout setting, the climate for partnerships and spontaneous discussions among different functional members became a way of life. This enabled design factors, engineering requirements, and newly-emerging marketing considerations to be integrated simultaneously into what was normally a sequential work flow. Here are some additional synergistic approaches that emerged from the new layout:

• The daily production meeting was attended by technical center leaders, design leaders, schedulers, and parts readiness personnel. The purpose of these meetings was to review progress along each design schedule, agree to priorities, and coordinate action to eliminate roadblocks. The meeting results were posted on the program status board so everyone could stay updated.

• The daily operations team meeting was led by Engineering. This took the output of the production meeting and coordinated the best use of all engineering resources.

• The design review was very participative. It was held in the open area with visuals being projected on a big screen and drafting boards. This meeting was attended by designers, product engineers, manufacturing engineers, service engineers, and others as required. Because of its high visibility, any executive or team member could easily participate in this meeting.

What were the results of Saturn's synchronous design process? Prior to introducing the office layout and design process, Saturn's design teams were late an average of 4 to 6 weeks per drawing. After introducing the new process, they cut that time to an average of only 1 to 2 weeks—a reduction in error-to-forecast of approximately 75 percent.

But, before you think rearranging offices is an end in itself, consider the finance manager in another firm who lamented that his company's new office facilities hadn't changed a thing. When his company built a new administration building next to its production factory, all occupants were placed "bullpen" style in one large room. Every manager and staff person were in the same room. "But," the finance manager complained, "the engineers still won't come around the corner to talk to us about their budgets." Without affecting one's paradigm, the many other changes we make may turn out to be only cosmetic improvements.

Indeed, new paradigms may be the only things that endure over time. With General Motors' move to establish global product platforms, the resources in the Saturn technical center have been reassigned to different groups. The culture of spontaneous, multifunctional collaboration has endured, however, as the Saturn team has found other ways to stay tightly connected with its partners. E-mail, virtual conferencing, frequent multifunctional reviews, and daily checks with each other are habits that have helped to overcome some of the barriers of geographic dispersion.

The Vizir Business Team

In the past two decades many organizations have used multi-functional teams to do more with less. These teams, the product of designing "one level up" from each function, capitalize on team resources to achieve synergistically what individual functions could not do alone. Exactly what do these teams look like and what do they do?

A multi-functional team brings together all who have a major role in delivering a product or service. In the early days these teams were simply made up of representatives of each functional department within an organization (research, engineering, operations, purchasing, human resources, distribution, etc.). More recently some have expanded the structure to include key outside stakeholders as well. The following model has been used by Procter & Gamble to illustrate the many relationships associated with some of its multi-functional teams:

Each functional group is illustrated by one of the "petals" on the flower. One representative from each function becomes a member of the core team—a mini board of directors for this piece of P&G's business. The core team is self-sufficient when it meets because it has access to everybody and everything that produce

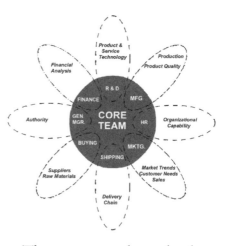

Pantene or Pringles or Pampers. The team members also have connections to every external stakeholder who contributes to their business. Thus, the Buying member brings to the table all of the Buying organization's resources and is linked to all the raw material suppliers as well.

You won't see this team on any organizational chart, however. It exists in parallel to the functional organizations and Global Business Units. Though it is informal, the team combines real authority with meaningful responsibility. The general manager has line authority (or can access it) for any issue that may arise. The team's "response-ability" comes from its linkages to all parts of the product network.

What do these teams do? They make important contributions in both product strategy and execution by virtue of their 360 degree perspective and mobilization of resources. Together, they can compensate for each other's blind spots. They can also integrate the many different action plans and timetables into one cohesive plan to cut time, expense, and error.

Strategically, these teams add value by doing such things as:
• Providing a 360 degree view of the brand's performance
• Proposing new products/services based on an understanding of the total marketplace
• Building competitive advantages across functional lines
• Integrating functional priorities
Executionally, they deliver fast, flexible, focused systems by:
• Coordinating functional action plans
• Launching new products
• Identifying and implementing cost savings
Let's examine the case history of one such team in Procter & Gamble's European operations.

• • •

In the early 1980s, P&G was facing enormous cultural barriers in its efforts to improve profitability in nine different countries. All European managers had been programmed for years to consider their country—and their consumers—as unique from their neighbors. Though each country was different, the complexity of having so many different products was keeping unit costs much higher than the business could tolerate. Something had to be done.

Some P&G managers began testing the concept of "Euro brands"—products that were basically the same throughout Europe. In 1982, they created Euro Teams—multi-functional teams as shown in the "petal" model. To reflect the added complexity of the European market, these functional team members came from four to six subsidiaries as well as the Euro center in Brussels to give the team geographical linkages. The charge of each Euro Team was to strategize and roll out a Euro brand plan across Europe.

One notable success story was the Vizir team. Vizir (now also known as Liquid Ariel in some countries) was an early European formulation of Liquid Tide that had been launched in Germany. To give you an idea of this team's diverse makeup, here is a look at the different members:

- General Manager (France)
- Advertising Managers (France, U.K., Germany)
- Research & Development Managers (Germany and Euro)
- Manufacturing Manager (Germany)
- Purchasing Manager (Euro)
- Sales Manager (Germany)
- Engineering Manager (Euro)
- Finance Manager (France)
- Team Consultant (Euro)

The first time the team came together all they did was share with each other what they knew about the Vizir business in each country. The Advertising people shared advertising copy strategies and marketing plans. The Sales manager shared shipment and market share data. Research & Development shared lab data on the product's performance and future improvements. Manufacturing reviewed plant efficiencies and quality data. Finance shared revenue and profit breakdowns for each country and for the whole of Europe. Each presentation filled in blind spots for many people in the room. At the end of the day the Sales manager summed up what everyone in the room was feeling: "I've learned more today about P&G's business than I have in 25 years in sales."

After that enlightening beginning, the team took on the challenge of developing a business plan for Vizir that would win in every country. Though research data indicated Vizir's formula would perform well in any country, many general managers had their doubts. The team worked with each subsidiary to understand what their issues were and what they needed the Vizir product to do in their market.

All of these efforts proved to be invaluable when a natural disaster dealt a serious blow to Vizir. One of the key ingredients in the liquid detergent was coconut oil. Approximately 90 percent of the world's coconuts are grown in the Philippines. In the summer of 1983, a combination of drought conditions and a sudden tropical storm decimated most of the Philippines' coconut crop. The now-scarce coconut oil had skyrocketed in price almost overnight, literally erasing Vizir's total profit margin.

The Vizir team met at the plant in Germany to consider what to do. In the warehouse they saw stacks and stacks of product that could only be shipped to certain countries because each had its own special label. In order to keep their efficiencies high, the plant production team had run a high volume of each special pack. The result was wasted space, capital tied up in inventories, and costly changeovers in production to accommodate over 40 labeling variations even though there was only one formula for Vizir throughout Europe.

With a clearer view of the situation, and relying on the trust they had built with one another, the team was able to overcome the crisis. More resources were allocated to agreed-upon cost savings projects to accelerate their payoff. New projects were identified, such as eliminating most of the special labels, quickly bringing additional savings to the bottom line. Literally, by the end of one working day, the savings now scheduled for that fiscal year fully offset the increased cost of coconut oil—in other words, the team had restored Vizir's profit margin. Additional savings of the same magnitude were also clearly identified for the following fiscal year. When all these events converged the next year, Vizir expanded across Europe faster and cheaper than before and profits more than doubled from the pre-catastrophe period. Abundance had emerged out of scarcity.

• • •

The Vizir story, though dramatic, was anything but unique. Each major P&G brand became a Euro brand. Every general manager wore two hats: as subsidiary business leader and as a Euro Team leader. By looking at the whole of Europe, these teams were able to see things differently and streamline company organizational structures, supply systems, manufacturing facilities, marketing approaches, and distribution channels. In the ensuing years the markets responded very favorably to the Euro brands; P&G's unit costs dropped and profits soared. Several years before the economic policies of 1992 took effect, P&G was already prepared for a common market in Europe.

Broward County Schools' Partnerships

No organization needs the synergy of partners more than our public schools. Enrollment is growing, the public wants lower taxes, and new technology offers exciting new instructional designs, but budgets are tight. If schools could build synergistic partnerships with others in their community, what would be the result? An exciting role model of designing "one level up" is the Broward County School District in the Fort Lauderdale, Florida area. Despite heavy influxes of immigrant students along with all the other issues any school system has to handle, Broward County schools have been outperforming many of their peers. How do these schools get such outstanding results? By getting the entire staff and student population to work with thousands of partners in their communities to face challenges and continuously improve the education process.

One of Broward's innovations is similar to the multi-functional business team. This innovation is called an Innovation Zone and includes the elementary, middle, and high schools that provide education to a given student population—an arrangement that is also called a "feeder pattern." Typically, the educational process is sliced up along school lines (elementary, middle, high school) as follows:

Elementary Schools	Middle Schools	High Schools
School A	School A	School A
School B	School B	School B
School C	School C	School C
School D	School D	
School E	School E	
School F		
School G		

Under this system, each level develops its students independently. Middle schools are not specifically responsible for the way they prepare their students for high-school work. At the same time, high schools seldom communicate their requirements to the middle schools and so forth. This fragmentation of the overall process is analogous to the "functional silos" that businesses have been working so hard to eliminate.

Broward County's Innovation Zones are a new paradigm. In each zone, representatives from all schools work together as a team to address zone-wide priorities and issues such as curriculum consistency and special programs. Other zones even share budget resources as they work to get training and spread knowledge throughout their "feeder pattern." The following diagram shows the change in thinking brought on by the Innovation Zones:

	Elementary Schools	Middle Schools	High Schools	
Student Population 1	School A School B	School A	School A	Innovation Zone 1
Student Population 2	School A School B	School A School B	School A	Innovation Zone 2
Student Population 3	School A School B School C	School A School B	School A	Innovation Zone 3

Innovation Zones have created partners from grades K-12 to deliver the best total education to each student. Equally important to Broward's success, though, has been its ability to create the same kind of partnerships with thousands of community citizens to provide mentoring, tutoring, the development of science and career labs, and participation in a host of multi-stakeholder forums. In the early 1990s, partnerships were sought in areas that related specifically to the eight system-wide priorities established by Superintendent Dr. Frank Petruzeilo, the School Board, and representatives of all stakeholder groups—parents, students, teachers, non-teaching staff, community and business organizations, as well as principals and other administrators. These eight priorities became a crucial part of the future direction for the entire district:

1. Improving student achievement and school effectiveness
2. Addressing growth
3. Achieving desegregation
4. Ensuring student and employee safety and security
5. Ensuring student and staff accountability
6. Developing and expanding partnerships
7. Attracting, retaining, and training the best teachers, principals and support personnel
8. Utilizing technology to improve student achievement and increase productivity and efficiency

"If we want people to share in our commitment to education, then we have to be committed to them," Dr. Petruzeilo said. "That means we have to listen carefully to them and take their input seriously—even if we don't agree with it at first." An example of this came from the early work to formulate the district's priorities. A student committee was asked to consider what they felt they needed in order to be prepared for the 21st century. As the discussion unfolded, technology became a dominant theme. The students felt that they were not learning to use computers as a way to get work done. They felt that technology needed to be more fully integrated into their classroom experience. None of the professional educators or business people had identified this as an issue. But the customers had spoken quite clearly. As a result, priority #8 was added to the list. Millions of dollars were directed to meeting those needs.

Dr. Petruzeilo didn't believe in giving mere lip service to his stakeholders. The entire district followed his example and still benefits today from the thousands of partners it has cultivated through forums like the following:

• *School Improvement Teams.* Although School Improvement Teams (SITs) have been mandated for every school in the state, Broward County schools have worked to do more than merely comply with this requirement. They've put the team to work to make things better. The SIT is composed of teachers, parents, administrators, people from the community, and students (in upper levels). Each team produces an annual School Improvement Plan (SIP), which outlines in detail the team's improvement objectives. The team then meets regularly throughout the year to discuss objective implementation, solve problems, and monitor progress toward their objectives.

• *The World of Baseball and The World of Hockey.* In these partnerships, professional sports league sponsors and corporate sponsors help fund and develop an integrated curriculum around the sports of baseball and hockey. Math is taught as a way to figure player statistics; writing as a way to write sports columns; and so forth. This emphasis on application has made learning more relevant to students and has increased their desire to participate in the learning process.

• *Florida Power and Light.* By involving the utility company in the process of bringing computers and other technology to the schools, the district has been able to shave $400,000 from its $23 million power bill.

• *Step-Up and Gateway.* Working with the local housing authority, Broward County has been able to help the less educated tenants of public housing earn GED degrees and receive vocational certifications as they work to improve their own homes.

• *Healthcare.* The district is working with hospitals to develop baseline health measures and to complement the efforts of medical services to promote healthy lifestyles among students and their families.

Mary Meyers, Director of Partnerships, summed it up well: "No one agency can do it all. If we don't collaborate and we don't foster that philosophy of sharing in a community, we will never be able to get the maximum value out of our investment of resources, whether they are people, buildings, money, or services. If we don't let go of the dividing lines, we'll fall behind."

The synergy emerging from all these partnerships is impressive. Here is just one of many examples you will find in Broward County:

• • •

When Margaret Underhill arrived as the principal of Nova Blanche Formann elementary school, she found that the school's fondness for experimentation had left it without a clear focus or strategy. Teachers pursued pet projects and collaborated on their particular interests, but the system as a whole was not organized for school-wide improvement. Rather than simply mandate a new direction, however, Margaret felt it was critical to create partners to shoulder the load. Working with Joanne Kralich from the district office, Margaret selected a process known as SAGE Analysis for the task.

The SAGE process seeks to identify those few factors that have the most impact on a school's performance. For Nova Blanche Formann, the process followed four distinct steps:

Step 1—Mission Statement Development. All stakeholders (parents, students, teachers, community leaders, etc.) were involved in creating a mission statement for the school.

Step 2—Validation. Using SAGE's method of "fault-tree analysis," all stakeholders worked to identify the barriers to accomplishing their mission. Throughout the next several weeks, parents, teachers, students, administrators, and interested stakeholders all wrote on a large (4' x 20') poster what they felt to be the key issues for their school. Participants were free to cross out, modify, or add to the poster anywhere they chose.

Step 3—Quantification. This multi-colored morass was then sent to SAGE Analytics, Inc. for study and analysis. SAGE Analytics submitted a report identifying those things that they found to be most critical to the school's performance.

Step 4—Implementation. Using this data, the School Improvement Team chose the issues they wanted to address and assigned multi-stakeholder "Primus Groups" to work on them. These actions were captured in the School Improvement Plan.

When Margaret's report came back, she was surprised to find that the number-one issue identified by stakeholders was school discipline. She did not expect this to be a priority because she felt the school was already pretty well-behaved. But the stakeholder analysis said the place to start was students' discipline. So Margaret trusted the 360 degree view and worked with her SIT.

The SIT designed and adopted a novel discipline program that, instead of making penalties stricter, focused on building strong shared values among students, educators, and parents. They call it a Proactive Discipline Program because it called for students to choose values consistent with the school mission and commit to live by those values.

The program was a tremendous success (including a 62 percent reduction in discipline referrals). Teachers reported that the environment was more conducive to learning and they were able to focus more effort on helping the well-behaved students learn rather than being distracted by those that were not well-behaved. More importantly, however, the whole process helped to renew the school's sense of direction and purpose. By involving everyone, Margaret helped create a school-wide plan that everyone could support.

• • •

Due in large part to these efforts, Nova Blanche Formann was awarded the Presidential "Blue Ribbon" award in 1994, an annual award that recognizes excellent schools across the United States. I salute Dr. Frank Petruzeilo, Margaret Underhill, their successors, and their many partners for their example in an area in which we all have a big stake.

A Global Network

A network is made up of many different organizations spread out over diverse geographies. The different organizations are usually a combination of functions and subsidiaries within the dominant company as well as external stakeholders. Networks potentially offer great operational flexibility to an enterprise operating globally. In their book *The Age Of The Network*, Jessica Lipnack and Jeffrey Stamps summarize their 15 years' research on networks into five organizing principles for the 21st century:

• *Unifying Purpose.* Purpose is the glue and the driver. Common views, values, and goals hold a network together. Purpose also drives the many contributions into an overall process that is focused, fast, and flexible.

• *Independent Members.* Each member of the network, whether a person, company, or country, can stand on its own while benefiting from being part of the whole. New members are invited into a network only because they can add value.

• *Voluntary Links.* The distinguishing feature of networks is their links, far more profuse and omnidirectional than in other type of organization. As communication pathways increase, people and groups interact more often. A network only needs to add links to grow and uncouple links to scale back with the market.

• *Multiple Leaders.* Fewer bosses, more leaders. Networks are leaderful, not leaderless. Each person or group in a network has something unique to contribute at some point in the process. Thus, each leader takes the lead for part of the process. With more than one leader, the network, as a whole, has great resilience.

• *Integrated Levels.* Networks are multilevel, not flat. Lumpy with small groups and clustered with coalitions, networks involve both the hierarchy and the "lower-archy," which leads them to action rather than to making recommendations to others.

Dr. Chris Bartlett of the Harvard Business School emphasizes the importance of looking at your business and carefully evaluating the need for global, regional, or local focus. An example of his thinking is captured in this framework:

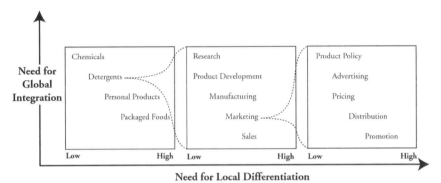

Need for Local Differentiation

In this example, chemicals need the most global integration of this company's many businesses, followed by detergents and personal products. Packaged foods need local differentiation because consumer tastes differ widely from country to country. Within the global detergent business, however, the functions of research and product development are highly global, manufacturing moderately global, with marketing and sales needing more local differences. Within the marketing function, product policy needs global integration, advertising and pricing moderate global integration, with distribution and promotion requiring local differentiation.

As you can see from the Bartlett framework, if you tried to globalize or localize any entire stream of business processes, you would miss the mark. The global marketplace is full of contrasting forces: consumer needs, competitive forces, economic differences, cultural diversities, and regulatory differences. Monolithic organizations that are either global or local might be simpler to administer, but they will invariably drift out of balance with the ecological order. A matrix organization offers the potential to balance the contrasting forces and allow you to fit into the order of things. The key, as Chris Bartlett has shown us, is to move your attention first to the global level and then analyze what makes sense globally, regionally, and locally. The synergies among all three levels will build your business.

The effective global market players are able to bring together many partners to research global market needs, develop products and services accordingly, and deliver them simultaneously around the world. This is what leaders such as Toyota, Sony, Procter & Gamble, and Philips have shown us. Now let's consider one outstanding example of a global product network.

• • •

For years, The Procter & Gamble Company had built its international business like most other companies. It opened a subsidiary organization in a foreign country and began to build its business from the ground up. As the business grew, the subsidiaries became larger and more self-sufficient. But, by the late 1970s, trying to manage dozens of organizations in the same regions was proving to be very complicated and expensive. More importantly, the company was missing the potential global leverage and profitability gains by simplifying its product offerings. Delivering one product in many countries was far more profitable than developing dozens of different products for more limited markets.

You have already seen how P&G began to address these issues with European business teams like Vizir. Through the years this approach has been refined to become a worldwide network delivering global brands.

In the pioneering days of this network, P&G associates learned by trial and error the importance of balancing global possibilities with local differences. Those who tried to standardize one global offering, when local preferences were very different, found they produced winners in some markets and losers in other markets. Those who exaggerated the significance of local differences missed out on the rollout advantages and economies of scale that came from a single global platform.

P&G's business has grown enormously in recent years as the product network has learned how to "think global and act local." This breakthrough occurred only after P&G leaders moved their attention "one level up" from their historical base. In other words, instead of trying to maximize each country independently, they looked first to the regional level and then ultimately to the global level to shape their product portfolio.

Today, P&G's network consists of Global Business Units (GBUs) focused on worldwide results, Market Development Organizations (MDOs) aimed at optimal product delivery in specific regions, and Global Business Services (GBSs) providing administrative integration and support for the other two.

Global Business Units divide up P&G's many businesses into manageable bits. GBUs are led by a president and include all strategic business functions (product development, advertising, product supply, finance, buying, etc.). The work of the GBU is to plan the development of its branded products for worldwide consumption. Each GBU has several product categories, each led by a general manager and a core team similar to the Vizir business team. The general managers have dual responsibility for a region (e.g., North America; Latin America; Asia; Europe, Middle East, and Africa) and a global category or technology platform (e.g., oral care, personal health care, or pharmaceuticals). Representatives of each category core team meet together periodically as a GBU team to coordinate the global business.

The Market Development Organizations deliver the GBU products and initiatives to their regions of the world. They are the ones who have to determine whether the global product platform should be modified to suit local preferences. Typical MDO functions include legal, marketing, manufacturing, engineering, and distribution.

The Global Business Services organization centralizes the support functions that cut across all GBUs and MDOs, such as information technology, security, and human resources. Their aim is to provide the most cost efficient support possible.

Let's get the overall effect of this dynamic organization. Market research, product development testing, and product launches, which used to be done in each country, are now organized in each region from a global plan generated by the GBU. As new consumer preferences are identified, and as new formulations are proposed, the network operates with the global end in mind. A global test plan is executed in each region. Advertising campaigns are shared and tested in several locations. Product tests, market results, cost breakdowns, and organizational innovations are generated and shared promptly throughout the network.

When the global team members gather from the corners of the world to meet and make decisions, all the learning and test results come together. When consumer responses to a shampoo/conditioner are favorable in every region, the team may decide to roll out a single formula everywhere. Based on past brand heritages, the product might be known in different countries as "Pantene," or "Pert Plus." If regional preferences require it, the MDO might execute some deviations to the global platform (such as color, perfume, or packaging). The company would finalize advertising campaigns and product supply lines regionally and locally. Then the company would synchronize a final worldwide launch plan in light of local needs and capabilities. As a result, dozens of countries could get a new product in a matter of weeks.

In the many countries where P&G does business, the fly on the wall frequently sees members of the GBU, MDO and GBS housed together in the same building. Their collaboration enables the regions to be self-sufficient in running the daily business while capitalizing on global leverage.

An important factor in the success of this network is P&G's practice of giving key leaders significant work experience in different parts of the network. It is not unusual to find a product development leader on a global team who has worked for years in a regional technical center. Most general managers have international experience.

Most important, however, is how this network has evolved from the inside out. Management's paradigms had to change before the global network could add any value. Each country's thinking "I am different" has changed to "we really are similar in many ways." Those who assumed "standardization is the goal" have learned that "standardization's potential must be justified by consumer testing." And the paradigm of "business teams are merely debating societies" has matured to "we are not ready to roll out a global brand until we have debated the facts locally, regionally, globally—and functionally." As you might expect, not everyone's thinking always coincides. There are still many debates about where a specific product offering should fit on the global standard/regional differences continuum. But, as Chris Bartlett suggests, this is healthy tension if it drives a thorough examination of all the issues prior to the product launch.

Ariel detergent is perhaps the finest example of Procter & Gamble's global network. Ariel (or Tide as it is known in the United States) is sold worldwide. But for years the laundry markets were thought to be fragmented by three main users: (1) those who hand wash their laundry in many developing countries; (2) those who wash their laundry in ultra high temperatures to disinfect their clothing like people in Germany and other parts of Europe; and (3) those who wash their clothing in cold water like many people in the U.S. and Great Britain.

Beginning in Europe, the researchers and product development staff began the quest for one chemical formula that would beat the competition in all three categories. Some people thought this would be impossible. But the regional product development director urged his colleagues to find one formula that would win in each category. In time they succeeded and Ariel's new formula earned its place as the best-selling detergent globally. The three user categories are basically the same worldwide—satisfy European consumers in these three categories, and you will be able to satisfy them in the other regions as well.

People may call it Tide in one country and Ariel in another, but the product platform can be developed and renewed faster, cheaper, and better if it doesn't require dozens of local variations.

• • •

As you can see, Procter & Gamble's global network has been carefully designed to get the results it wants. I must note that if you were to try to operate such a network under the rules of bureaucracy (find the one best way, unity of command) then you would not have similar work units who were bound together by a common factor. Telling the GBU president what he/she wanted to hear would skew the P&G system—thereby eliminating the crucial dialogue between those people closest to the consumers and those thinking globally.

Conclusion

I hope you feel excited about your own potential to create synergistic partnerships. Whatever your current results are, your most significant improvements in the future will come through your work with your committed "volunteer" partners.

As we have seen, just calling them "partners" doesn't accomplish anything. You must see your stakeholders as the fly on the wall sees them: as literal partners in your work process. You both must value each other as true partners. Their missions must be as compelling to you as your own and vice versa. Your systems must require fast, flexible, and focused action from all those involved.

The following are three examples of results you can expect if you organize yourself and your network of partners according to high performance design principles.

• Ritz-Carlton has seen revenues grow by $125 million over two years with 800,000 fewer work hours in those hotels who have moved "one level up" to make work process improvements and create self-sufficient team structures. Customer satisfaction and employee satisfaction have both improved in these hotels.

• Saturn has shattered the myth that American automobiles can no longer compete with the Japanese. J. D. Power consumer research shows Saturn is ranked right behind Lexus in terms of customer satisfaction. Saturn is ranked number one in sales satisfaction.

• Procter & Gamble has grown to be a $40 billion company in 140 countries fueled by its global network. In 1999, each of its four regions had double-digit earnings growth despite severe economic crises in Russia, Brazil, and many parts of Asia. And the rate of new brand launches continues to accelerate year after year.

You can't get results like these through coercion or better supervision. You can only get them by developing thousands of partners who care as much about your results as you do.

• • •

Applying what you have learned:

Here are some suggestions to put into action what you have learned in this chapter:

1. Map out the hidden costs and missed opportunities in your organization's "Hidden Enterprise."

2. Identify some "latent" partners (either inside or outside your organization) who possess the talents and resources to help you significantly improve your results. Now ask a member of your organization, one customer, and one supplier to identify some latent partners for you. Ask yourself why they aren't full partners with you right now.

3. Identify some things you could do to build trust with each of the stakeholders you identified in #2.

4. Design "one level up" from your core operation by reshaping your interdependent work processes with some key stakeholders. Map out the inputs, work processes and outputs for both sides.

5. Think about how each of the following could be employed in your organization to increase trust and synergy:

• Co-location of some partners (How could you get the same benefits Procter & Gamble, Wal-Mart and Saturn did?)

• Multi-stakeholder forums (How could you do what Broward County Schools have done?)

Section

5

Leading a High Performing Culture

12
Embracing Change

"There is nothing more difficult to take in hand, more perilous to conduct, or more uncertain in its success, than to take the lead in the introduction of a new order of things, because the innovator has for enemies all those who have done well under the old conditions, and lukewarm defenders in those who may do well under the new."

—Machiavelli

"Whatever can be done, will be done. If not by incumbents, it will be done by emerging players. If not in a regulated industry, it will be done in a new industry born without regulation. Technological change and its effects are inevitable. Stopping them is not an option."

—Andrew Grove

THE PREVIOUS CHAPTERS HAVE GIVEN YOU THE opportunity to consider your own leadership in light of what effective leaders have done throughout the ages—and what will be required in the Global Age. Through your application of each chapter's learning, you can see how you can reshape your organization to get the results you want. But all of this doesn't come without cost or sacrifice. The elements of Leadership for the Ages will require some existing paradigms, values, and habits to change. See if the following items would require significant changes in your work culture:

• Every person centering his/her life on a personal mission that is aligned with natural laws

• Acting as stewards rather than subordinates; exercising "intelligent disobedience"

• Regularly gathering stakeholder feedback to understand their moments of truth—and then fulfilling them

• Shaping a compelling mission and then using it as your Constitution

• Uprooting your bureaucratic practices and putting natural laws to work every day

• Creating synergistic partnerships

This list really presents you with two challenges. First you need to change what your are doing, then you need to help others change what they are doing. How will you and your associates enthusiastically embrace such changes? Your investment in reading this book won't amount to much unless you successfully answer this question.

The Broken Contract

"I've been in research my entire career," stated a veteran manager in a world-class research organization, "but the rules of the game are changing. It used to be you had money, people, equipment—and time to do your work. It was like sitting down by the cozy fireplace for a game of chess. Nowadays things are very different. Money is tight. Staffing levels have been decreased. Equipment is supposed to last longer. And the new global competition doesn't give you any time. It's more like ice hockey today than chess. Our people are getting bumped, bruised, and shoved around. But the worst part is they still think the game is chess. They think everything they have to contend with today is unfair."

This manager's situation is shared worldwide. Some individuals wish for the "good old days" when their job was more stable, when they could expect to work for the same company from start to retirement, when they could count on their employers to look out for everybody's welfare, and when they could trust one another. The term for such expectations is a "psychological contract." Though never formally written down and signed, this "contract" is a series of expectations that everyone seems to share. Fulfilling these expectations builds trust; violating them erodes trust.

As we have seen, the Global Age is wreaking havoc with the organizational status quo—and the traditional psychological contract. Product lifecycles are shorter than ever. Consequently, work processes must change frequently. Our recent history of downsizing, restructuring, and "the program of the month" has eroded trust in leaders and institutions. All of these phenomena have produced a reflexive, negative reaction to any change that might come along. And on top of everything else, you are now motivated to introduce more change into the picture after having read this book! Machiavelli's quote at the beginning of this chapter is a sobering one. How will you earn the trust of battle-weary associates for yet more change?

Consider how nature responds to tumultuous change. Think back to the devastating eruption of Mount St. Helens in 1980 in the northwest United States. This spectacular explosion spread lava and ash for many miles around. But in the ensuing two decades, natural elements have flowed together to create new life. A good example is Spirit Lake, five miles away from Mount St. Helens. Spirit Lake was right in the lava flow path and was inundated with thousands of trees and tons of volcanic debris. All forms of life from fish to plants to plankton were destroyed. Today, Spirit Lake has new life. The trees have decayed. The debris has settled. The water is clear again. Birds and wind have brought back plankton to sustain life in the lake. In fact, Spirit Lake now has more nutrients than before the eruption. Whereas the lake previously had to be artificially stocked with fish for sport fishing, it now naturally supports a thriving fish population. The ecosystem is actually stronger than before the catastrophe.

And so it can be for your organization if people will keep their eye on ecological order rather than personal comfort, act with purpose instead of emotion, and avoid distractions in times of change.

The Roots of Lasting Change

In approaching the challenges of change, there is one consolation: *natural laws govern*. Let's explore some of the universals that can guide you and others along the way. Here is an illustration of some of the critical dynamics.

• • •

Principal Bruce Miller thought he had seen everything in his 25 years of education, but he could scarcely believe what he was seeing this time. Someone had left bright red lipstick smudges all over the mirror in the girls' restroom, presumably by "kissing" it. Bruce thought, "It's just someone having a little fun. It'll blow over."

But it didn't blow over. Day after day the mirror in the girls' restroom was covered by the bright red lip marks. After 10 days of mirror kissing, Bruce had seen enough. At the end of the morning announcements the next day he gave one last notice to the home rooms: "For some time now vandals have been at work in the girls' restroom by kissing the mirror with bright red lipstick. This has gone on long enough! Anyone caught kissing mirrors in the future will be subject to disciplinary action." The gauntlet had been cast down.

The next day the mirror was completely covered with red lipstick marks. Bruce acted swiftly, placing faculty monitors in the girls' restroom.

The next day the mirror in the boys' restroom was covered with lipstick. Faculty monitors were placed in both the boys' and girls' restrooms.

The next day the mirror in the teachers' lounge was covered with lipstick.

Bruce was getting panicky. Nothing was stopping these kids from having their fun. How could he reassert his authority as principal? He called for a faculty meeting to discuss the problem. During the faculty discussion, George, the head custodian, volunteered his help. "Mr. Miller, if you will give me 10 minutes in the next pep assembly, I will solve your problem." Bruce and the faculty decided George couldn't do any worse than they had—so he got his 10 minutes in front of the student body. The following Friday Bruce announced at the pep assembly, "Now we are going to hear from George, our head custodian." Then Bruce held his breath as George walked out to the microphone with a scrub brush and mop bucket.

"For the past few weeks some of you kids have been having fun decorating the mirrors in the restrooms," George began. "I asked Mr. Miller for some time to impress upon you how hard it is for us custodians to keep your school clean." George then dropped down on all fours and began scrubbing his brush over the gym floor. "While you kids are still asleep in the morning, your custodians are scrubbing the restroom floors on our hands and knees," he said from his crouching position. The students began to laugh and gave a cry of mock sympathy. Bruce began to clench his fists. Why had he agreed to this? George was only making things worse!

Undaunted by the students' response, George continued: "Then while you kids are eating your breakfast, we custodians are hand scrubbing every toilet." Again the brush flashed around the imaginary commode as the students chuckled and mocked.

"Then, as you kids are arriving on the school grounds, we scrub and polish the mirrors." The same brush that had cleaned the floor and toilets now swished across the imaginary mirror. A stunned silence permeated the gymnasium, immediately followed by shrieks of genuine horror as George's message registered with the students.

• • •

Needless to say the problem was solved—no student's lips ever touched the mirrors again. What George understood better than any of the professional educators is that *a lasting change in behavior always develops from the inside out; from a paradigm shift that changes our view of the world, our situation, and even our-*

selves. The faculty couldn't force these high school students to stop kissing the mirrors; something had to change from within before the problem could be solved. Paradigm shifts cause us to re-examine our purposes, strategies, values, and behaviors. From paradigm shifts come "inside out" commitments to change.

Inside out commitments are the very essence of self-control. Once the students had changed their paradigms of the mirror (and the mirror's cleanliness), they controlled their behavior themselves. When this same dynamic becomes part of a work culture, performance standards rise dramatically. A former Hewlett-Packard manager relates this example of a self-controlling culture:

• • •

"I was down on the manufacturing floor one day, standing, observing the assemblers, when one of them clipped some copper wires and dropped them on the floor. Another assembler seated several rows ahead saw this and came back and said, 'Excuse me, are you the one who put the copper wire on the floor?' And the second assembler said, 'Yes I was.' The first assembler said, 'Well, see that bin over there? That's where the excess copper wire goes because we sell that. We turn that back in. And besides that, if you leave it on the floor it makes it look like a mess.'

"And the second assembler looked kind of annoyed by this and the first assembler said, 'What's the matter with you? Haven't you heard about profit-sharing? That's not the way we do things here.' The second assembler didn't drop any copper wires on the floor after that."

• • •

We all envy such cultures, especially if they are purposeful in exercising their self-control. How do you cultivate such a culture? How do you help people rethink their paradigms? Think for a moment about the many incomplete or faulty paradigms operating in organizations today: the bureaucrats who blindly follow procedure even though it moves away from meeting the goals. The smothering supervisors who look over everyone's shoulder because they are convinced this attention will cause people to do better. The employees who stubbornly refuse to go along with their team's decision because they have a better idea. The inventors who ignore customer feedback about the new product because they believe that "customers don't understand" the product's new technology. The students who skip over Algebra because they don't see its relevance to their future. Senior managers who lay off thousands of employees because they are convinced such a drastic step is required to save the rest of the organization.

You may say, "Each of these actions could produce the exact opposite of what is intended." And you may be right. However, it doesn't matter what you or I think of the situation. All that matters is what the person thinks will come from his/her efforts. *In order for people to change their paradigms, they first have to understand how these mental models are self-defeating.* That's what George accomplished in the school assembly.

Explaining Why Individuals Change

Despite Machiavelli's warning at the beginning of this chapter and our own frustrations with changing a culture, the fact remains that people do change. What if we could better understand the dynamics that cause people to actually embrace change? Consultant David Gleicher developed a formula years ago to help us understand why people change. Notice how this simple formula summarizes the critical elements of inside out change that I have discussed so far:

$$C = f(A, B, D) > X$$

where C = the change to be accomplished

A = a dissatisfaction with the status quo

B = a clear vision of the desired future state

D = some practical first steps

X = the cost of making the change

This formula says that people will change if they feel the advantages are stronger than the costs of making the change. Here's the way the formula works:

1. "C" is any change you or others are struggling to make.

2. Now develop an understanding of the X factor. What will it cost you or others to make the change? (Think of the many aspects of cost: financial, political, comfort, ego, physical.) Resistors always perceive a high personal cost for changing.

3. Finally, identify how they perceive the strength of the three factors "A, B, D." Dissatisfaction with the status quo, vision, and practical first steps are the real drivers of change.

Until you understand how other people would fill out this formula, your attempts to influence them to change their behavior will be frustrating—and frustrated. Initially you may not have much factual information with which to complete this formula. Without facts, your first task would be to understand how people feel about the changes they are being asked to make. Through your discussions, you may come to realize:

• Some may not be dissatisfied with the status quo.

• Some may be dissatisfied, but have no vision.

• Still others may be dissatisfied and have a vision of the future, but aren't sure what steps to take to improve things.

Part of your leadership task is to identify and strengthen any of the missing elements until they weigh more than X. The Gleicher formula is simple, yet powerful. I once used it to help a senior executive understand a puzzling situation:

• • •

I was approached once by a senior vice president of a Fortune 500 company who couldn't understand why many senior managers were resisting a restructuring of the sales organization to better fit the emerging needs of the market place. While all the sales managers thought it was the greatest improvement to be made in decades, the general managers were fighting it tooth and nail. As we discussed the situation, we filled in the change formula for the general managers and the sales managers from what we knew about each group:

General Managers

A: They wanted more sales volume but didn't see the need for restructuring Sales.

B: They had been through many presentations on the new organization but still didn't agree it was ideal.

D: They didn't spend much time in the Sales organization and therefore didn't understand how conditions were changing and how the pilot structure really worked.

X: They felt they would lose control of their Sales force. This was a huge concern.

Sales Managers

A: They wanted more volume but were under pressure from the general managers to get it faster and with fewer people.

B: The vision was understood and embraced enthusiastically by all.

D: The pilot project was clearly understood. It was proving to be a big improvement in the process of taking products to market.

X: Very little cost; many advantages. Everyone in Sales was getting more with less.

Once I made this analysis, the vice president understood why the new Sales organization was running into opposition.

• • •

Now consider a similar situation in your own organization. Think of an individual or group who is resisting an important change effort. Use the change formula to help you understand why the resistance is perfectly logical to them and what you might do to earn their commitment to the needed change.

Leveraging the Drivers of Change

Let me review some approaches that have been successful in a number of situations to help people embrace change. I will focus on the drivers from the change formula: developing greater dissatisfaction with the status quo, reconnecting to vision, and developing some practical first steps for making the move from the status quo to the vision.

Dissatisfaction with the status quo. Too often leaders try to shield their associates from bad or disturbing news. Yet it is frequently the bad news that motivates the leaders to seek changes. Imagine how associates must feel if drastic changes are being proposed, but their paradigm says "business as usual." No wonder they resist change.

General Electric's CEO Jack Welch offers this advice: "How do you bring people into the change process? Start with reality. Get all the facts out. Give people the rationale for change, laying it out in the clearest, most dramatic terms. When everybody gets the same facts, they'll generally come to the same conclusion. Only after everyone agrees on reality and resistance is lowered can you begin to get buy-in to the needed change."

Remember that the first step in the OP Model diagnosis process is to compare today's results with current and future stakeholder needs. The gaps identified in this step are a powerful way of developing a healthy dissatisfaction with the status quo. In fact, I have never had a group resist change when they emerge from step one.

Don't forget to help people assess the cost of not changing when you are addressing their dissatisfaction with the status quo. Resistors may choose to follow you if obsolescence is the other alternative.

The hidden ingredient in the change formula is mutual trust. When a large auto assembly plant was closing down some years ago, an all-employee assembly was held to share the facts with everyone. The plant manager went through a detailed review of the parent company's sliding market shares, decreased profitability, dropping stock prices, and downsizing plan to restore fiscal health. "There you have it, ladies and gentlemen," the plant manager said at the conclusion of this presentation. "The figures don't lie." Next on the agenda was the local union president who began by saying, "That's right, ladies and gentlemen. The figures don't lie. But just remember, liars figure!"

If trust is low in your organization, you will need to arrange for some skeptics/thought leaders to get firsthand exposure to the "bad news" through direct discussions with customers, shareholders, company executives, and others. Once they have seen the facts for themselves, they will be able to influence other people to see things as they really are.

Commitment to a compelling vision of the desired future state. Chapters 6 and 7 explored how to get commitment to a compelling mission or vision. It is this very vision of the future that can add to one's dissatisfaction with the status quo. For instance, supervisors of would-be self-sufficient teams often resist change for fear of losing their job. However, when they are introduced to the boundary management role and are able to identify the tasks and projects they would be doing to address their team's interface issues, they get excited about the new prospects. This greatly increases their dissatisfaction with being a supervisor.

In many cases, part of "letting go" of the status quo is to make a symbolic commitment to the new order of things. If there is strength in numbers, then a ceremony demonstrating united commitment to the new plan can help everyone strengthen their resolve to change. An oath of citizenship, a political oath of office, and the Alcoholics Anonymous pledge are all examples of this symbolic commitment to change.

Through the years I have seen many organizations seek this symbolic commitment. Leaders attempting to gain commitment from a critical mass of organizational members have organized meetings or small discussion groups around a symbolic theme. Some themes they have used include:

• "A Call to Arms" (Based on the wartime signal given to drop everything and prepare for the fight.)

• "The train is leaving the station." (Everyone get on board or get left behind.)

• "The Burning Platform" (Think of yourself standing on a burning platform high in the air. Your survival depends on your taking the plunge—implementing the new plan. Once you leap from the burning platform, there is no going back.)

• "The Constitutional Convention" (Similar to the Vision ratification process used by Shell Oil as described in chapter 6.)

The aim for each of these meetings and discussions is to align everyone's expectations of what will change and what will remain the same—and to seek an internal commitment from each member to "let go" and "take the plunge."

I am not implying that by simply having a mass meeting or pep rally you will earn everyone's commitment to make changes in their culture. Remember the significance of the words "inside out." People must commit from the inside out if you are to be successful. Any approach you use should help individuals commit from the inside out. Otherwise you will find yourself in the impossible situation of trying to supervise a change in culture. As we saw in the Hewlett-Packard example, self-control is the best supervisory mechanism.

Practical first steps. Many years ago, circus troupes thrilled audiences with wing walking exhibitions. A performer would climb out on the wing of an old biplane and move from tip to tip while the plane did some loops and other tricks. This death-defying act was very popular. The first rule of wing walking was simply: "Never let go of what you have until you have a hold of something better." Keep this metaphor in mind when thinking of element "D" in the change formula: practical first steps. We may not be thrilled with our current position and we may have a clear vision of where we want to go. But until we get "a hold of something better," we must remain frozen where we are.

Everyone needs a plan of action, a strategy for moving ahead. One of leadership's most valuable contributions, therefore, is to help everyone see not only what they must *stop* doing, but also what they must *start* doing.

• • •

Once a corporate change agent came to me with a dilemma. The pilot restructuring program was proceeding well, but was being criticized by people who didn't understand or who assumed the worst concerning the changes it would bring. In our discussion of the problem, we hit on the idea of painting a very detailed picture of what the new restructured work experience would be like. The change agent constructed a few visuals of what a typical month would look like in the future: how these managers would be spending their time, the balance between in-the-office and in-the-field, the type of problems and issues they would handle, the nature of their communication with the head office, etc. Once managers saw this level of detail of the restructuring, they all agreed it would be much better than their current job. The program was successfully expanded throughout the company.

• • •

Practical first steps are important in spelling out what the change is—what must stop, start, and continue into the future. If you can't articulate what the practical first steps are, you probably haven't thought everything through sufficiently to make the change successful.

Conclusion

In this chapter I have summarized some hard-earned lessons of those who have been trying to change their organizational cultures to keep up with the new Global Age demands. The price paid to understand these dynamics has been enormous. Acting on these lessons can make all the difference for you. Remember:

• Resistance to change is the only reasonable course when you view things through the eyes of those who are resisting.

• A lasting change in behavior always develops from the inside out—from shifting our own paradigms of the situation.

• People change their paradigms, beliefs, and habits once they understand these elements are self-defeating. They must see the advantages outweighing the costs of making the change.

• People will let go of old practices only if they have something better to hold on to as they move forward.

The Change Formula is a wonderful tool to help you get in touch with each of these dynamics.

• • •

Applying what you have learned:

An exercise to apply what you have learned in this chapter:

1. Interact with those who are resisting change in your organization to discover how they perceive the various elements of the change formula. Fill in the formula for each element and strategize how to increase A, B and D and how to decrease X.

13
Leading Change

"Any real change implies the breakup of the world as one has always known it, the loss of all that have one identity, the end of safety. And at such a moment, unable to see and not daring to imagine what the future will bring forth, one clings to what one knew, or thought one knew, to what one possessed or dreamed that one possessed. Yet it is only when one is able, without bitterness or self-pity, to surrender a dream one has long cherished or a privilege one has long possessed, that one is free . . . that one has set oneself free, for higher dreams, for greater privileges."

—James Baldwin

"The reasonable man adapts himself to the world: the unreasonable one persists in trying to adapt the world to himself. Therefore, all progress depends on the unreasonable man."

—George Bernard Shaw

SOME YEARS AGO THE EXECUTIVES OF A MAJOR metropolitan transit system were dissatisfied with the performance of their busses. Passengers complained frequently about the busses being late and taking too long to reach their destinations. The executives commissioned a study of bus lines and transit system efficiency. They surveyed their customers to see what was most important to them. They benchmarked their system against other metro systems. They concluded that customer service and productivity both needed improvement.

Accordingly, many bus routes were redrawn to reduce travel time. Managers spent hours talking with employees about the need for greater efficiency and customer service. As the new bus timetables and revised routes were rolled out, the leaders thought their job was done.

Imagine their surprise when it was reported that bus drivers were speeding past queues of people with a smile and a wave of the hand. The bus drivers were questioned about the incidents. "Why on earth would you not stop to pick up those passengers?" the executives asked. Their reply was simple. "It's impossible for us to keep to our timetables if we have to stop for passengers!"

This experience carries some serious messages. First of all, it reminds us that planning how the organization *should* operate doesn't always guarantee that it *will* operate that way in real life. Second, it illustrates that everything that has gone on before in the change process is meaningless unless leaders effectively face the tests under fire. This chapter will consider the characteristics and interventions that enable leaders to face such tests.

Leaders of Change

Let's begin by learning from the experts who have actually led a change in culture. Take a moment to recall who some of these leaders are. Who has actually led a change in an organization's culture and made it last at least 10 years? Here is one such leader who made a great impact.

• • •

Misha recalled how his grandfather, a good communist, occasionally removed the pictures of Marx and Lenin from the living room walls to reveal religious icons taped on the back sides. Despite the State's ban on religion, Misha's grandparents, like many of their neighbors, refused to deny some of their beliefs and traditions. His grandparents' example greatly impressed Misha and shaped his paradigm of life. Despite all the government's rhetoric, Misha knew you could be a good party member and have some different values than those dictated by the State.

One day in law school, Misha caused a disruption in class. A professor was delivering a two-hour monologue without any comment or discussion. Misha and a classmate wrote a note of protest: "We are university students. We can read the material by ourselves. If you don't have anything to add, please take this into consideration." They slipped the note anonymously to the professor. To their surprise, the professor exploded and said the note showed hostility to Marxism. "Who wrote this?" he demanded.

Misha rose and said, "I wrote it." Then his colleague also stood up.

The professor left the room and within minutes Misha and his co-author were summoned to the administrator's office. Many of the students feared for their two classmates' well being. After some time, Misha returned from the meeting and said that the committee had accepted the students' criticism. Everything was all right.

In time Misha—Mikhail Sergeyevitch Gorbachev—used his values and courage to lead significant change in his homeland. He legitimized opening the doors of communication with the west (glasnost), sanctioned religious worship again throughout the USSR, and led the perestroika (restructuring) movement to begin reshaping a badly decaying bureaucracy. Though the opposition was strong to many of his reforms, Mikhail Gorbachev continued to push ahead.

• • •

Mikhail Gorbachev's experience is a wonderful illustration of how the inside out process really works on leaders and organizations. His personal paradigms and values (who he is) drove his actions (what he did) as head of the Soviet Union. Without such personal transformations, what would have motivated Mr. Gorbachev to "stay the course" for glasnost and perestroika when the keepers of the status quo challenged his leadership? And what is Gorbachev's legacy in his country? His popularity in the polls gradually dropped, he resigned the presidency when communism fell from power, and he hasn't always agreed with his successors on economic policies; but his fundamental freeing up of political and cultural systems has continued under his successors.

Mikhail Gorbachev was one name that came to my mind when thinking of leaders of change. Some other great leaders of change are: Margaret Thatcher, Jack Welch, Martin Luther King, Jr., Anwar Sadat, Walt Disney, and Mother Teresa.

Perhaps some other leaders you thought of were Chrysler Corporation's Lee Iacocca, Southwest Airlines Herb Kelleher, India's Mahatma Gandhi, or UCLA basketball coach John Wooden. Some of the leaders that we have already studied in earlier chapters are Scandinavian Airlines' Jan Carlzon, Saturn's Skip LeFauve and Mike Bennett, Ritz-Carlton's Horst Schulze and Wal-Mart's Sam Walton. All of these leaders ushered in new cultures that endured at least 10 years.

In our world there have been few real leaders of enduring change. Many people talk about it, but few have actually done it. What elements have enabled the few true leaders to succeed where many others have failed? Here is a profile that is common to Mother Teresa as well as Jack Welch:

1. They are visionary. They have a vision of a future state that compels them to action and helps them stay the course when adversity comes.

2. Their vision becomes the center of their work. These leaders become so committed to making their vision a reality that they subordinate their personal comfort and short-term popularity for their cause.

3. They believe in themselves. Regardless of how others respond to them, they stay on course. Any moments of doubt they may have they keep to themselves.

4. They are controversial risk takers. As Machiavelli said, introducing "a new order of things" is risky business. These leaders are not deterred by the risk or controversy of their vision.

They view themselves as standard bearers for a better way. Other people may view them as radicals and non-conformists.

5. They are passionate, courageous, persistent, and even ruthless in pursuing the vision. Sometimes we forget how "ruthless" Mahatma Gandhi's unwavering standards were to the order he was trying to establish. A leader's passion is contagious. Followers are bonded together through their passion to the vision.

6. They inspire trust and confidence in others. Leaders of enduring change have a charismatic effect on others. The trust they inspire in others is the seed that helps any leader attract enthusiastic followers, but it also grows to produce leadership capacity in others. Charisma leads people to share the leader's values and employ the same behaviors.

7. They are great communicators. Whether it is Mother Teresa's quiet example or Martin Luther King, Jr.'s "I have a dream" message, leaders are able to connect their vision with others in a motivating way.

8. They align their followers. This characteristic is just as important as charisma. Once people are following the leader's lead, they are able to reshape and align their collective efforts to deliver a different level of performance. The leaders actually introduce a new order of things and this new order endures beyond temporary euphoria or sacrifice to make a lasting contribution.

9. They turn their dream into reality. Despite all the odds against them, these leaders and their associates succeed in adapting the world to their dream. They produce turnarounds from the status quo by overcoming great adversity.

It is natural to feel somewhat intimidated by these nine attributes. They are an exclusive leadership standard, but only because most individuals decline to adopt them. However, each of us has fulfilled these attributes, at least in part, in different dimensions and at different times in our lives—in families, in community roles, or in specific work situations. Put aside your sense of intimidation for a moment and consider a few questions:

• As you look at your personal mission statement, do you feel it deserves to take center stage in your life? Is it worth sacrificing some personal comforts?

• Consider the trusts your stakeholders have placed in your organization. Will it require some "intelligent disobedience" from the current rules and policies to fulfill their moments of truth?

• As you read your organizational mission statement, is it worthy of becoming the Constitution for your work life?

• Review the diagnosis you made after reading chapter 9. What are the consequences for yourself and others if you do nothing about what you uncovered?

• Look over the design plans you made after reading chapter 10. What would it be worth to you to actually see this design come to life every day?

• How important is it to you to convert the latent partners you chose at the end of chapter 11 into synergistic partners?

Now for the payoff question: does your dissatisfaction with the status quo, your sense of mission, and your commitment to your high performance design all outweigh the cost and risks of stepping off the beaten path? If so, you are committing yourself to become a leader of change. If you do not feel compelled to take this step, at least you will be able to empathize with the countless others who have made the same choice. Read on as I describe some of the ways leaders have turned their conviction into a new order of things.

Change from the Inside Out

At the beginning of this book I made the point that leaders earn enthusiastic followers by working from the inside out—by developing trust personally before trying to align things organizationally. This inside out formula is also required for enduring culture changes.

Sustainable organizational change begins when individuals change their paradigms and practices, becomes mainstream when a critical mass of people change what they do, and fulfills

its purpose when the organization becomes aligned with the new order of things.

This crucial process has been misunderstood and neglected by many organizations in the past 40 years as they sought to improve their results. In the 1960s, the emphasis of organization development was on personal growth, values clarification, team building, and improved communication. This is the "inside" approach to change. Although this approach may have benefited some individuals, past experience tells us the inside approach has had minimal impact on changing an organization's culture and results.

While the foundation of lasting change starts inside with changes in people's paradigms, vision, and values, working on the inner circle alone isn't sufficient to guarantee greater effectiveness. The inside out approach means "inside out"—it is not complete until it has reached the outer circle.

Many who have questioned "inside out" are proponents of the "systems approach." This approach gained momentum in many organizations in the 1970s and sought to improve organizational performance by changing systems, structures, and processes. Work redesign, self-sufficient work teams, and most approaches to Total Quality are examples of the "outside in" paradigm. Conceptually, this approach begins at the organizational level and then attempts to cascade down to impact each individual at the personal level. Although the "outside in" approach has led to some positive processes, it is apparent that something is missing in the way most companies have gone about it. Consider this track record:

• The American Quality Foundation found that only 30 percent of companies with Quality programs say they are successful. Most Quality programs last only two or three years.

• The success rates for self-directing teams, reengineering, and mergers range between 20 and 30 percent.

• Only 30 percent of new incentive plans, such as gainsharing, achieve their desired outcomes.

• The effectiveness of downsizing efforts is even bleaker. An American Management Association study of 700 firms who downsized between 1989 and 1994 reported that 86 percent saw employee morale collapse, 66 percent saw no improvement in productivity, and only 50 percent improved their profits even as long as five years after they downsized.

Let's zero in on one of these approaches—re-engineering—to understand why the "outside in" paradigm fails so often. Hammer & Associates researched some of the leading factors in the poor success rate of re-engineering efforts. Here are some of their findings.

1. Indicated resistance to change—60%
2. Limitations of existing systems—40%
3. Lack of executive consensus—40%
4. Lack of a senior executive "champion"—40%
5. Unrealistic expectations—30%
6. Lack of cross-functional project teams—28%
7. Lack of team skills—25%
8. Late staff involvement—18%
9. Project charter too narrow—16%

Reid Moormaugh & Associates add some insight to the picture with research identifying the most common errors in trying to re-engineer the work process.

• Trying to fix a process instead of changing it
• Not focusing on the business process

- Ignoring everything except process design
- Neglecting people's values and beliefs
- Being willing to settle for minor results
- Quitting too early
- Placing constraints on the definition of the problem and the scope of re-engineering
- Trying to make it happen from the bottom up
- Picking someone who does not understand re-engineering to lead the effort

Notice in both sets of issues that the software issues far outnumber the hardware issues. The failure of the "outside in" approach lies in the old axiom, "Those convinced against their will are of the same opinion still." In other words, people cannot and will not change their behavior, their work systems, or their relationships with stakeholders if such changes are incongruent with their conviction of what the situation requires. No one can act outside of their paradigm or value system for very long and still maintain their integrity. Look at any organization that has experienced an enduring shift in culture and performance and you will see evidence of the inside out process.

• • •

Dr. W. Edwards Deming taught the Japanese the principles and methodologies of continuous improvement and Total Quality. Dr. Deming was one of a handful of individuals who pioneered Quality management during World War II. In the factories that employed Quality methods, the production results were at an all-time high—even with an inexperienced work force. As many employees returned to reclaim their former positions in these factories after the war, Dr. Deming and his colleagues taught them the methods that had brought such impressive results.

These new methods were rejected by a post-war America focused on mass production, not quality. When Dr. Deming was asked to assist Japanese companies rebuild themselves after the war, he vowed he would never again teach the methodologies of Quality management without first teaching the principles and paradigms upon which it was based.

• • •

Today we can see the fruits of these two approaches: Deming's inside out approach in Japan versus the outside in approach used by many of the industrialized Western nations. Quality is a way of life in Japan, while many companies in the West are still struggling.

Inside Out Vs. Outside In: A Third Alternative

The debates rage on today about the best approach to change culture. Customer focus and competitive strategies require an outside in process, yet people don't always respond to outside in pressure. Even if you launch an inside out process, external changes will demand your attention immediately. How can you balance these two forces? The answer lies in what Stephen Covey calls a Third Alternative—a new solution that is more synergistic than existing proposals.

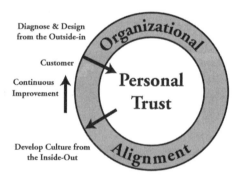

The Third Alternative is continuous improvement: an iterative cycle of diagnosis, design, and development. Study the organizations that have made enduring culture changes and you will find they employ a process in which they diagnose and design from the outside in and develop their culture from the inside out.

The systems advocates are correct when they say organizational diagnosis and design are outside in processes. As noted in chapter 9, the first step in organizational diagnosis is to look outside to the customers and other stakeholders' needs. Ideally, this diagnostic process would move steadily inward (toward each person), helping each individual diagnose the fit between their mission, strategy, tasks, resources, systems, and processes against their critical stakeholders' needs. Through this process the larger unit provides the necessary context for effective planning by the subunits. Then the organization would design (or redesign) itself to align 100 percent of what it does within the framework of stakeholder needs and natural laws. As I outlined in chapter 11, the outside in design process requires you to focus "one level up" from your unit to better fit into the order of your ecosystem. The bottom line of diagnosis and design is that every person has a clear line of sight between what they do and how it fulfills the stakeholders' moments of truth.

Developing actual performance is where the crossover must occur between the outside in and inside out approaches. As the change formula demonstrated, we resist change if we feel the costs outweigh the benefits. A person's commitment to change is just as individualistic and critical to culture change as it is to choosing which leader to follow. If you want the changes to last, you must spend time and energy to connect with many individuals and earn their support.

Many managers don't feel they can take the time to earn this support. After all, market pressures are strong, time is short, and the new design and culture have been carefully crafted by a well-qualified task force. "It is their job to do as we tell them. So implement the new design."

The only problem is 70 percent of the time people don't do as they've been told. Some time ago the CEO of a Baldrige award-winning company told a visitor, "If we relaxed the pressure from the top for one instant, our culture would bounce back to where it was before we started the quality program." This very thing occurred later in another celebrated Quality company when a new leader replaced the CEO. As the new CEO made the rounds to get to know people, employees complained about many requirements of the quality system. This led the new CEO to believe the quality program was distracting and burdensome. He abolished many of the quality practices and, unfortunately, this company's Quality performance settled back to more traditional levels. Both of these companies failed to build Quality from the inside out.

In reality, something will always come along to cause the pressure from the top to relax—short-term gains, executive retirements, sharp market changes—and then the true underlying values and behaviors of the culture will reassert themselves. Organizations who violate the dynamics of the continuous improvement process simply are unable to be effective when the heat is on. The critical needs are not aligned: external stakeholders have been ignored, lip service only is given to the defined strategies, and everyone copes by working primarily on their personal agendas. The organization winds up disappointing many of its stakeholders.

Contrast this level of performance with that of Ritz-Carlton, Saturn, Procter & Gamble and others cited in this book. When outside in diagnosis and design come together with an inside out culture, it spells competitive advantage.

This means if you are serious about earning others' followership you must first see the world through their eyes and then try to expand their view. An often-overlooked byproduct of outside in processes is the impact they can have on shifting paradigms— the necessary first step of the inside out process. A thorough diagnosis usually creates a healthy dissatisfaction with the status quo. Development efforts, therefore, should focus on helping individuals choose their paradigms, visions, and priorities to be aligned with the realities uncovered in the diagnosis/design processes.

Once individuals have shifted their paradigms, they still have to become skilled in the practical first steps of living in the new culture. The following pages contain a summary of ways that some leaders have been able to accomplish this.

Becoming the Change You Seek in Others

There are research findings that support the notion that an entire company tends to take on the personality of its founders. In other words, if you want to understand much of what makes IBM what it is today, study the life, values, and work behaviors of Tom Watson. Want to better understand the culture at Apple Computer Corporation? Observe Steven Jobs for a while. As we have already seen, the Ritz-Carlton Hotel Company is a mirror image of what Horst Schulze and his leadership team value above everything else.

This means that if you want to see the culture make lasting changes, you yourself must become the change you seek in others. You must personally live the new standard and set the example for others to follow. For those who don't fully trust you or the new system, your behavior will be their first clue that the new culture is "for real." Here are some things you can do:

• *"Walk the talk" yourself.* John H. Feldmann, Jr. was my first plant manager at Procter & Gamble. He epitomized many of the attributes of change leadership. When he had the opportunity to start up the paper products plant in Albany, Georgia, he was excited to shape an organization that would break all the molds—and all the production records. One of John's deep convictions was that most work systems underutilized people's capacity to contribute. The plant's mission and operating principles were a reflection of John's personal mission and values. The organization design was based on many of the high performance design principles outlined in chapter 10. John was committed to bringing out the best in a diverse work force. The Albany plant had committed itself to hiring a demographic profile matching the surrounding area, meaning 40 percent would be Black and 20 percent would be women. In southwest Georgia in 1972 this was considered truly radical. When some managers on John's team and some people above him in the hierarchy suggested the plant might have to back off these targets for start up, John was "unreasonable." He refused to back away from his dream. The plant culture John created also minimized status symbols. John came to work every day in casual clothes. He arrived at the plant early each morning to get a close spot to the plant entrance because there were no reserved parking places. Coincidentally, John's unreasonable organization did break all the production records. Every product the Albany plant started up established a company record. John Feldmann died many years ago, but his influence can still be felt at the Albany plant today.

• *State clearly what the vision is and is not.* It is usually not sufficient to merely communicate what the organization's vision is. You must be able to state clearly what it is not. For example, your associates may interpret a vision of empowerment to mean many different things. Some associates may believe this means they should be self-sufficient and operate without any management supervision from day one. Other associates may believe a supervisor will always be part of the picture. For such issues, it is important to paint a picture of the ultimate destination and the milestones you will be passing along the way.

• *Manage the consequences for desired and undesired behaviors.* The way you manage the consequences of people's behavior is one of the most powerful reward systems in your organization. Your associates take their cues for what is important and what is okay and not okay by what you pay attention to, follow up on, and measure. In shaping culture this means you need to (1) replace negative consequences for the needed behaviors with positive consequences, and (2) replace positive consequences for the undesired behaviors with negative consequences.

• *Teach others step-by-step what the needed behaviors are.* An old German proverb says, "The devil is in the details." This is true with changing culture. People may understand and agree with the vision, but unless they become skilled in the daily behaviors required to fulfill it, the new culture will develop very slowly. For instance, in the matter of customer service, you must model to your own associates how you would like them to treat your customers. You must coach and correct what you see happening every day. Horst Schulze practices the three steps of service with everyone he comes in contact with during the day. John Feldmann once said as he passed by a department manager operating a piece of equipment on the production line, "Contribute any way you can!" This was John's not-so-subtle reminder that he believed a manager added value by working on the system, not just by operating in it.

• *"Celebrate" in the organization when employees behave as needed.* Developing a new culture is a challenging undertaking. Many people will sacrifice and go through painful moments as they work at it. It is important to celebrate the occasion as they achieve certain milestones. For instance, one organization was struggling to become more innovative in its work. A diagnosis study had shown that too many people were trying to figure out what senior management wanted instead of developing their own solution and then pressing forward. When one courageous project leader exercised intelligent disobedience and championed a solution that saved the company millions of dollars, the division vice president sent a memo throughout the company praising the project team not only for the winning solution, but also for demonstrating how everyone should be going about his/her work.

Leaders who set the example for the new cultural behaviors earn the trust of employees and also provide an anchor point to help them do the same. One of the most paralyzing forces in a culture is the sense that the direction may change after people have sacrificed to make it happen. By becoming the change you seek in others, you actually lead the way to the new vision. But the work is only half done. In order to fulfill the inside out approach, you have to work on the organizational circle to institutionalize the new way of doing things. You have to work on the system. We already covered much on this side of the equation in chapter 10. In addition to such system-wide changes, you may need to make some design changes to help key individuals change their paradigms through new experiences. Make this design work consistent with natural laws, and the benefits will soon become self-evident.

An Example of Inside Out, Enduring Culture Change

Leaders who successfully change culture from the inside out leave their impact on the organization that lasts long after they have left the scene. A good example of this is a partnership that was forged between a government agency (ALPHA) and a contractor (BRAVO). Thousands of such relationships are in operation every day, but few of them actually produce synergy. Some years ago, however, the leaders of both organizations tried to create a true win-win partnership instead of the typical "arms-length" compliance relationship. In this memo, the new organizational culture is spelled out:

• • •

The government-industry partnership that began with the first generation of WHITECAP has grown and evolved over the past 40 years. The largely continuous team of ALPHA, contractors (e.g. BRAVO), and subcontractors has created a unique "culture" in which business is conducted. The tenets of that culture (though often unwritten) are as fundamental to the success of both day-to-day and long-term operations as are the principles, objectives, and unique WHITECAP business processes. The following describes (in abridged form) what each team member expects of all team members:

1. Ethical Behavior at All Times.

2. Open Communication.

3. Trusting Communications. Identify problems early and don't shoot the messenger. Work on solutions. We are all in this together. Communications are not rank conscious nor stove-piped.

4. Win-Win Interactions. Understand each other's world well enough so that required compromises allow each party to be successful in their world.

5. Make and Fulfill Commitments.

6. Lock-step Together. No surprises to the partners. Joint and continuous discussions of key program and personnel issues.

7. Comprehensive Long-Term View. Short-term expedient decisions are bad; we both expect to be in the business for the long term. We are willing to take short-term pain for long-term gain.

8. Team Work.

9. Fault-Tolerant. We manage risks, but we accept that mistakes will occur. We have a disciplined systems approach to handle mistakes and to learn from them.

10. Tailored Processes. We expect that most bureaucratic processes (acquisition, contracting, financial, etc.) will require tailoring (including waivers) to be appropriate for WHITECAP.

• • •

The significant thing about the ALPHA-BRAVO partnership is that this document is used to orient new supervisors and team members in both organizations to "how we do things at WHITECAP." This document has become a tool for developing the inside out commitment to keep the relationship going. Through its use, the culture is maintained. The leaders' contribution of many years ago is still alive today.

Conclusion

Leaders of change must undergo a personal transformation before they attempt to transform their organizational culture. Their personal transformation is fueled by a vision or dream of a better future and is evidenced by their paradigm shifts and behavior changes. Thus, leaders of change must first become mission-centered themselves.

Next, these leaders embark on the task of transforming their organizational culture. They do this by diagnosing and designing the new organization from the outside in, using market/customer needs and natural laws for their design criteria.

Then these leaders earn the followership of other mission-centered people by working from the inside out. They influence others to commit to the same mission, paradigms, and behavior changes. They don't rest until the vast majority of associates spontaneously do whatever is needed to fulfill the mission.

This is how mission-centered people create mission-centered organizations. When this process is repeated to stay in touch with evolving stakeholder needs, the result is continuous improvement. The legacy of such leadership is an organization that perpetually fits into the order of things through the ages.

You should not assume all of the foregoing will happen automatically. Changing a culture is not like changing an automobile's spark plugs. It is far more like an experience I had while whitewater rafting on the Clark Fork River near Missoula, Montana.

• • •

On one of our leadership program expeditions, our five rafts were approaching "Fang," a challenging set of rapids that can give you a real roller coaster ride if you hit the wave train just right. Each raft crew spaced themselves far enough behind the boat in front of them to allow for the proper positioning to take on "Fang." The first boat moved forward and hit the wave train perfectly. Then the other four rafts came through in succession. Although every raft was positioned correctly and the crew was paddling together, only half of them hit the waves just right and got the full up-and-down ride. The others hit the waves just a split second off their peak. As we analyzed our "system's" performance, we realized that once the five boats were in formation and moving with the river's current, each boat had a very small margin for error to synchronize with the waves. Each guide had to calculate factors such as wind, the water flow, and the raft's speed in an instant and adjust accordingly. Only more experience in taking on "Fang" could have helped us get the feel of the river and time our approach with split-second accuracy.

• • •

When changing cultures, as in whitewater rafting, timing can mean everything. Even successful leaders of change don't always hit the organizational peak with their interventions. Sometimes their timing is wrong: they have the right principles, but the organization simply isn't ready to shift what it is doing. Sometimes their strategy for change is flawed: they overlook something important in the culture and are unable to assemble critical mass. Sometimes the whitewater environment changes drastically at a critical stage in the change process: supportive leaders leave, finances collapse, or natural disasters impose their own agenda of change. Sometimes success is a combination of what the leader brings, good fortune, and good timing. But successful leaders of change aren't put off by the odds against them. They may try and fall short—but, like our raft guides, they keep at it until they develop a feel for the ecosystem and find the right timing. This is their most important characteristic—they get up every time they fall.

• • •

Applying what you have learned:

1. List the initiatives that have been used in your organization:
• Inside: focusing on individuals and team building.
• Outside in: changes in mission, strategy, structure, systems.
• Inside out: personal changes in paradigms and purpose leading to organizational realignment.
   What impact have these initiatives had in actually changing what people do every day?

2. Consider your culture change strategy:
• What paradigms, values, or behaviors must you first change in yourself?
• How will you personally demonstrate your new paradigms and values to others with whom you work?
• What work do you need to do on systems to help others make the transition to the new order of things?
• Now sequence your answers to the three previous bullets into an action plan that lays out who (you and others) will do what (specifically) by when. Set some milestones to monitor your progress over time.

Section

6

Leadership That Lasts

14
A Legacy for the Ages

"Our deepest fear is not that we are inadequate. Our deepest fear is that we are powerful beyond measure. It is our light, not our darkness that most frightens us. We ask ourselves, Who am I to be brilliant, gorgeous, talented, fabulous? Actually, who are you not to be?"

—Marianne Williamson

"The life of a small group of people who live true to their convictions does more and more certain good than all writing. Let us, therefore, young and old, direct all of our actions, as much as possible, toward the realization of our convictions."

—Leo Tolstoy

LET'S REFLECT ON THE POTENTIAL IMPACT OF THE information we have covered in this book. This chapter is to encourage you to carry through with the resolutions and action plans you have chosen to shape something that can last for ages.

Leadership for the Ages is not some utopian, ivory tower view of management. Leadership for the Ages is a practical idealism because it is a formula that great leaders throughout history have intuitively followed to accomplish extraordinary things. This formula is practical because it works. This formula is idealistic because it leads people closer to the quality of life they would like to have. Chapter by chapter we have explored the various elements of Leadership for the Ages:

1. Being mission-centered, making a deep personal commitment, and sacrificing for your values

2. Focusing your company's values into a compelling, common purpose

3. Shaping organizational processes and systems to put natural laws to work

4. Living in a culture of mutual trust and commitment in which each individual sees what needs to be done and then simply does it

5. Delivering results that exceed expectations, especially in trying situations

These elements do not appear out of thin air. They are nurtured and developed by leaders who work from the inside out to earn the trust of others before aligning their organizational ecosystem.

Some people will say, "I know many managers who get great results without being mission-centered, or without using the OP Model or high performance design principles." I won't debate this point. Managers can get great short-term results (short-term meaning several years) and not do everything described here. *Any market will tolerate aberrations for a time, but only alignment with natural laws will allow you to prosper through the ages.* This means managers can coax or coerce employees to meet targets long enough to get promoted. Managers can even string together enough such experiences to make a successful career. But after they have left the scene, these individuals will have produced very little that is long lasting. If drastic changes disrupt the status quo, the organization's survival will be in peril. Don't take my word for it—just ask the few remaining top 100 companies from 1909!

Leadership for the Ages can match other approaches for meeting short-term needs, but it adds value beyond the here and now by contributing some intangibles that are longer lasting. These intangibles alter the relationships of those who work together and align their efforts with natural laws:

• *Your intangible commitment to your own personal mission* causes you to see yourself, your organization, and your world differently. Your commitment produces different and better responses to the environmental challenges you face.

• *Your view of yourself as a steward, rather than a subordinate,* leads you to seek a win-win relationship with all stakeholders. This produces a different level of energy and commitment from them toward the common purpose. *Everyone thinks of survival for self, group, and the larger organization(s). This enables everyone involved to fit into the order of things.*

• *The diagnosis and design processes* help you see the tangible and intangible sides of your organization as they really are and harness the power of high performance design principles to make things better. This causes the same people and resources to work together very differently. *These processes establish a steady state and allow for more specialized and complex functions over time without blunting your abilities to mobilize against threats and adapt to challenges and opportunities.*

These new relationships produce the synergies that propel you further up the lifecycle. The acid test will come, of course, when the next "Age" emerges. Agrarians laid the foundation for the industrialists who have paved the way for today's globalists. We would be naïve to believe that another new age will not follow in our footsteps. In fact, the lifecycle of an "Age" appears to be decreasing as technology explodes. When the next seasons of change hit, the organizations that possess all of these intangibles will be able to embrace the leading edge of change.

Take a moment and ponder this important intangible: what will be the truly lasting results of your life's work? How will it affect future stakeholders, even those who haven't been born yet? What is your work's potential legacy?

These questions will put you in touch with elements that are important to improving your current performance. This is the value that Leadership for the Ages adds. Leadership for the Ages addresses the tangible issues to improve your results today and taps into the intangibles to build a legacy for tomorrow. Let me give you some examples.

The Legacy of Being Mission-Centered

Caught in the midst of Russia's transition to a free market economy, Krasny machine tool company became a privatized industry as the Gross National Product declined by more than 10 percent year after year and inflation jumped at approximately 10 percent per month. Of the 400 Russian machine tool companies that were in business in 1990, less than 100 are still in business today. Krasny is one of them.

• • •

Director General Yuri Kirillov placed natural laws ahead of Russia's conventional wisdom and government edicts to keep Krasny a viable organization. The process began with Yuri and his leadership team members each drafting their own personal mission statement. They considered what was important to them at work and in other areas of life. Then the leaders collaborated to produce a common mission for Krasny. At first glance, their "Philosophy of Management" may not seem earth shaking to you:

We build our relationships as a team of people driven by common values in an atmosphere of trust and respect, based on the principles of integrity, fairness, equality, and mutual assistance. This is the only way that leads to the common goal.

These words were crafted by a senior management team that had merely filled government contracts prior to 1991. None of these men and women had any feedback on what their customers thought of their products. They managed their departments in isolation. Their revenues were provided entirely by the State. Krasny's 6,000 workers had a job for life. Their business had moved along as a classic federally-controlled bureaucracy. By most standards, it was a most inefficient organization!

The "common goal" referred to in the company's philosophy was to make Krasny a successful enterprise in a free market economy; to win loyal customers through superior quality and service; and to stay in business as government props were withdrawn. The commitment to become a true "team" was a revolutionary idea for these managerial isolationists. Their commitment to "integrity, fairness, equality, and mutual assistance" went much deeper than typical Communist propaganda. Their vision was to be a successful business by earning the partnership of all stakeholders.

Two very atypical leaders helped Yuri Kirillov and the Krasny management team. Elena Kishinets was the company's newsletter editor and a former school teacher. Because of her fluency in English, Elena became part of the steering team working with me and John Simmons, founder of Participation Associates, a Chicago-based consulting firm. Another member of the steering team was Maxim Iliin, an internal management specialist hired from the university to help Krasny become a free-market competitive organization.

The Krasny change project embodied many of the elements described in previous chapters. The OP Model guided their diagnosis and design processes. They structured their operations into self-sufficient departments. Each department developed a win-win relationship with its partners. Departments used quality principles to help realign some core processes. Elena and Maxim conducted leadership training ("The Seven Habits of Highly Effective People") for every Krasny work group. But in early 1993, Russia's declining GNP and spiraling inflation had seemingly brought Krasny to its knees. "Our customers tell us they love our products and that they want to buy more," Yuri reported, "but they don't have any money."

Their business environment appeared to be squeezing them out of existence. How could they fit into this new order of things? What would a typical bureaucracy do in the face of this dilemma? How would a mission-centered culture respond?

Krasny's leaders faced their predicament with courage and creativity. Fulfilling their mission was more important to them than anything else. They were prepared to even question what business they were in. As they did this soul searching, they came to realize that what they needed were some different products that customers needed and could afford. Having learned brainstorming techniques from their American consultants, Krasny's leaders now launched a brainstorming initiative to solicit from the workers some alternative products that could be produced and sold at a profit in their environment. The alternative products, the workers were told, should meet three criteria:

- Capitalize on our technical expertise
- Be affordable to the desired customers
- Deliver immediate profits

The old company culture would have ignored such a request. In Russia, only the leaders concerned themselves with such matters. But Krasny had invested in the empowerment process. Brainstorming, Seven Habits, quality principles, and basic economic principles were widely shared. Paradigms had been shifting over a three-year period. As evidence of how Krasny's culture had changed, the different work groups supplied nearly 200 product ideas! A small task force screened the ideas and eventually recommended 12 new products, including such things as a portable, self contained brick-making plant; oil pipeline equipment; steel doors; nails; consumer lathes; and even toys. While many other firms were going out of business, the sales of these new products enabled Krasny to meet its payroll and expand its marketing research to identify new potential customers for its traditional machine tools.

• • •

Krasny did not escape these desperate conditions without considerable pain. The company has downsized to approximately 1,500 employees today. Its product lineup is very different than when it began operating in the 19th century. But, thanks to its mission-centered leadership team, it is still very much alive and well.

The key point emerging from the Krasny experience is that when the common mission is tied to people's values, it will supersede other self-interests in times of crisis. The Krasny employees' commitment to the mission and their survival instincts are the intangibles that caused them to subordinate personal comforts, traditions, and policies to a higher cause and get on with the needed changes.

The Legacy of Stewardship

In the book *Schindler's List* by Thomas Keneally, we can observe the paradigm shift that wartime entrepreneur Oskar Schindler experienced. Somewhere in the process of running his company, Oskar transitioned from being an army pots and pans vendor to being the steward of his workers' livelihood. His mission shifted from making money to serving those who had placed their trust in him. We celebrate Schindler's courage and resourcefulness in saving the lives of his 1,100 workers. The bonds of loyalty that Schindler and his people experienced are an intangible byproduct that comes to any steward leader. One of my Procter & Gamble colleagues, Tony Turnbull, stepped up and assumed the steward's mantle when he was plant manager of a P&G soap plant in Newcastle, England.

• • •

As Procter & Gamble's business evolved in Europe, new technology and changing market conditions made some manufacturing locations obsolete. The Newcastle City Road Plant, part of P&G since the early 1950s, was targeted to be closed. This meant its 250 employees were to be transferred to other locations or laid off. A few were to move to a newer plant in the same city, but most would be offered assignments in other parts of the U.K. Tony and his leadership team knew how their associates would respond to the offers. Most of these men and women were natives of the area and would be very reluctant to move. This presented Tony and the rest of his leadership team with a personal dilemma. They said to each other, "These people have been told for 30 years that there are no layoffs at Procter and Gamble. How can we face our people and tell them they no longer have a job?"

Such dilemmas cry out for leadership. Fortunately, Tony was equal to the challenge. "Before we face our people," he said, "we first have to face ourselves. We can't defend an action that we ourselves don't believe is right." So the leaders planned a retreat to discuss the situation.

(Let me interject a question here: do mission-centered organizations ever have layoffs? Do such organizations have an inherent right to exist any more than any other organization? It depends on the order of things in the environment. There are no guarantees. In this particular case, the environment dictated the need to close the plant, but not how the plant should respond.)

Emotions among the plant leaders ran high. In their discussion, they tried to separate folklore, tradition, and practice from principle. "No layoffs" was a practice, they concluded. They dug deeper to find the principle underpinning the practice. Finally someone reminded the others of former CEO Richard R. Deupree's time-honored statement, "The interests of the company are inseparable with the interests of the employees." They decided that was the real principle upon which the practice of "no layoffs" had been based.

So Tony said, "If the principle is, 'our employees' interests are inseparable with the company's interests', how do we handle the fact that we are closing the plant? We can't deliver on the practice anymore. How do we do this in a principled way?" The team began thinking how they might align their shutdown process with the principle. "Their need is to have a job," they reasoned, "so our job is to see they are well placed."

Most companies would have said at this point, "We gave every person an opportunity to move and each one turned it down. We've done all we can do." This wasn't good enough for Tony and his team, though. Partners wouldn't treat each other so casually in such a serious situation. They made it their business to help their partners find another good job.

"If these people failed to show up for work today without warning, we would have felt betrayed," the leaders reasoned. "What kind of energy would we expend if one of us were being laid off?" This question led them to a far more proactive stance. They set up an out-placement office in the plant. They used company time to counsel people. They personally visited other employers, saying, "We have a situation where people, through no fault of their own, are losing their jobs. These are good people. We have nothing to hide. With their permission, we will open the personnel files and let you look through them to see exactly what has been going on with each person."

Amazingly enough, a new employer was coming into the area to build a new plant. Because of the leadership team's involvement, this company came into the City Road Plant and interviewed all 250 employees. The new plant hired about 90 percent of the employees. The other 10 percent found good jobs elsewhere.

The bottom line of Tony's leadership was measured by what the people going out the door said to those few who remained. They essentially said with one voice, "I wish I were staying with P&G. I love it here. But you can be proud of your company—they have done it the Procter Way."

• • •

Tony Turnbull's stewardship actions actually increased trust in what most people would have called a no-win situation. Procter & Gamble did improve its bottom line significantly by closing the City Road plant, but because of a steward-leader, its roots remain strong, its transplants are blooming elsewhere, and it has successfully handled the challenges that have followed.

True stewards like Tony Turnbull are able to win and maintain high trust in a world full of cynicism toward authorities and institutions. People who have this intangible high trust will stick together when they come under fire.

The Legacy of High Performance Partnerships

If your personal contribution and the organization in which you work are to endure beyond your immediate involvement, other people are going to have to supplement what you can do. In other words, you need partners. Partners last longer than subordinates, associates, or even colleagues. Not only that, partners can help create synergy—multiplying exponentially what your talents can provide. Here is a great example of a leader whose synergistic partnerships have extended several corporate lifecycles.

• • •

Ritchey Marbury is owner and principal of Marbury Engineering (ME), a small civil engineering firm in Albany, Georgia, started by his father many years ago. Though the firm for decades had enjoyed a strong reputation for quality work, several events brought it to the brink of closing down.

When the financing collapsed on a leveraged buyout of another engineering firm, ME was forced to return the purchased firm to the original owners at a significant financial loss. Through no fault of its own, ME's financial resources suddenly were depleted, debts were high, and the banks cut off its line of credit until the firm could show a full year of successful operation.

The prospects for the next 12 months were bleak. Most of ME's work was for municipal governments, who paid only after the job was completed. The average timeline for most existing projects was 18 months, meaning there would be very little cash in the next 12 months if ME conducted business as usual. To make matters worse, another firm approached all 12 ME employees and offered them a job with a raise in pay. To Ritchey's surprise, all of his employees turned down this attractive offer.

"I knew we would never get out of this situation by using traditional approaches," Ritchey confessed. "We had to have a radical change. I decided our only hope was to build such strong relationships and trust with everybody that they would want to help me make the changes before it was too late."

Because ME needed a radical improvement in the bottom line, Ritchey first focused his attention on his staff. He convened a meeting to share the situation with everyone. "It's no secret we're in serious financial trouble," Ritchey began. "Each of us is going to have to take an immediate salary adjustment to help us get through. If we continue as we've been doing, we'll all be out of a job in a few months. We need to come up with some radically different approaches."

He then passed out envelopes containing a substantial salary increase for each employee! After everyone had opened their envelopes, they stared at Ritchey in disbelief. "We thought you said we were in serious financial trouble!" they said.

"We are," Ritchey replied. "But I'm counting on each of you to do much more than before. So I'm paying you up front for what I expect you to do. If we do what the business needs, you will all earn this increase." There was a method to Ritchey's madness. "These people had all turned down a better paying job to stay with me. Now I was asking them to put out more for our firm than ever before. No one should make less because they stayed with me."

Together Ritchey and his associates developed a Vision and Mission that sought win-win outcomes for everyone:

Mission
"Marbury Engineering Co. serves its clients, its staff, and the public by improving their economic well being and quality of life through engineering, surveying, planning, and information systems."

Vision
"The vision of Marbury Engineering Co. is to be recognized and respected as a leading provider of quality engineering and related services; to work in an attractive, highly professional and committed environment in which we are financially sound; to be a unified team with a goal of improving the economic well being

and quality of life for our staff, our clients and the public; and through shared commitment grow personally and professionally, increasing in size and developing new innovations."

Marbury Engineering's three governing values were "integrity, quality, and service."

With his staff committed to do more with less, Ritchey turned his attention to the other stakeholders whose support was crucial, starting with the bank. He knew he couldn't expect any additional line of credit, but Ritchey needed some help in reducing his existing monthly loan payment. He went through the financial picture with the bank's officers. He told them what level of payments he could sustain. Since ME had never missed a payment in the past, the bank agreed to a longer-than-normal loan repayment schedule to give Ritchey a chance to pull things together.

Given this new lease on life, Marbury Engineering went about creating radical new ways of doing business. With full energy and commitment from everyone, here's what they did:

• They streamlined their work processes by challenging who had to do what. Their basic engineering survey process was streamlined from 21 steps to 13; a loan survey process (for home mortgage approvals) was trimmed from 15 steps to eight.

• Everyone developed multi skills to enable the firm to handle more projects at one time. Lunchtime became class time for everyone as Ritchey shared what he was learning from seminars on Quality management, leadership, and technical skills, such as storm drainage design and subdivision layout. This empowered drafters to become project team members, CAD operators to do drainage analyses, and secretaries to do subdivision plat research.

• Rather than steer all the projects personally as he had in the past, Ritchey took advantage of the multi skills being developed by creating small self-sufficient teams to manage all project phases: client contact, correspondence, most design decisions, and billing.

Next, Ritchey worked to establish partnerships with some of his customer/suppliers—survey companies who occasionally brought jobs to ME. "We again relied on the principle that a trusting relationship will be more productive for both parties," Ritchey said. Marbury began charging selected survey companies lower fees for the work ME did for them. This win-win arrangement immediately brought more business to ME. In fact, the volume work nearly doubled in the ensuing months.

Then Ritchey took the next step by forming a partnership with seven of these surveying companies—Marbury Associates, Inc. (MA, Inc.). Each partner in this enterprise maintains his/her own name and independent business, but owns a piece of MA, Inc. as well. By combining their crews on some projects, the partners could take on larger projects for public clients. One partnership alone won contracts to build six golf courses. The relationship with each of these partners has been win-win. For instance, when one partner was having financial difficulties, Marbury Engineering covered some of the partner's expenses until things turned around.

Marbury Associates, Inc. is a network organization that ebbs and flows according to the opportunities. As Ritchey says, "We have gained the advantages of a 70 person organization with a payroll of only 22."

What did this radical new way of doing business accomplish for Marbury Engineering and its stakeholders?

• In the critical first year, ME met every payroll, made every bank payment on time, and saw a 30 percent increase in its revenues.

• In the longer term, ME's revenues more than tripled and profits have doubled. The revenues from the golf course projects alone were equal to ME's total revenues before the crisis. All MA, Inc. partners have prospered at the same rate of growth.

• ME employee salaries doubled over the same period.

• Quality increased dramatically and costs plummeted even though the owner (and most competent engineer) was less involved in each project.

• Better alignment proved to be the key to doing so much more with less. Projects that used to take up to seven days to complete are now done in one or two by the project teams using streamlined processes.

• • •

Notice how many intangibles came together from the inside out to prolong Marbury Engineering's lifecycle. The foundation was the trust established by Ritchey's father who built the firm on character and competence. This foundation was strengthened by the trust that Ritchey earned with his stakeholders in the moment of crisis because he sought their benefit as well as his own. The new design reshaped the business and put natural laws to work. And the partnerships produced abundance for everybody, far exceeding what any one firm could produce. In the end, Marbury Engineering and Marbury Associates succeeded in adding value to a bureaucratic world. They found a way to do more with less, with everyone winning in the process.

Only Your Legacy Is Lasting

The leaders profiled here—Yuri Kirillov, Elena Kishinets, Maxim Iliin, Tony Turnbull, and Ritchey Marbury have all left a lasting legacy. A dying Krasny manufacturing organization is alive and healthy. Procter & Gamble is still a trusted name in Newcastle despite having closed down an entire plant. The hard work and vision of Ritchey Marbury's father lives on in his son's synergistic partnerships. In every case the stakeholders are better off because of what these organizations have been able to produce. Incomes are up. Work is more challenging and exciting. Products and services have improved the quality of life for many people. These organizations will prosper for generations because of what a few leaders have done today.

Despite all the good you might do for your organization, though, your organization might not survive in its current form in the evolving market place. What will be left as your legacy then? Consider the case of the Hoechst Celanese Corporation (HCC), once a Fortune 100 producer of chemicals and specialty fibers. HCC was owned by Germany's Hoechst AG, one of the world's largest chemical companies. Every year HCC hosted a leadership values conference for 250 of its senior managers. Traditionally one afternoon of the conference schedule was devoted to recreational golf and tennis.

• • •

At the conclusion of one Values Conference a few years ago, certain participants were bold enough to comment on the conference feedback sheet, "Some of us don't play golf or tennis. Wouldn't it be nice next year if we had some activity that we could participate in together?" Dave Williams, one of HCC's conference planners, raised the issue with his colleagues. "We call it a Values Conference," Dave said. "Why don't we have a group activity that embodies one of our corporate values?" One value was to be a good citizen in the community. One of Dave's colleagues had seen a video from the Shell Corporation about a community service project Shell managers had done as part of a corporate program. One idea led to another and at the next Values Conference held in Charlotte, North Carolina, nobody played golf or tennis during the "open afternoon." Instead, everyone (including myself) took part in a service project at a work center for mentally handicapped adults. It was truly an inspiring experience!

We were organized into small teams of about ten, each with our specific assignments. When we arrived at the work center, we were unprepared for what we saw. The 170 men and women (called "clients") who worked at the center had lined the path to the center's doors. Even the clients who weren't scheduled to work that day had come to greet us and thank us for coming to help them. They patted us on the back or hugged us. Each of us was a different person by the time we made it through this welcome party.

These clients reminded me of the movie character Forrest Gump, someone who doesn't know any better than to show love openly; to work hard; to be appreciative of what people do for him; and to sacrifice himself for those he loves. Such individuals do not understand that there are alternatives to doing the right thing; they just naturally follow their conscience. We had 170 Forrest Gumps as our clients that afternoon.

We worked for five hours in our small teams and here's what we did:

- We painted the walls and ceilings in the work center.
- We laid down carpeting in most of the rooms.
- We built storage closets.
- We built a deck on the back of the building so the clients could have lunch outdoors.
- We built a shelter for the bus stop so the clients wouldn't have to wait unprotected in the rain.
- We smoothed and paved a parking lot.
- We planted shrubs and bushes.
- We constructed picnic tables and put them in the yard.

While we were doing this, our clients served food and drinks to us, helped us with many of the tasks, and provided us with plenty of pats on the back and hugs. We were supposed to end at 5 P.M., but everyone stayed until after 6:00 to make sure the work was completed.

After one afternoon the building was transformed—and there were 250 transformed people. We rode back on the bus and one of the managers sitting next to me said, "You know, when they told me they weren't going to have golf this year, I was mad! I work plenty hard for this company and when we have something like this, I like to relax and have some fun." He said, "Let me tell you something, Dave. We can play golf any time! Today I am proud to be a member of this organization!"

The spirit of the project was truly contagious. In Charlotte, as the planning committee ordered paint, lumber, tools, carpeting, and other materials, every supply company volunteered to donate the materials at no cost. Some companies even sent a couple of their own employees to lend a hand and give instructions on how to use the tools or how to build things.

• • •

As this experience illustrates, when the mission is compelling enough, enthusiastic followers flow to you from unanticipated sources. Not surprisingly, the service project became a regular feature of Hoechst Celanese's values conferences. As part of a worldwide restructuring initiative a few years later, however, the parent company decided to break up the Hoechst Celanese Corporation into separate spin-off entities. But the legacy of the company values lives on today, as one former HCC manager told me:

"I remember my boss coming back from the Charlotte conference and telling us in glowing details about the service project. Her enthusiasm and pride in the company excited us. We were proud to be part of a company that took its values seriously. When the company broke up and parts were sold off, I decided to find another job rather than relocate. A top priority in my search process was to find another company who lived its values like Hoechst Celanese did."

The Hoechst Celanese story reminds me of a powerful insight shared by Herbert Fisk Johnson, Sr. in 1927 shortly before he retired as CEO of S. C. Johnson: "When all is said and done this business is nothing but a symbol; and when we translate this we find that it means a great many people think well of its products and that a great multitude has faith in the integrity of the men who make this product. In a very short time the machines that are now so lively will soon become obsolete and the big buildings for all their solidity must some day be replaced. But, a business which symbolizes can live so long as there are human beings alive, for it is not built of such flimsy materials as steel and concrete, it is built of human opinions which may be made to live forever. The goodwill of the people is the only enduring thing in any business. It is the sole substance. . . . The rest is shadow!"

The Hoechst Celanese Corporation is no more, but the goodwill it generated lives on in its products; in communities like Charlotte, North Carolina; and in the lives of those who continue to live by its values. The ongoing legacy of Dave Williams and his conference planning team cannot be measured. The Shell Oil Company could not have anticipated the widespread impact its initial community service project would have on others.

Experiences like these reveal the true potential of human organizations. Machines are systems, but they just sit there. Animals are living systems, but they are highly dependent on their environment. A human organization can cycle up and down like a machine; or it can merely respond to its environment like an animal. It is only by tapping into that part of us that is uniquely human that we can make a contribution that no other system can make. We, the programmers of our organizations, can dream, live consistent with our convictions, and use our independent will to put real purpose into our work. As Ritz-Carlton's Horst Schulze says, "A chair fulfills a function; people need a purpose. It is immoral to ask people to work without purpose."

Oskar Schindler's wife, Emilie, commented on how real purpose affected her husband's life. She noted that Oskar had done nothing astounding before the war and was unexceptional thereafter. He was fortunate, she said, that during the war he had met people who summoned forth his deeper talents. If you had your choice, would you rather be associated with an organization that produced excellent results only, or would you like to have that and a situation that called forth your deeper talents?

Leadership for the Ages calls forth our deeper talents! It builds the bottom line today and builds a legacy for tomorrow. But legacies require time to emerge. As you begin implementing the plans you have developed in these chapters, your efforts may seem small at first. You may not hit every wave at its peak on your first attempt. But, as you persist over time, your efforts can lead to a new order of things. Like the many leaders described in this book, your legacy will be evident in everything that is done for many years to come—long after you are gone.

In the meantime, don't let your concerns extinguish your vision or deprive you of your legacy. Remember the words of a teen-age girl who was depressed by her circumstances:

"That's the difficulty in these times: ideals, dreams, and cherished hopes rise within us, only to meet the horrible truth and be shattered. It's really a wonder that I haven't dropped all my ideals, because they seem so absurd and impossible to carry out. Yet I keep them, because in spite of everything I still believe that people are really good at heart. I simply can't build up my hopes on a foundation consisting of confusion, misery, and death. . . . In the meantime, I must uphold my ideals for perhaps the time will come when I shall be able to carry them out."

The young girl who wrote these words had a vision of what she wanted to do in life. She wanted to be a writer who would influence the world. Her name was Anne Frank. This excerpt from the July 15, 1944 entry in her diary was written some eight months before her tragic death at age 15 in the Bergen-Belsen concentration camp. Anne clung to her vision and ideals to sustain her through unspeakable horrors. Though she didn't live to see it, she left a powerful legacy. She is a writer who influenced the world.

Winston Churchill once said, "To every man (or woman) there comes in his lifetime that special moment when he is figuratively tapped on the shoulder and offered the chance to do a very special thing, unique to him and fitted to his talent; what a tragedy if that moment finds him unprepared or unqualified for the work which would be his finest hour."

It is my hope that reading this book has prepared and will qualify you for that work which will become your finest hour.

For Further Reference

Chapter 2:

1. Durant, Will and Ariel, *The Lessons of History*, New York: Simon & Schuster, 1968. A great summary of civilization lifecycle dynamics. Condenses volumes into a few profoundly-impactful pages.

2. Wasson, Chester R., *Dynamic Competitive Strategy & Product Lifecycles* (Third Edition), Austin: Austin Press, 1978. Nicely summarizes the product lifecycle dynamics.

3. Wheatley, Margaret J., *Leadership and the New Science*, San Francisco: Berrett-Koehler Publishers, 1992. An excellent overview of control, chaos, and order. Applies these scientific principles as metaphors for how organizations might operate for greater effectiveness.

4. De Geus, Arie, *The Living Company*, Cambridge: Harvard Business School Press, 1997. A retired Shell executive cites research and his own experiences to support the theme in this chapter: organizational longevity is enhanced by operating consistently with natural laws.

5. Kotter, John P. and James L. Heskett, *Corporate Culture and Performance*, New York: The Free Press, 1992. A well-researched study of the impact of organizational culture on the bottom line. Cultural attributes of high performers are contrasted with attributes of low performers.

6. Collins, James C. and Jerry I. Porras, *Built To Last*, New York: HarperCollins Publishers, Inc., 1994. An insightful review

of the successful habits of visionary companies—those who preserve their core beliefs amidst changing business conditions.

Chapter 3:

1. Covey, Stephen R., and A. Roger and Rebecca R. Merrill, *First Things First*, New York: Simon & Schuster, 1994. Not as well known as *The Seven Habits of Highly Effective People*, this book goes into more depth on the processes of detecting what your personal mission is and aligning your daily activities with these priorities.

2. Albom, Mitch, *Tuesdays With Morrie*, New York: Doubleday, 1997. The true story of a successful young journalist who learns life's greatest lessons from his dying teacher. It will cause you to reflect on your own life's priorities.

3. The Arbinger Institute, *Leadership and Self-Deception: Getting out of the Box*, San Francisco: Berrett-Koehler Publishers, Inc., 2000. A very insightful look into one of the main causes of poor individual and organizational performance—our tendency to treat others as objects rather than as people. Shows how this underlying dynamic hinders personal and organizational performance.

4. Melohn, Tom, *The New Partnership*, Essex Junction: Oliver Wight Publications, Inc., 1994. An in-depth case study of how one leader earned the trust of employees at North American Tool & Dye and led a dramatic turnaround in the company's results. Full of practical ideas and anecdotes.

Chapter 4:

1. Anderson, Kristin and Ron Zemke, *Tales of Knock Your Socks Off Service*, New York: AMACOM, 1998. Inspiring case studies of outstanding customer service—all coming from the steward paradigm.

2. Read biographies of leaders whose legacy you admire. You will find they acted out of the steward paradigm, not the subordinate paradigm.

Chapter 5:

1. Carlzon, Jan, *Moments Of Truth*, New York: Ballinger Publishing Co., 1987. A refreshingly practical history of Jan Carlzon's experiences at Scandinavian Air Lines (SAS). The leader's role is explored in relating to different stakeholders (particularly boards, union, employees), setting strategy, aligning information and rewards, and shaping culture.

Chapter 6:

1. Graham, John W. and Wendy C. Havlick, *Mission Statements: A Guide to the Corporate and Nonprofit Sectors*, Garland Reference Library of Social Science, Vol. 900, 1994. A good summary of research and practice on the writing of mission statements. Includes 622 actual mission statements.

2. Parker, Marjorie, *Creating Shared Vision*, Oak Park: Dialog International Ltd., 1990. An interesting case study of a large Norwegian company's effort to establish a common, compelling purpose.

Chapter 8:

1. Senge, Peter M., *The Fifth Discipline*, New York: Doubleday/Currency, 1990. A thought-provoking presentation of what it means to be a learning, synergistic organization. Senge outlines the five disciplines of a learning organization: personal mastery, mental models, shared vision, team learning, and systems thinking.

2. Friedman, Thomas L., *The Lexus and the Olive Tree*, New York: Farrar, Straus and Giroux, 1999. An excellent overview of globalization and its impact on society, government, and organizations. The Lexus symbolizes the global market. The olive tree symbolizes the cultural roots of individual nations. Friedman shows how globalization puts pressures and strains on both.

3. Hanna, David P., *Designing Organizations for High Performance*, Reading: Addison-Wesley, 1988. The first published description of the OP Model with examples of its use for diagnosis and high performance design.

Chapter 9:

1. Goldratt, Eliyahu M. and Jeff Cox, *The Goal,* 2nd edition, Croton-on-Hudson: North River Press, Inc., 1992. A unique book for teaching principles of total systems diagnosis. This is a novel about a manufacturing plant manager and his struggles to improve his organization's results. An intriguing consultant teaches this manager how to see things as they really are and how to connect the streams that make up his current results. Entertaining and profound at the same time.

Chapter 10:

1. Porter, Michael E., *Competitive Advantage,* New York: Free Press, 1985. A classic in strategic thinking. Covers the structural analysis of competitive advantage, value chains, and possible approaches to gain competitive advantage.

2. Hamel, Gary and C. K. Prahalad, *Competing For the Future,* Cambridge: Harvard Business School Press, 1996. Contrasts "maintenance engineers" who reengineer today's system with true strategists who see future opportunities and follow the path wherever it leads.

3. Kohn, Alfie, *Punished By Rewards,* Boston: Houghton Mifflin Co., 1993. A paradigm-busting book that presents you with research to show that artificial inducements cause people to lose interest in what they are being induced to do.

4. Hanna, David P., *Designing Organizations For High Performance,* Reading: Addison-Wesley, 1988. Gives a more detailed description of some of the high performance principles reviewed here.

5. Jaques, Elliott, *Requisite Organization,* Arlington: Cason Hall and Co., 1989. Based on the career learnings of one of the Tavistock Institute's founders, this book examines the structuring of organizations based on the logic of the work to be performed. If you really believe form should follow function, this book is a must read!

Chapter 11:

1. Lipnack, Jessica and Jeffrey Stamps, *The Age Of The Network*, Essex Junction: Oliver Wight Publications, Inc., 1994. A good summary of globalization's organization template.

2. Bartlett, Christopher and Sumantra Ghoshal, *Managing Across Borders*, Boston: Harvard Business School Press, 1989. A must-read for those organizing global organizational efforts.

3. Hanna, David P., *Designing Organizations For High Performance*, Reading: Addison-Wesley, 1988. Chapter 4 elaborates further on designing from the outside in.

4. Ashkenas, Ron, Dave Ulrich, Todd Jick, and Steve Kerr, *The Boundaryless Organization*, San Francisco: Jossey-Bass, 1995. Global age organizational concepts brought to life through corporate case studies and tools that illustrate how to overcome barriers vertically, horizontally, externally and geographically.

5. Ohmae, Kenichi, *The Borderless World*, New York: HarperBusiness, 1990. An insightful review of the realities of the global age and its implications for leaders of organizations.

Chapter 12:

1. Bridges, William, *Managing Transitions: Making the Most of Change*, Reading: Addison-Wesley, 1991. An insightful and practical discussion of the issues involved in managing the change process. The author distinguishes between change (the new situation) and transition (the psychological process of coming to terms with the new situation). Many critical issues are addressed in a way that's easy to understand. The book is full of real-life organizational examples.

2. Conner, Daryl R., *Managing At The Speed Of Change*, New York: Villard Books, 1993. A well-presented case for the nature of change, the process of change, and how leaders can keep their organizations moving synergistically in our global age.

3. Beckhard, Richard and Reuben T. Harris, *Organizational Transitions: Managing Complex Change*, second edition, Reading: Addison-Wesley, 1987. A short, but profound review of the

change process and the leader's role in managing its complexities. A must read!

Chapter 13:

1. Walton, Mary, *The Deming Management Method*, New York: Dodd, Mead & Co., 1986. A very practical and understandable review of the philosophy and approach of Dr. W. Edwards Deming, the man who taught the Japanese all about quality. It reveals the real wisdom of Deming: his inside out approach to quality.

2. Freiberg, Kevin and Jackie, *Nuts!: Southwest Airlines' Crazy Recipe for Business and Personal Success*, New York: Broadway Books, 1998. A behind-the-scenes look at Southwest Airlines CEO Herb Kelleher—his passion, vision, and actions to reinvent the airline industry.

About the Author

 **David P. Hanna** is the founder of Confluence Consulting, whose mission is to partner with leaders at all levels, helping them to align people, systems, and natural laws to create an enduring standard of excellence.

A former senior consultant with Franklin Covey and Procter & Gamble, he has worked with clients in North and South America, Asia, Europe, Australia and Russia. He has consulted with executive teams, manufacturing plants, foreign subsidiaries, Research & Development technical centers, and corporate staff groups.

Dave is experienced in the areas of principle-centered leadership, strategic planning, organization diagnosis, high performance work design, executive development, and team development. His list of clients includes Merck, Eastman Chemical, General Motors, Hoechst, Allied Signal, Conoco, Xerox, Saturn, Siemens, Shell, S. C. Johnson, Deloitte & Touche, Trammell Crow, Beverly Enterprises, Novell, Metro Cash & Carry, and Philips.

A native of Albuquerque, New Mexico, Dave received his B.A. in Communications and his M.A. in Organizational Behavior from Brigham Young University. He is the author of *Designing Organizations for High Performance* (Addison-Wesley, 1988), considered one of the top 50 Quality books in America.

Other Books by
Executive Excellence

193
201